FULLNESS
NO MATTER WHAT

FULLNESS NO MATTER WHAT

Juicy Living From The Inside Out

Ulla Mentzel, M.A.

iUniverse, Inc.
New York Lincoln Shanghai

Fullness No Matter What
Juicy Living From The Inside Out

Copyright © 2005 by Ulla Mentzel

All rights reserved. No part of this book may be used or reproduced by any means, graphic, electronic, or mechanical, including photocopying, recording, taping or by any information storage retrieval system without the written permission of the publisher except in the case of brief quotations embodied in critical articles and reviews.

iUniverse books may be ordered through booksellers or by contacting:

iUniverse
2021 Pine Lake Road, Suite 100
Lincoln, NE 68512
www.iuniverse.com
1-800-Authors (1-800-288-4677)

ISBN: 0-595-34081-4

Printed in the United States of America

Dedicated to my sisters Fine, Marita, and Rike.

Contents

I THANK YOU ALL	XV
INTRODUCTION	1
Invitation to a Journey	3
Travel Guide for this Book	4
My Pleasure Language	7
What About Those Breathing Reminders?	8
And What About Editing Mistakes?	8
How to Let This Book Work for You	9
BASIC ASSUMPTIONS	11
The Grand Experiment	13
Holographic Universe	14
An Offering versus the Right Way	15
Remembering is the Key	16
Balance	16
Miscellaneous	17
MORE	19
FULLNESS METER	21
Fullness Questions	24
Pleasure Meter	26
Acceptance Opens the Door	27
1 LOVING FULLNESS	29
BODY	31
Breathing Exercise: Color of Loving Fullness	31

  Pleasure Exercises 36
    Solo: Balancing Your Heart and Your Jewels 36
    Partnered: Giving and Taking Touch .39
 MIND 40
  Loving Fullness in the Body 40
  The Journey of Selfhealing 41
 SOUL 43
 MORE 44

2 COMMUNITY FULLNESS 45
 BODY 47
  Breathing Exercise: Peace Room and Ray of Community Fullness . .47
  Pleasure Exercises 51
    Solo: Wave Breath 51
    Partnered: Toning on Your Partner's Body 53
 MIND 55
  Finding Community within Us 55
 SOUL 58
 MORE 60

3 INSPIRATIONAL FULLNESS 63
 BODY 65
  Breathing Exercise: Vessel of Inspirational Fullness 65
  Pleasure Exercises 69
    Solo: Cobra Breath for One 69
    Partnered: Inspirational Lovemaking for Two 71
 MIND 72
  Inspiration at its Best 72
  To Be of Service 73
 SOUL 74
 MORE 76

4 GRATITUDE FULLNESS 79

BODY 81

Breathing Exercise: Fountain of Gratitude Fullness 81

Pleasure Exercises 84

Solo: Touching My Own Body with Gratitude 84

Partnered: Touching Your Partner's Body with Gratitude 85

MIND 86

Surrender to Saying Yes 86

The Attitude of Gratitude 87

SOUL 88

MORE 92

5 HEAVENLY FULLNESS 95

BODY 97

Breathing Exercise: Inverted Tetrahedron of Heavenly Fullness 97

Pleasure Exercises 100

Solo: On the Edge Pleasuring 102

Partnered: Taking Your Partner for a Pleasure Ride 103

MIND 106

Heaven on Earth 106

High Energy States 107

Characteristics of High Energy States 108

Upper Limits 109

Safe Ways to Integrate High Energy 111

SOUL 113

MORE 115

6 GUIDANCE FULLNESS 117

BODY 119

Breathing Exercise: Sofa for Guidance Fullness 119

Pleasure Exercises 122

Solo: Inviting the Spirit Realm 122

    Partnered: Left Eye Pleasuring 124
  MIND 125
    May I Introduce to You…? 125
    Understanding 127
    The Bigger Picture 128
  SOUL 128
  MORE 130

PARADOXING 131
  BODY 133
    Breathing Exercise: Paradoxing Stretch in a Sphere 133
    Pleasure Exercises 137
      Solo: Breathing the Bow and Arrow 137
      Partnered: The Crowning of the Jewels 139
  MIND 140
    Left Foot versus Right Foot 140
    Contrary Medicine Man 142
    My Story 143
    The Shadow 145
  SOUL 146

7 CONNECTING FULLNESS 147
  BODY 149
    Breathing Exercise: Web and Jewel of Connecting Fullness 149
    Pleasure Exercises 152
      Solo: Pleasurable Connections in Nature 152
      Partnered: Loving Touch of Your Partner's Jewels 154
  MIND 156
    My Old Story 156
    A Friend's Story 156
    My New Story 157
    Separation 158

    Dominator Culture 159
    Rationalism 160
    Patriarchy 160
    Divide and Conquer 161
  Integrity 161
  Right Action for All Living Things 163
Soul 165
More 166

8 EARTHLY FULLNESS 167
Body 169
  Breathing Exercise: Tetrahedron of Earthly Fullness 169
  Pleasure Exercises 172
    Solo: How to Enjoy Eating Delicious Food by Yourself 172
    Partnered: Playing with your Food! 173
Mind 174
  A Day in the Arms of the Earth 174
  The Sorcerer's Apprentice 176
Soul 178
More 180

9 LAUGHTER FULLNESS 183
Body 185
  Breathing Exercise: Bubbles of Laughter Fullness 185
  Pleasure Exercises 188
    Solo: The Effects of Laughter on Turn-on 188
    Partnered: Stunny Fuff! 189
Mind 190
  I Love to Laugh 190
Soul 191
More 192

10 SECURITY FULLNESS 193

BODY 195
- Breathing Exercise: Seat of Security Fullness 195
- Pleasure Exercises 198
  - Solo: Awakening the Rosebud 198
  - Partnered: Loving Attention for the Rosebud 201

MIND 202
- Breastfeeding Patterns and Social Implications 202
- Security and Vulnerability 204
- Added Benefits for Men 205

SOUL 206
MORE 209

PLEASURE FULLNESS 211

BODY 213
- Breathing Exercise: Three Spheres of Pleasure Fullness 213
- Pleasure Exercises 219
  - Solo: The Three Pleasure Spheres 219
  - Partnered: Honoring the Divine in Each Other 221

MIND 222
- Definitions First 222
- My Pleasure Story 224
- The Politics of Pleasure 225
- Some Pointers 226
  - The Road to Feelings 226
  - For Women in Particular 227
  - What DO Women Want? 228
  - For Men in Particular 229
  - Communication—Communication—Communication 230
  - Social Ramifications 231
  - Transcendence 232

    Soul 234

    More 236

11 FEELING FULLNESS 239

    Body 242

        Breathing Exercise: Anemones of Feeling Fullness 242

        Pleasure Exercises 246

            Solo: Add Sexual Pleasure into Your Feelings 246

            Partnered: Gibberish Releases 248

    Mind 249

        The Five Attitudes of God 250

        A Guide to Feelings 251

        Through the Body into Feelings 256

        The Tunnel of Not Knowing 257

            Symptoms 258

            What to Do 259

    Soul 261

    More 264

12 KNOWING FULLNESS 265

    Body 267

        Breathing Exercise: Caves of Knowing Fullness 267

        Pleasure Exercises 270

            Solo: High Energy Oracle for One .271

            Partnered: Washing Your Partner's Jewels 272

    Mind 274

        Knowing—An Inquiry 274

    Soul 275

    More 278

THE DONUT 281

    Body 283

    Breathing Exercise: Whole Body Breath 283
    Pleasure Exercises 287
        Solo: Mandala Pleasure Breathing 287
        Partnered: Sensuous Whole Body Pleasuring 290
  MIND 293
    The Organizing Principle behind the Twelve Aspects of Fullness . .293
  SOUL 296
  MORE 297

JUST FULLNESS 299
  MORE 306

ART NOTES 307
    Technique 307
    Design Elements 307
    Individual Mandala Designs 308

APPENDIX 313
    A Word Concerning the Verbal Gems in the Soul Sections 313
    Contact Information 313

I Thank You All

I thank you all
Who danced with me
In all these years
Of different dances
Just full of everything
I needed to be here

I thank you all
Who gave so much
Of life and love to me
The dancer in the dark
With so much light in me

I thank you all
Who saw in me
More than I ever dreamed
And helped me step by step
To be who being wanted me to be

I thank you all
You are in me
And we are all in one

~~ Ulla! ~~

- ❖ Ingrid von Krosigk, my mother, for having given me a body, for having raised me with all the love you had for me, for modeling generosity to me, and for letting me find my own way into fullness, even though it did not look at all like what you had in mind for me;

- ❖ Adolf Lorenz von Krosigk, my father, for loving me always and all ways from the day I was born until today, even though I followed my path to fullness so far away from you; and for having been able to become my very good friend once I did not need a Father anymore;

- The Sex-Positive community in the Bay Area, for having opened your arms to me so that I could experiment with and also experience many different forms of relating and loving, thus allowing me to move on out of an external fullness into the complex simplicity of the internal fullness;
- All my wonderful lovers over the years (you know who you are), who assisted me on my journey to discover my passion in loving, my joy in being loved, my ecstasy in lovemaking, and my depth in relating;
- Lori Grace, for having brought so many new ideas, experiences and people into my life allowing me to translate my personal fullness into a fullness for everyone who is open to it;
- Zeya, Tali, Deja, Christopher, Matt, Errin, and Danny for letting me be your friend while you were friends with my children Felix and Emily;
- Robert Gerrard, for having shown me that there is another one like me, for offering me everything I ever wanted from a man, and for then vanishing conveniently from my life, so that I could find this fullness within me by myself without a partner;
- Audrey, for letting me be there for you towards the closure of your life;
- Pamela Joy, for having created "Food For People" 10 plus years ago so that over the last year and a half I have been able to enjoy free ingredients for many delicious meals that have kept my body well nourished during the writing of this book;
- Brent Bolton, you wonderfully sweet and steady friend, for having brought Lisa into my life;
- Lee Hayden, for 13 years of loyal friendship, generous financial support, and whimsy meistering—boy, can we laugh together;
- Harbin Hot Springs, for being my spiritual home where I can always find clarity again, no matter how confused I believe myself to be;
- Sabina Cass, for loving me so joyously and generously from your big heart—I have always felt and still feel so supported by you and held in your love;
- Peta Lynne, you wonderful mother and imp, for all your loving support with graphics, editing, and most of all for the joy you reflect in my life;
- Andre Angerman, for creating the fullness graphics for the Art Notes;
- Dominique Gauthier, for creating all the illustrations that clarify my words, and for being my friend;
- Glenn Meader, for help in editing and web site setup and design;

I Thank You All

- Sarah Bly, for mirroring my joy so perfectly in your wonderfully bright blue eyes and light blond curly hair, for having given me a new joy in my teachings by bringing all of your gifts to our classes, and letting them so easily and effortlessly combine with mine;
- David Irvine, for having offered your home to house sit, ripe cherries, plums, peaches, and pears to pick, fresh roses that grace my computer desk, and your friendship on top of all of that;
- The dogs Heidi and Amy who have been calling me constantly outdoors for new inspiration, energy and pure joy, and have taught me more about boundaries than any human teacher so far did;
- Barry Feinsmith, for knowing how to make me laugh, for having let me loose myself in loving you so that the Madness could visit me to bring me into fullness, and for still being my friend;
- Clint Housel, for having held up a light so large that I could find my way back out of the Madness;
- Patti Taylor, for many years of love, support, effortless friendship in the face of possible drama, and for lots of laughter in our creative German lessons;
- Iver Juster, for a depth of connection that is independent of physical contact, for your wildly imaginative space trader stories, for your quirky sense of humor, and for helping me remember my kinesthetic way of touching ("can you feel me feeling you feeling me?")
- La Principessa Bianca or Kitty, for just being here with me, often sitting next to me curled up in your basket while I was writing;
- Chris Mentzel, my wasband, for all the support you have given me over 20 plus years, as lover, husband, co-parent, computer specialist, and friend; and all the love you taught me and showed me including the longest declaration of love I know of: a CD-ROM full of "I love you's" strung together with "Ulla" at the very end;
- Felix, my wonderful son, for exploring and finding your very own way in the world, for being who you are in spite of me, and for letting me stay connected with you;
- Emily, my beautiful daughter, for lending me your Pink Mac to write this book on, for having had the courage to follow your path into high school graduation on your very own terms, for letting me go, so that I could move to Ashland and follow mine into fullness and into this book, and for being who you are in the face of having me as your mother;

- All the Spirit Guides around me, never to interfere, always available when I need encouragement, reminders, a specific word, a concept, or a story, reminding me that all I ever need is available to me for The Asking, once I let go of The Need;
- Dr. Peebles, as channeled by William Rainen, for many years of loving encouragement, gentle and insightful teachings, and for a bigger picture that slowly but surely helped me remember to grow into with you daily on my side, until fullness is blessing me, once more;
- Sunanda, for reminding me constantly and gently that I could not reach for the stars, if I did not already know that I actually could go there;
- Lisa Bleier, for having held the position of the witness during my blossoming into this book and into fullness, for being such a strong and open woman friend, and for being able to make crème brulee show up on your car roof after a long and exhausting hike, even with two spoons;
- All the brilliant sunsets full of different colors every night, the wind turning the leaves into my nightly rustling lullaby, the blue jays for waking me up early in the morning to sunrises full of soft hues of dawn colors, the myriads of far away stars for watching over me, the Ashland Creek for washing my emotional body clean most mornings on my hikes through Lithia Park, and many, many more companions around me in nature;
- My Beloved, for already knowing and loving me in Spirit long before we meet in person at exactly the right time;
- Fullness, for having found me, finally, after so many years of deeply, painfully longing for you, and, once I had come through the Madness, for gracing my life with all I ever wanted and much more.

~~~~~~~~~~

Introduction

Fullness No Matter What

Come Celebrate With Me

Come celebrate with me
All that there is to live

Come dance with me
Right on the razor's edge

Come sing with me
Of pain and pleasure
Joy and grief

Come call with me
Into this world
The mighty wind
That fullness brings

Come celebrate with me
Till all we know is gone

~~ Ulla! ~~

Introduction

Invitation to a Journey

Let me invite you on a journey into a realm I call fullness. Allow me to help you into my open horse carriage for a tour of this magical realm that is very real. This realm is both far, far away and just around the corner. It feels both very familiar and utterly strange. We can spend a whole lifetime (and if you believe in reincarnation—many, many lifetimes) searching for it and never finding it. And we can stumble across its entryways all of a sudden and fall into it totally unexpectedly.

We all have come from that realm, and eventually will return to it. Even though this is an invitation into the exploration of possibly new realms, this journey might easily feel as if it is just one big reminder of what we already know. And when we get there, it feels like we have finally come home. At the same time we might be feeling just as excited as if we are making a completely new discovery.

This journey into fullness for me has been and still is a very precious experience. It has asked me to tear down any structure I created to find shelter from the wind of change blowing through my life and to slaughter every single "holy cow" I was trying desperately to hold onto. It has led me into the darkest moments of my life without a sense of ever being able to return. It also has brought to me a joy and peace and so much laughter in the oddest moments combined with a sense of purpose and fulfillment I could hardly dream possible.

Interestingly enough, while living in this materially oriented Western world, I found that this journey full of riches and wonders can happen independently from having any money. Money is one of the commodities I needed the least of to embark on this journey.

Once again, my invitation here is to open up to new possibilities and thus new lives. All that is needed is the willingness to stray a bit from the worn out grooves of our habits and to try on different and new ways to be, think, and do, just for the sake of the journey.

~~~ A deep belly breath in ~~~

Travel Guide for this Book

This is a very practical book. It is both a handbook and a journey into fullness. Imagine a circular journey in a horse-drawn carriage with twelve sites to be visited. The twelve sites are the twelve aspects or twelve chapters of fullness. I am using these twelve aspects as a compass to my ideas, experiences, and suggestions exploring fullness. They are based on an ancient organizing principle. If you want to know more about that organizing principle, please go to the Mind Section of the Donut chapter.

There are six chapters that have no numbers because they do not fit in the order of twelve. Remember my invitation to a journey? Here are all the different components of that journey put together:

- The **Twelve Fullness Chapters** are the twelve sites to be visited on this circular journey.
- The **Basic Assumptions** are the six wheels of the carriage (four to keep it rolling and two spare ones—you never know!).
- The **Fullness Meter** offers a way to take inventory at the start of your journey.
- **Paradoxing** is both you, the traveler, and the carriage.
- **Pleasure Fullness** is the horse that keeps the carriage in motion.
- The **Donut** is the map to the journey.
- **Just Fullness** is all of it, the journey, the watching, you on the journey, me creating the journey. All of it.

Most of the chapters offer six different entry points into each Fullness aspect:

- **Art:** One of my art pieces as Fullness Mandala
- **Poetry:** One of my poems
- **Body:** Various exercises offering experiences through the body
- **Mind:** Concepts, ideas, tools, and techniques
- **Soul:** Inspirational messages, insights, and poems
- **More:** Books, teachers, videotapes, audiotapes, web sites etc.

Introduction

The **Art** entry points present you with a visual gateway into each aspect of fullness. I created all of the Mandalas specifically for this book. If you want to know more about the Mandalas and their creation, please go to the Art Notes at the end of the book.

The **Poetry** entry points are examples of my own poetry. I have been writing poetry since I was 15 years old. I first wrote poems in German and actually self published a volume of German poetry in my twenties. In the last 14 years the poems have come out in English, and a number of the "Girls" quite definitely wanted to be included in this book (I borrowed that attitude from Tori Amos who calls her songs "the Girls".)

The **Body** entry points offer an experiential way into each aspect of fullness with two different suggestions for exercises. These exercises invite you to explore a particular fullness aspect on a practical basis:

- **Breathing Exercise:** Breathing and imagination as gateways into the world inside our bodies
- **Pleasure Exercises:** Pleasure as a guide into sexual, sensuous, and transcendent explorations through our bodies

The **Breathing Exercises** are invitations to explore the world of imagination right inside our bodies, always accessible, and unlimited in scope. The following quote by a channeled entity called Abraham offers you a context: "Anything that you have the ability to imagine—you have the ability to have a physical manifestation of." Our breath becomes the guide into the world inside our bodies and anchors any imaginative experiences into our daily reality as the one thing we all do for sure is breathe every day, every minute, as long as we are alive.

Each **Pleasure** Exercise is offered in two variations, as we are pleasure beings no matter if we are single or in relationship:

- **Solo:** When you are by choice or default single and still want to relate to yourself as a sexual, sensuous, and transcendent being.
- **Partnered:** When you want to explore sexuality, sensuality, and transcendence with your significant other.

Most traditions that teach the use of sexual energy as a gateway into spiritual or mystical experiences offer two paths: one for singles (often as a preparation for the partnered path), and one with a partner. If your are currently with a partner, feel free to explore any of the Solo Exercises by adjusting the instructions to your needs. If you are single, reading the Partnered Exercises most likely can serve to inspire and prepare you for a more expanded relationship in the future.

For the **Mind** entry points I put together various ideas, insights, and concepts as an offering into a different way of looking at the world we live in. I have been blessed with an unusual perspective into both the workings and failings of our modern day society, while keeping in mind that all is perfect just the way it is. I present them here for your perusal. If they ring true for you, use them as a fresh way to look at the world around you. If they sound strange and too far out, consider them just my particular fancy. I sure had fun discovering them.

The **Soul** entry points are verbal gems that I have been collecting since I was 15 years old. First I wrote them down in my special little notebook, and carried them around with me. Later they have often spent time in printed form taped to my bathroom mirrors, the steering wheel of my car, and on the backs of my notebooks. Here is a poem that expresses the function of the verbal gems beautifully:

~~~~~~~~~~

SPIRIT'S HANDS

They
can be a great help—words.
They can become Spirit's hands
and lift and
caress
you.

Meister Eckhart (Landisky Translation)

~~~~~~~~~~

The **More** entry points at the end of each chapter direct you to a wealth of resources to keep exploring a particular subject more in depth. Because of the scope and breadth of this book, I have not gone into much detail concerning

Introduction

the ideas, concepts, and perspectives I present. My intention here is to just open doors, to awaken your curiosity.

~~~ *A deep sigh out* ~~~

My Pleasure Language

Our language associated with pleasure, and particularly with sexual pleasure, is either very graphic (like cunt, bush, cock, or wiener), or very clinical (like vagina, penis, or cunnilingus). I my opinion there is absolutely nothing wrong with using graphic sexual terms in the bedroom to create a particular lusty turn-on.

In the context of fullness, though, I am not looking for words that create turn-on. I am rather seeking ways to express and honor the sexual and pleasure force at its fullest. For this book I am therefore using words either from other cultures that have a different attitude towards sex (like India) or from a more lustrous context (like precious jewels) to describe sexual organs and activities. Here is my dictionary of sexual terms for this book:

HONORING TERMS	FAMILIAR TERMS
Lovemaking, make love	Any sexual interaction
Sexual Union	Intercourse
Jewels	Genitals (male or female)
Yoni (East Indian for Pleasure Grotto)	Vagina
Pearl	Clitoris
Female Sacred Spot	G-Spot
Lingam (East Indian for Wand of Light)	Penis
Twin Globes	Testicles
Male Sacred Spot	Prostrate
PC muscles	Pubococcygeus muscle
Rosebud	Anus
Honoring him orally	Fellatio (Going down on him)
Honoring her orally	Cunnilingus (Going down on her)

If you sense some awkwardness in reading about sexual pleasure in these unfamiliar terms, my suggestion is to stay with it and let it guide you into a possibly unknown territory. The awkwardness is just a sign of something unfamiliar and new. Once you get used to the unfamiliar terms, you might just get ushered into a different relationship with your own sexuality.

<p align="center">~~~ *A deep belly breath in* ~~~</p>

What About Those Breathing Reminders?

Maybe some of you are thinking, why does she have to remind me about breathing, as for example at the end the last section: "~~~ *A deep belly breath in* ~~~" This is so didactic, so schoolteacher like…

I am offering these reminders to breathe in and to breathe out as an invitation to stay connected to our bodies while dwelling in the world of words and concepts. So often when we are hearing, reading, or discussing mental concepts, we literally lose touch with our bodies. We end up having only a partial experience, because much of our focus stays in our minds. That is a great place for thoughts, but a limited place for experiences.

If these reminders help you feel more connected to your body, keep following the suggestions. If you feel irritated, just pretend they are either mistakes or meaningless subdivides.

<p align="center">~~~ *A deep sigh out* ~~~</p>

And What About Editing Mistakes?

This book has found some loving support from a number of friends who helped me both edit and proofread it. But it has not been professionally looked at, as I decided to self-publish this book for a number of reasons. You most likely will find a number of spelling mistakes, some strange use of the English language as English is not my native language, and some formatting errors. This is a perfect book just because it was written, and is out there and available. But it is not a perfect book in terms of a professionally published book. Please keep that in mind while reading it. And may the errors that successfully evaded all the eyes looking for them not distract you from the content.

<p align="center">~~~ *A deep belly breath in* ~~~</p>

Introduction

How to Let This Book Work for You

There are several ways you can let this book work for you and with you. This journey offers a number of ways to travel, depending on what you enjoy most, what tickles your fancy, or what drives you:

- ❖ This book and its journey can be read and traveled from cover to cover, page by page, just for the enjoyment of its content and its flow.
- ❖ If you want to get serious (what a funny idea) about experiencing this journey into fullness, my suggestion is to devote the next fourteen months of your life to this exploration, taking a whole month for every fullness aspect. Check my website (www.FullnessNoMatterWhat.com) to find out when a whole support system for that approach will be available to help you stay on track towards a life of fullness.
- ❖ Another route to travel through this book is to take the Fullness Meter Test (see chapter called Fullness Meter). There you will find out where you already feel pretty full, and where you could open up to more fullness. Then just focus on those chapters where you want to expand your degree of fullness.
- ❖ Three of the four Sections (**Body, Mind,** and **Soul**) can be used as special entry points into the various aspects of fullness:
  - ➢ If you like delving into experiences first and find understanding later, then start with the **Body** Section and its Breathing and Pleasure Exercises as entry points.
  - ➢ If you like exploring ideas and concepts first to get oriented, starting with the **Mind** Section is a good idea.
  - ➢ If you are in the mood for some inspirational reading, start with the **Soul** Sections. Peruse them just after you wake up or before you go to sleep. These gems are meant as balm for busy days, inspiration for lazy days, or plain soul food for any days.
- ❖ Don't forget that this book also can just be opened somewhere by chance and voila!, there is a magical entry point into something unexpected, new, or familiar.
- ❖ You can also just put this book underneath your pillow (make sure it is centered exactly in the middle), count the number of windows in your house, and go to sleep remembering that number. This is a variation on an old German saying my mother Ingrid taught me as a child.

❖ A combination of all the approaches might lead to some very complex results!

No matter what road into fullness you decide to take, it will be the perfect one for you, at the right time, and with the right outcome. That is one of the magical properties of fullness!

~~~ A deep sigh out ~~~

Basic Assumptions

Yes We Designed A Life

Yes we designed a life
To birth a knowing
Called for in times of need
And we created me
The human vessel to live here
On earth and as a fellow being
Right in the midst of all

I lived the life that we foresaw for me
And I became the woman
We wanted me to be
With every grace and scar in place
Through which the knowing
Has been birthed and shaped
Into a perfect jewel
So that the seeing in the light
Turned into knowing here on earth

~~ Ulla! ~~

Basic Assumptions

This journey into fullness is based on six Basic Assumptions (remember, four wheels for the horse drawn carriage and two spare ones), which represent the underpinnings for the book as a whole.

- ❖ The Grand Experiment
- ❖ Holographic Universe
- ❖ An Offering versus The Right Way
- ❖ Remembering is the Key
- ❖ Balance
- ❖ Miscellaneous

The Grand Experiment

In the Mind Sections of this book you will find a number of references to the Grand Experiment. Using these words is my way to keep reminding myself as the writer, and you as my readers, of a couple premises that I don't want to have to spell out every time:

In looking at life from a perspective of fullness I have naturally found a number of aspects in our Western culture that are not conducive, to say the least, to that fullness. In pointing out these aspects in several of the Mind Sections of this book I want it to be clear that this is not meant as a general critique of Western culture. My intention here is not to point a finger and judge the experiments of the Western mindset as faulty, erroneous, and overall detrimental.

I am more interested in observing and describing a stage of human development that had and still has its benefits, its reasons, and its purpose. In other words, my invitation is to see these observations as expressions of a whole range of long term "experiments", independently from any apparent shortcomings.

I believe that everything we humans have ever come up with and lived through, no matter how inappropriate it seems in looking back, has been necessary in and for the growth and change of us humans here on Earth. I believe that there is method to the madness we are and have been experiencing, especially in the last 90 to 100 years. Examples of this madness include technological acceleration, two world wars, the potential for worldwide nuclear destruction, large scale environmental damage, the extinction of species, etc.

There is a Bigger Picture here that I am not quite able to put into detailed words yet, but I know it exists and I know it points to wholeness, to balance, and to fullness. From that perspective of fullness, all and everything is and has always been perfect just the way it is.

~~~ *A deep belly breath in* ~~~

Holographic Universe

You will notice throughout this book that in my universe there is a definite connection between the workings of our external world and the workings of our internal worlds. I believe that how we see events, people, and things on the outside will be reflected on the inside filtered through the particular facets of our personality, psyche and our bodies. The reverse is true too. Whatever we believe to be true based on personal experiences and inherited or acquired belief systems on the inside, this universe we live in will reflect it back to us. If we believe we live in a dangerous world, all we see and experience is danger. If we believe we live in a benevolent and peaceful world, all we see and experience is peace.

One answer I came up with for this connection is that we live in a Holographic Universe. If you look at a holographic photograph of a water faucet projected onto glass, it sticks out like a three-dimensional object although it is only a flat piece of glass. If that piece of glass breaks, you can take any of the broken shards and see the whole water faucet, if you turn it and look into it. The whole is always visible in any part of it. In a normal photograph if you cut off a corner of the photograph, all you see is the part that was cut off. In other words, every part of a hologram contains all the information possessed by the whole.

The human body and our world to me are both holographic in nature. That means, humans are part of the holograph Earth. An example is that the earth is made up of 70% water just as the human body. To me the holographic aspect of humans as part of the Earth and the universe around us explains why I believe that whatever we human do on the external level is mirrored on the inside.

In my research I came across a physicist and mystic, David Bohm (1917-1992) who as a child already had a special talent for solving complex mathematical problems. He saw himself as a microcosmic reflection of the universe as a whole, and by exploring his own thoughts and feelings in response to the universe around him, he was able to come to a deeper understanding of the workings of nature. To David Bohm all laws of the universe have the same source, and everything under the sun and beyond is interconnected, including the human mind.

David Bohm put into words what I sensed inside myself: that it is time to reconnect to all aspects of our selves, both internally and externally. When we experience connection on the inside it spills over on the outside into action. One very simple way to experience connection inside ourselves is through the breath. In this book there are twelve equal aspects of fullness all connected through the breath in the various Breathing Exercises. Another way is through pleasure as all aspects are also connected through Pleasure Exercises offering fullness experientially in our bodies. Action will invariably follow once the inside fullness has been found just as much as a pitcher will invariably spill over once it has been filled up to the brim, and then some.

~~~ A deep sigh out ~~~

An Offering versus the Right Way

Just to put it right up front, I do not believe in The Right Way as in the "The Only Right Way". I believe in an offering, suggestions, invitations. In this book I put together all the ideas, concepts, techniques, practices, sayings, poems, art pieces etc that over the years have helped me grow into more and more aspects of my own fullness. All of it has been tried out by me, used by me, and explored by me. As I have a complex personality, there are many different aspects presented in this book. I am offering all of this to you to try on and play with. If it does not work for you for whatever reasons, toss it and try something else. Just because it worked for me, does not mean it will necessarily work for you.

And it is working for me. I am so glad that I said Yes to this opportunity to put onto paper a selection of my experiences, ideas, and insights. The most wonderful aspect is that it is reminding me of what I do know, and how many tools I do have available when my own journey gets a bit rocky. By putting what I know into this book, I am reminding myself in challenging moments how to be with myself.

~~~ A deep belly breath in ~~~

Remembering is the Key

Here are two important assumptions that are kind of entangled with each other: number one is that I do not see myself as The Teacher (both with a capital T) who has all the right answers (see last assumption). Instead I have been gifted with a very bright, fast, and curious, but very quirky mind. I am able to use my curiosity to explore ever deeper layers of meaning, having been blessed with a good dose of courage. All of that has allowed me to turn my life into one big exploration no matter how afraid I have been feeling concerning some of these explorations. And—I love sharing the treasures I find with anyone willing to hear or read what I have to say.

Which leads me to number two: I believe that everyone of us has all the answers within us and available to us. The only thing we are invited to do is to remember what we do know. Got That? By sharing my fullness through insights, stories, art, poems, and exercises I see myself as being the spark that helps you to remember, just as I had countless sparks in my life that helped me to remember. And then you can go forth and help others to remember…

~~~ A deep sigh out ~~~

Balance

To live a life from fullness a multitude of aspects are invited to be present in various degrees at different times. So much of our history shows trends of living only certain aspects of our human wholeness while excluding others. For example for centuries most religions declared human sexuality as something bad, destructive, sinful—you name it. Other factions declared the logical mind as the only basis relevant to human life. Others again excluded the non-physical angel or spirit realm as superstition and focused on only the five senses of human perception.

I believe and have found in my years of explorations, that the more inclusive I can be with the various aspects of my humanity, the more balanced I feel and the more fullness I am able to experience and express. My personal emphasis here is on balance and inclusion rather than imbalance and exclusion.

~~~ A deep belly breath in ~~~

Basic Assumptions

Miscellaneous

You will not find a lot of references to support the concepts and ideas I present. This is neither a Ph.D. thesis nor a scientific research paper. You will also not find great detail in my ideas, theories, or concepts due to the wide scope of this book. And you will not find a sense of separation between my personal life and its process and the ideas and concepts I offer. Here is a list of what else you will not find in this book:

- How to find your lifelong perfect partner, husband, wife, soul mate!
- How to have a lot of money in a very short time!
- How to redecorate your home, office, or closet!
- How to manage your seemingly recalcitrant teenage children!
- How to fix any and all of your problems once and for all and live happily aver after!

This book offers a different invitation instead:

- Find out how rich our lives are just by being accepting of and grateful for what is;
- Let new or unusual perspectives brighten up our daily existence; and
- Open ourselves up to as many different aspects of our humanness in ourselves and in others as we can possibly experience.

There is a wealth of choices, perspectives, and explorations available to us—let's get drunk on them just as Rumi celebrates getting drunk in this poem:

~~~~~~~~~~

Gone, inner and outer,
No moon, no ground or sky.

Don't hand me another glass of wine.
Pour it in my mouth.
I've lost the way to my mouth.

The wine we really drink is our blood.
Our bodies ferment in these barrels.

Fullness No Matter What

We give everything for a glass of this.
We give our minds for a sip.
I used to be shy.
You made me sing.

Rumi (Coleman Barks translation)

~~~~~~~~~~

Basic Assumptions

More

David Peat. *Infinite Potential: The Life and Times of David Bohm.*
Bohm himself strongly believed himself part of the universe and that, by giving attention to his own feelings and sensations, he should be able to arrive at a deeper understanding of the nature of the universe." Quote by David Peat

Michael Talbot. *Holographic Universe.*
"Talbot explains the theory advanced by physicist David Bohm and neurophysiologist Karl Pribram that despite its apparent tangible reality, the universe is actually a kind of three-dimensional projection and is ultimately no more real than a hologram, a three-dimensional image projected into space." Book News, Inc. Portland, OR.

Jalaíāl al-Diíān Ruíāmiíā. *The Essential Rumi. Translated by Coleman Barks.* (All the Rumi poems in the Coleman Barks translation quoted in the rest of the book were taken from this source.)

Natan: *Rumi Sings.* Download Natan's musical renditions of some of Coleman Bark's Rumi translations at:
http://www.rabbinathan.com/music_songs/music_songs.asp

Daniel Landinsky. *Love Poems for God.* (All the poems translated by Daniel Landinsky quoted in the rest of the book were taken from this source.)

Fullness Meter

A Grandiose Fool

Am I a grandiose fool waiting to be fooled
Again and again by reaching out
For the seemingly unattainable
In terms of normal wisdom all around me?

Have I created this one way street
In every aspect of my life right now
For the sole purpose of no way out
Just by my own devices?

I am hanging on a precipice
Far out there without hold
I am willing to let miracles
Come out and get me so hard
That doubt no longer holds me back
From being all I came to be

~~ Ulla! ~~

Fullness Meter

The Fullness Meter is an invitation to find out what your current level of fullness looks like visually. The important aspect here is to find out how full your life already is. Try to focus on the blessings, and not so much on the shortcomings. If you have a sense of falling short of your own goal, just redefine what you consider a shortcoming as lots of room to explore, to open up, or to still get excited about something!

Here are the instructions for you Fullness Meter:

- ❖ Find a piece of paper, some crayons, color pens and/or felt markers.
- ❖ Draw two circles inside each other about 1/4 inch apart, which are at least eight inches wide, either by freehand, by following the outline of two different sized plates with a pen, or by using a compass.

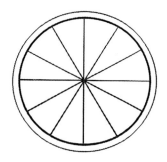

  - ❖ Draw six lines through the circle so that you will end up with twelve, more or less equal segments. The easiest way to do six lines through the circle is to do the following:
    - ➢ Start by drawing one line though the middle of the circle to create two halves.
  - ➢ Draw two lines that divide each half again into thirds.
  - ➢ Draw three more lines, each halving the existing segments.
  - ➢ You end up with twelve segments.
- ❖ On the line that separates segment #12 from segment #1 write the numbers 1 through twelve on or next to the line, starting with 1 at the center and 12 at the first circle.
- ❖ Write the following captions on or inside the segments, one caption per segment:

1. Loving Fullness
2. Community Fullness
3. Inspirational Fullness
4. Gratitude Fullness
5. Heavenly Fullness
6. Guidance Fullness
7. Connecting Fullness

8. Earthly Fullness
9. Laughter Fullness
10. Security Fullness
11. Feeling Fullness
12. Knowledge Fullness

Fullness Questions

Now comes the fun part! Take one segment at a time and check in with yourself: how full are you right now in your life in regards to this area? Just answer the following questions, one a time, and fill in a dot at the appropriate segment. One dot per question. Remember that the center of the circle, where the twelve segments meet, represents one, and the circumference of the circle represents twelve on the Fullness scale.

1. Loving Fullness

- ❖ How familiar am I with love, that is, how well do I know what love feels like, looks like, sounds like?
- ❖ How much do I experience myself as being loved in my life?
- ❖ How much do I feel my loving is being received?

2. Community Fullness

- ❖ How much do I experience myself as part of a community with a sense of belonging?
- ❖ How much are my particular creative gifts being received in my community of like-minded and like-hearted members?

3. Inspirational Fullness

- ❖ How much is inspiration a part of my daily life?
- ❖ How well am I able to contribute to an idea, a community, work etc, where I am able to be of service to something larger than myself?
- ❖ How much can I align myself with a larger vision to give my life more meaning?

4. Gratitude Fullness

- How much gratitude am I able to feel and express in my life?
- How much do I know that there is something larger out there called God, Yahweh, Source, the Universe, Nature etc?
- How much do I know that I am part of something larger than myself like God, Yahweh, Source, the Universe, Nature etc?

5. Heavenly Fullness

- How open am I to the idea of a Heaven on Earth instead of a Heaven after death?
- How willing am I to experience a Heaven on Earth?

6. Guidance Fullness

- How often do I feel guided in my life by an inner voice, angels, spirit guides, God, Source etc?
- How much do I rest in that connection and its source of information, knowing it is always and all ways available to me?
- How well do I know that in challenging times I am not alone, even if I feel lonely as I have lost my support system, my friends, or my family?

7. Connecting Fullness

- How connected do I feel to myself, the people around me, the Earth I am living on?
- How much do I sense being in integrity with myself at work, in my social life, and my relationships at least some of the time?

8. Earthly Fullness

- How much am I aware of the fact that the Earth is a living, breathing entity, and that by living on this Earth, breathing the air, eating the food grown in its soil, drinking the water, I am intricately connected to that entity?
- How much do my daily actions reflect that sense of connection?

9. Laughter Fullness

- How well do I know how to laugh about myself, even in challenging times?
- How much can I see the humor even in really serious circumstances?
- How much do I enjoy making others laugh?

10. Security Fullness

- How well do I know, deep within myself, independently from external circumstances, that I am physically and emotionally taken care of, no matter what?
- How full am I in terms of my living situation, my work situation, and my financial situation?

11. Feeling Fullness

- How comfortable am I with my feelings?
- How well am I able to feel my emotions, and express them in a safe way?
- How much can I let myself experience a whole range of feelings?
- How much do I know myself blessed by my ability to feel?

12. Knowledge Fullness

- How much room have I created in my life for new concepts and ideas?
- How open am I to the concept of Universal Knowing, that is do I believe that I can tap into a deeper knowing beyond what I have learned from books and classes?

Once you have placed your appropriate dots in the twelve segments, connect all the dots in one line and Bingo! Here is your visual fullness map. My suggestion: delay trying to interpret this map. Later in the text are my suggestions on how to use this map.

Pleasure Meter

Pleasure Fullness, of course, has its own rules. Here they are:

- First the question: On a scale of one to twelve, how much pleasure can you stand in your life? Or put differently, how pleasurable can you really have it?
- Just pick the first number between one and twelve that you either hear in your head or that pops into your mind.
- When you have come up with your number, just be with that number. It is not a good nor a bad number, not a right nor a wrong number. It is just a number.
- Now pick a color, your pleasure color.
- Go back to your Fullness Meter.
- Looking at the rim around the segments, if you start counting at Loving Fullness and call that number one, then Knowing Fullness would be number twelve.
- Color in as many top segments as your number calls for. For example, if you picked six as your pleasure index, color in the first six top segments.
- That's it! You have your pleasure fullness added into the Fullness map.

Acceptance Opens the Door

When you have completed your Fullness Meter, look at it as a whole by softening your eyes into a kind of blurry vision. Give yourself a minute or two in that blurry vision. Then close your eyes for a moment and just be with your map. Relax into and around it. Let the questions and answers and dots and colored-in areas just stand on their own, without interpreting them or giving them meaning as in "My map says that I am…" or "My answers mean that I am not…" Or anything like it. Just wrap them in a soft layer of acceptance. Just breathe very gently and slowly into your belly. Accept your answers just for this moment for what they are: a snapshot of fullness in your life right now.

Interestingly, this being present through acceptance opens the door for change. A change on softly padded feet that sneaks in through the backdoor when you least expect it. A change that surprises you sweetly or wildly. All you need to do is as much as possible accept what is happening, what you are thinking, what you are seeing—just accept it for that moment (you are not accepting anything for the rest of your life, just for that moment) and the door opens.

~~~ *A deep belly breath in* ~~

1

Loving Fullness

The Grandeur of the Heart

It is the heart alone
That speaks to me
Of wondrous meetings with the Soul
Unnoticed often
Quite forgotten mostly
But always and all ways just there for me

Let me take comfort in the heart
In all these times of daily challenges
Let me take comfort from the heart
That I am walking on the rightful path
Let me take comfort with the heart
And just be still and listen
To my own heartbeat
Wherever I go
Whatever I do
Whoever I am

It is the heart that soothes me
It is the heart that knows me
It is the heart that loves me
Always and all ways

~~ Ulla! ~~

Body

Fullness starts with the heart. The physical heart in a human body is located at the crossing between our torso, which turns food into energy and waste, and our arms, taking that energy out into the world. It is the meeting point between earth, our feet on the ground, and heaven, our head in the clouds. Love, which we typically associate with the heart, to me is way more than just the feelings experienced with lovers, partners, friends, parents, children and family. It is a state of beingness. It is the starting point for fullness.

Breathing Exercise: Color of Loving Fullness

This breathing exercise is an invitation to explore our own fullness from the perspective of the heart, how to find it, enjoy it and let it work its magic inside of us.

Preparations

This Breathing Exercise is designed to be experienced while you are reading it, preferably out loud to yourself, if you are in a position to do so. If not, at least mouth the words; it will help you slow down and stay focused. If you are with a partner who is open to sharing this exercise, take turns reading it out loud to each other. Make sure you are in a position to relax while you are reading, without falling asleep too quickly.

If you want to intensify this exercise, invite your spirit guides and angels, known or unknown, seen or unseen, to join you in this experience.

Exercise

- ❖ I focus my awareness into my chest cavity by placing my hands on my heart.
- ❖ If I feel any discomfort or tightness in my chest cavity, I notice it, and then totally accept it by directing my very own Loving Color into the tender or tight area.
- ❖ I bring that Loving Color of acceptance into every area of discomfort, one after another, until my chest cavity is glowing with acceptance.

~~~~~~

- I focus my breath into my chest cavity, slowly counting to five on the inbreath, and again slowly counting to five on the outbreath.
- I sense the inbreath slowly raising up my chest.
- I sense the outbreath slowly letting my chest come down.
- I continue watching the raising of my chest on the inbreath, and the falling of my chest on the outbreath for about four to six long slow breaths.

~~~~~~

- When I am comfortable with that slow breathing in and out, I bring my awareness to my chest area, to where my physical heart does its wonderful job of pumping blood through my whole body.
- I appreciate my physical heart for doing such a wonderful job.
- If I feel any discomfort, pain, or tightness in my chest area or my heart, I notice it.
- I totally accept it by directing a soft breath of acceptance into the tender or tight area. I bring that breath of acceptance into every area of discomfort, one after another, until my chest area and heart are glowing with acceptance.

My Very Own Color of Loving

- I imagine a light glowing deep inside my physical, pumping, pulsing heart.
- It is an imagined light source, which has always been there and will always be there. All I need to do is become aware of the existence of this light.
- This light comes in a color, and it is my very own color. I can ask the light what the color is.
- I listen for the first impulse that might bring the answer. Or I can sense the color, or see it with my inner eyes.
- The color deep inside my heart can have a particular texture:
  - ➤ It can be like fast and light liquid.
  - ➤ It can be of a slow and heavy viscosity.
  - ➤ It can have a bright crystalline texture.
  - ➤ It can have my very own texture.

- ❖ I can also sense its quality:
  - ➢ Is it like a soft, slow, warm glow?
  - ➢ Does it feel like cool running water?
  - ➢ Does it have a fiery hot quality?
- ❖ I can also sense its shape:
  - ➢ Is it like a ball glowing and expanding?
  - ➢ Is it like a six pointed star radiating out in all directions?
  - ➢ Is it like a lighthouse beam slowly turning a magnified ray of light all around me?
  - ➢ Is it all of the above?
- ❖ And I might not know the answer right away as to what color, texture, quality, or shape that light has. The answer will come to me sometime in the next few minutes, hours, or days.
- ❖ Whatever the responses, they are what make that color inside my heart my very own.
- ❖ I bask in my very own color.

Selfhealing

- ❖ This color in my heart is the color of selfhealing.
- ❖ It is always available to me inside myself.
- ❖ All I need to do is ask.
- ❖ I am now ready to have my color of selfhealing activated.
- ❖ From now on I am on the path of selfhealing.
- ❖ My very own color knows what the next step is that I need to further my healing.
- ❖ When it is done, the next step will be brought to me.
- ❖ And the next step.
- ❖ And the next step.
- ❖ All I need to do is be open to the opportunities brought to me.
- ❖ I appreciate myself for being open to the opportunities for selfhealing.

Spreading my Very Own Color

- I once again sense the color, the texture, and/or the quality of my color.
- I imagine it slowly expanding beyond the limits of its hidden space within my physical heart.
- I imagine it slowly expanding into my chest cavity all the way up to my neck and into my head until it reaches the top of my head.
- I imagine it slowly expanding all the way down to my diaphragm, into my belly, through my Jewels into my legs and all the way down to the soles my feet.
- I come back to my physical heart, and imagine my color slowly expanding through the shoulders into my arms, into my hands, and all the way into the tips of my fingers.
- I flood my whole body with that rich light of my own. I bathe in my own fullness, enjoying it just for the sake of knowing myself fully loved.

~~~~~~

- I notice any changes in my body, in my sense of well being, in my breathing.
- I once more focus my awareness into my chest cavity.
- I breathe into my chest cavity, slowly counting to five on the inbreath, and again slowly counting to five on the outbreath.
- I sense the inbreath slowly raising my chest up.
- I sense the outbreath slowly letting my chest come down.
- I continue watching the raising of my chest on the inbreath, and the falling of my chest on the outbreath for about four to six long slow breaths.
- Anytime now I can access my own color of loving and the power of self-healing and experience their effect on my life in the hours, days, and months to come.

Completion

- When I am complete, I bring my awareness back to the world outside of me.
- I wiggle my toes and fingers.
- I stretch my body like a cat with a few lazy, long, full body stretches.
- I am back in my waking reality.

Loving Fullness

Suggestions

This color inside your physical heart, your very own Loving Color, is yours to explore with at any time. This kind of suggestive way of working with our imagination receives its actual power from repetition. The more often you use it and remember to apply it, the more powerful its effect to bring optimal change. So play with it and use it to infuse situations or objects with your very own energy, for example:

- ❖ I infuse my food with my very own color, especially restaurant food. Food then can change its vibration to match my very own.
- ❖ I send it to parts of my body that are hurting. There might not be an immediate change, but over time painful circumstances tend to feel better.
- ❖ I clean up unpleasant energies in a room or at my workspace by projecting the color from my heart into the world outside of me.
- ❖ I send it out to people I would like to send love to but am not close enough to express it in words.
- ❖ I send it to animals or plants that I would like to infuse with my love energy.

Mandala Breathing

If you want to make sure that you experience more of a particular Fullness in your life, try this: read through the exercise at least once, exploring it in your body through your imagination and your breath. Then make photocopies of the Fullness Mandala you find at the beginning of a chapter, and place them on strategic places like your refrigerator, your bathroom mirror, on top of your computer screen, the steering wheel of your car, above your kitchen sink, or across from your toilet. Any place where you spend a significant amount of time. Every time you become aware of the Mandala, take three deep slow breaths into your heart while staying completely focused on the Mandala. And then watch what happens…

Pleasure Exercises
Solo: Balancing Your Heart and Your Jewels

A woman's pleasure energy typically starts at the heart and then moves down into her Jewels. Imagine an upside down triangle with the long baseline at your heart level and the point on your Jewels. For most women any form of lovemaking is more satisfying when her heart and love energy are awakened before the sexual energy is aroused. Typically a woman will say to a man: "First you open up your heart to me and then I will open up my Yoni for you." That means she wants to feel safely held in an emotional heart connection before her pleasure spills over and over and over again.

 A man's pleasure moves in the opposite direction. It is has its base at your Jewels and then moves into you heart. This time imagine a triangle with its long baseline on the Jewels and its point in his heart. Men tend to want to be sexual before they want to feel connected and loving. Typically a man will say to a woman: "First you open up your Yoni to me and then I will open up my heart for you." A man's sexual energy is quick to rise, meanwhile the heart energy takes it's sweet time.

One of the reasons men and women feel attracted to each other is that these two triangles balance each other out by forming a star when they come together. They hold a useful polarity to create and maintain attraction based on opposites. These opposites can easily be managed as long as we accept the polarities as just two different expressions of the same basic needs: to feel loved and to experience pleasure. That balance is easier to maintain when both partners have access to both modalities that is each partner is able to move energy in either direction of the two triangles. Finding that balance within each of us also creates less of a dependency on each other, and therefore avoids some of the push-pull games that are the result of feeling dependent.

The following pleasure exercise gives both men and women a chance to balance out their individual energy triangles in a self practice.

Preparations for both Men and Women

- ❖ Lie on a flat surface, either your bed (remove all pillows underneath your head) or the floor
- ❖ Wear comfortable and loose clothing or no clothes

Exercise for Women

- ❖ I place one hand on my heart.
- ❖ I breathe into my heart and ignite my very own Color of Loving inside my heart through my breath (see Breathing Exercise: The Color of Loving Fullness).
- ❖ I imagine letting my Color of Loving expand till it fills my whole chest.
- ❖ I breathe my Color of Loving into my chest for about ten long slow breaths until my heart feels fully charged.

~~~~~~

- ❖ I might have a sensation of warmth, or feel a sweetness, or just experience an overall sense of wellbeing by igniting my heart through my breath.
- ❖ I now imagine sending that charged heart energy down into my Jewels.
- ❖ I place my other hand on or close to my Jewels, my Pearl and my Yoni.
- ❖ I breathe my Color of Loving down into my Jewels, that is I start by breathing into my belly and noticing my belly rise on the inbreath and fall on the outbreath.
- ❖ On the inbreath I bear down to push my breath all the way into my Yoni.
- ❖ On my outbreath I squeeze my PC muscles (the muscles that stop the flow of urine) to contract the muscles in my Yoni.
- ❖ I keep breathing in and bearing down and breathing out and squeezing for about ten breaths or until my Jewels feel nicely charged up.

~~~~~~

- ❖ I might notice sexual turn on in my Jewels or experience a sense of warmth and general pleasure.
- ❖ I now imagine sending my Color of Loving fully charged with my sexual pleasure back into my heart.

Fullness No Matter What

- I focus my breath back into my chest area for about ten slow breaths.

~~~~~~

- I just breathe normally and notice how my body feels.
- I simply rest in the sensations of my body, whatever they may be.

Exercise for Men

- I place one hand on or around my Lingam.
- I breathe into my Lingam, that is I start by breathing into my belly and noticing my belly rise on the inbreath and fall on the outbreath.
- I imagine bearing down on the inbreath to push my breath all the way into my Lingam.
- On my outbreath I squeeze my PC muscles (the muscles that stop the flow of urine).
- I keep breathing in and bearing down and breathing out and squeezing for about ten breaths or until my Lingam feels nicely charged up.

~~~~~~

- I might notice sexual turn-on in my Lingam or experience a sense of warmth and general pleasure there.
- I now imagine sending my sexual pleasure energy up into my heart.
- I place my other hand on my heart.
- I breathe into my heart and ignite my very own Color of Loving inside my heart (see Breathing Exercise: The Color of Loving Fullness) through my sexual pleasure energy.
- I imagine letting my Color of Loving expand till it fills my whole chest.
- I breathe my Color of Loving into my chest for about ten long slow breaths until my heart feels fully charged.

~~~~~~

- I might have a sensation of warmth, or feel a sweetness, or just experience an overall sense of wellbeing by igniting my heart through my breath.
- I now imagine sending my Color of Loving fully charged with my sexual pleasure back into my Lingam.

- ❖ I focus my breath back into my Lingam and belly for about ten slow breaths.
- ❖ I just breathe normally and notice how my body feels.
- ❖ I simply rest in the sensations of my body, whatever they may be.

Suggestions

Try doing both breathing exercises. If you are a woman doing the male triangle, just substitute Yoni whenever you read Lingam. If you are a man doing the female triangle, just substitute Lingam whenever you read Yoni.

Notice if you feel a difference. Which one feels more comfortable, natural to you? Which one feels harder to do? Do you feel comfortable with either one? Have fun exploring these two different modalities.

Partnered: Giving and Taking Touch

There are two different kinds of touch for pleasure, both equally enjoyable, but very different in intent: there is the **Giving Touch** and the **Taking Touch**.

The intent of the **Giving Touch** is to give pleasure (or relief) while touching. The focus of the person touching is on the person receiving. This is the way most of us touch. We want to achieve a specific result through our touch. This kind of touch lends itself well for sexual arousal, especially when being focused on a Pearl, a Lingam or a Sacred Spot. It also is the basis of most stress relieving massages.

The intent of the **Taking Touch** is to feel and stay connected with our own pleasure while touching our partner. Here we are focusing more on our own sensations than on the other person. The sensations could be the texture of the skin being caressed, the effect of my partner's hairs on the skin of my palm, or the feel of the curves and hills and valleys of someone's body. This kind of touch is usually slower that the Giving Touch and more sensual than sexual. Women especially enjoy being touched in that slow and aware way, especially as a way to be invited into lovemaking.

The Taking Touch is also a great way to stay present and in the moment. Sometimes in lovemaking we feel our minds drifting off into the future, or getting too focused on achieving a specific goal like an orgasm. Using the Taking Touch is like an instant switch into being present. It is also a great way to stay connected with each other after orgasm.

If you want to explore these two kinds of touch, take turns playing with either touch. Make sure you share your experiences with each other. Notice the difference in effect either form of touch has on both you and your partner. If you want to explore further, add your own Loving Color into both the Giving and the Taking Touch. Again, share the sensations and feelings that come up.

Mind

Loving Fullness in the Body

I find loving in my body. I find it not as a feeling like anger or grief, but as a state of deep relaxation and openness in which feelings like anger or grief come and go. In that state of openness my shoulders drop down into a more relaxed stance. My head and neck move back a few inches to a place more above my torso than far ahead in front of my body. A deep and open soft sigh-like breath happens. My belly relaxes and becomes soft. My breath reaches all the way into that soft belly. The muscles in and around my Yoni let go. I am at home in my body. Interestingly, all of this happens in only a few seconds, much less than it takes for me to describe it here in words.

With that sense of being at home in my relaxed body comes an openness to "what is" in that moment. My worries drop away (even if just for a minute). I am present right now right here. Something else happens and I can feel it right now writing about it: a very soft sweetness gently permeates my whole being, sometimes so much that I sense tears coming up.

I have also found that it works both ways. When I am in a loving state, my body relaxes and I am at home in it. When I consciously relax into my body, I become a loving person.

An important point to make here is that this kind of loving is not restricted only to romantic relationships. It encompasses everything:

- ❖ from the loving for my two children ready to explore being on their own two feet,
- ❖ to the loving for my parents and sisters far away in Germany,
- ❖ to the loving for a gnarly old big tree I pass by on my way into town,

- ❖ to the loving for the full moon rising just above the horizon in all her silvery white splendor,
- ❖ to the loving for my white princess cat sitting next to me in her basket all curled up and purring while I am writing,
- ❖ to whatever my loving happens to fall upon or be ignited by.

It is a loving that rises up in the moment just for the sake of loving and the pure joy of loving.

~~~ A deep belly breath in ~~~

The Journey of Selfhealing

There is one aspect of Loving Fullness that has asked me to be part of this book in more detail: the Journey of Selfhealing. I believe selfhealing is a form of Loving Fullness. It is a way to love ourselves, just because. There is a trust implicit in the belief that selfhealing can take place. I am not saying we are doing it. I am saying that we are open to letting it find us.

My friend David Irvine pointed out to me that we as humans would not have survived as a species for roughly 4000 years if we would not have had an enormous capacity to heal ourselves. Neanderthal man and woman had no physicians, therapists, psychiatrists, massage therapists, hospitals, etc available to get healed in case of physical or emotional wounding. They possibly had a shaman who might have been able to help, if he or she was intuitively good. The point is that our capacity for selfhealing is much greater than we have allowed ourselves to experience yet.

Let me sketch out here a possible scenario for how I believe the Journey of Selfhealing operates. We all need some form of healing, be it physical, emotional, psychological, or even spiritual. You name it, at some point in time we need it. Once we become aware of that need we typically try to locate an expert for the form of healing that we would like. Once we find that expert, we receive some form of treatment, and it either works or it doesn't. If it doesn't, we go to the next expert, and the next, and the next…

I am not trying to discredit the healing profession and its experts here. I know there are a great number of qualified, caring professionals and healers available. I would not be who I am without some of them. I only am offering a different approach here, one that starts within ourselves and reaches out to receive support from the experts where and when needed, but it always comes back to ourselves as the ultimate authority. I believe that **each** one of us has the capacity to be the main source who knows what supports us in our own and very personal healing journey towards fullness. The alternative is and has been to hand over our own knowing to the experts who have a tendency to only fix certain aspects without necessarily looking at the whole.

Here is my offer: if we believe in the Journey of Selfhealing, or are open to exploring it in an area that is not life threatening, we can invite our selfhealing capacity to bring to us opportunities to heal that which is in need of healing. Once we have said Yes to that next opportunity, and have explored it to its fullest, we are offered the next step. And the next step. Most likely we will not be able to see the whole healing process lined up in front of us. All we get to see is the next step. And only when that step has been completed, can the next opportunity for healing show up.

Here is what these opportunities might look like:

- A deep and intimate conversation with a friend or loved one that allows me to experience feelings I have been holding back for a long time, which results in a deep release of tight areas in my body.
- Someone suggests seeing a massage therapist that is particularly skilled and is able to help open up areas of my body that have been shut down for many, many years.
- A relationship develops, that is not exactly what I had hoped for, but I feel compelled to open up to it. Over time find out that it brings up opportunities for exactly the kind of emotional healing I had asked for.
- I overhear a stranger in the park talking about a particularly gifted healer or doctor. I sense a connection here for me, and approach the stranger to ask about a way to get in touch with that healer or doctor.
- An encounter with a stranger, a friend, a child reminds me of a childhood memory I had completely forgotten, and it opens up a whole new line of insights into the workings of my mind.

The important thing to remember here is that we never know where the Journey of Selfhealing will lead us and what opportunities it will bring to us. All we do know is whether we trust that power or not. Actually, the question here is whether we love ourselves enough to enter into the Journey of Selfhealing.

~~~ *A deep sigh out* ~~~

Soul

Pale sunlight,
Pale the wall.

Love moves away.
The light changes.

I need more grace
Than I thought.

~~ Rumi (Coleman Barks translation) ~~

~~~~~~~~~~

When you do the easy thing,
when you decide to come from,
to be who you really are,—
which is pure love, unlimited, and unconditional—
then your life becomes easy again.
All the turmoil disappears,
all the struggle goes away.
This peace may be achieved any moment
by asking a simple question:
What would love do now?

When you ask that question, you will know instantly what to do.
In any circumstance, under any condition, you will know.
You will be given the answer.
You are the answer and asking that question
brings forth that part of you.

~~ Neale Donald Walsh, Conversations With God ~~

~~~~~~~~~~

Fullness No Matter What

Love can never be sin.
It can only be a blessing.
Even if you are not loved in return—
to love is a proof of life.
Indeed, it is the only proof,
for once you can't love another human being,
you are not alive.

~~ Pearl S. Buck, Mandala ~~

~~~~~~~~~~

Nature abhors dimensional abnormalities, and seals them neatly away so that they don't upset people. Nature, in fact, abhors a lot of things, including vacuums, ships called the "Marie Celeste", and the chuck keys for electric drills.

~~ Terry Pratchett, Pyramids ~~

~~~~~~~~~~

Every beat of your heart
is the rhythm of your soul.
The voice of your soul
is your breath.

~~Quote on a Yogi Tea Bag~~

More

Institute of Heartmath: a Change of Heart Changes Everything—an institute teaching biofeedback techniques based on an open heart.
www.heartmath.org

The Journey to Wild Divine is the first "inner-active" computer adventure that combines ancient yogic breathing and meditation with modern biofeedback technology for total wellness. You can build stairways with your breath, meditate to open doors and juggle balls with your laughter to deepen your mind-body awareness with over 40 events.
http://www.wilddivine.com

2
Community Fullness

Fullness No Matter What

My Fullness Song

Fullness is my sole purpose and inspiration
And from that ample viewpoint
Everything falls into place
Offering a sense of balance
Right on the razor's edge

Now every choice I daily make is measured
Against this grand intention
What furthers fullness passes muster
What hinders fullness is no more

I am held sweetly in that vast endeavor
Surrendering into this state
Not yet quite comfortable with its speed
Like lighting and so full of joy

It's not the one relationship
Or business or my art
Or raising children or a family
Or passionate sex or fame
Or wealth or peacefulness
And yet it's all of it

It's fullness at its most expansive
An all-encompassing reaching
Without a shape or plan or definition

It's both direction and a coming home
It's movement and the center both
It calls me and I have arrived

~~ Ulla! ~~

Body

"It takes a village to raise a child" is an African saying, which to me says that it takes more than just two parents and maybe some grandparents to raise healthy children. I have turned it into my version of "It takes a community to live a life from fullness". Community to me only happens in an atmosphere of peace, that is, in the vulnerable openness to meet one another, in the willingness to listen, and in the safety to be heard. It then becomes the supportive container for creativity to flow into and enrich each one of us and the whole of community around us. Wherever the Ray of Creativity can come forth and be seen publicly, there is community, and wherever there is community, the Ray of Creativity shines for all to see.

Breathing Exercise:
Peace Room and Ray of Community Fullness

This breathing exercise is an invitation to explore our own fullness in our shoulder and throat area, the bridge between the body and the head. Here is where to me community and connection happens in our bodies: community between the various parts inside of ourselves, connection between the thinking head and the processing torso, and connection between the processing torso and the acting arms and hands.

Preparations

This Breathing Exercise is designed to be experienced while you are reading it, preferably out loud to yourself, if you are in a position to do so. If not, at least mouth the words; it will help you slow down and stay focused. If you are with a partner who is open to sharing this exercise, take turns reading it out loud to each other. Make sure you are in a position to relax while you are reading, without falling asleep too quickly.

If you want to intensify this exercise, invite your spirit guides and angels, known or unknown, seen or unseen, to join you in this experience.

The Peace Room

- ❖ I bring my awareness to my upper chest area to where my collar bones, my shoulders, and my neck create the structural connection between my head and my torso in the vertical line, and my torso and my arms on the horizontal line.

- ❖ I place my hands on my chest just below the collarbones in a comfortable position.
- ❖ I am appreciating my collarbones, my shoulders, and my neck for doing such a wonderful job of connecting different parts of my upper body.
- ❖ I bring my breath into the upper parts of my lungs, and open up my collarbones, my shoulder and my neck area.
- ❖ If I feel any discomfort or tightness in my upper chest area, my neck, or my shoulders, I notice it
- ❖ I totally accept the pain or discomfort by directing my very own Loving Color into the tender or tight area. I bring that Loving Color of acceptance into every area of discomfort, one after another, until my upper chest area, my neck, and my shoulders are glowing with acceptance.
- ❖ I feel my upper lungs rise and my shoulders stretch with the inbreath, slowly counting to five, and fall with the outbreath, again slowly counting to five.
- ❖ I continue watching the rise and fall of my upper lungs for about four to six long slow breaths.

~~~~~~

- ❖ I imagine a room inside my upper lung cavity. A very safe, protected, quiet room.
- ❖ This room has the outside dimensions of my upper lung cavity. Its inside dimensions are that of the most comfortable and homey living room you can imagine.
- ❖ I imagine an open circle of the most comfortable chairs, sofas and pillows around the room.
- ❖ I imagine the room furnished with plants, an open fire place or a wood burning stove, a water fountain, side tables, ottomans for feet to be propped up on, anything that makes this room very comfortable and inviting for meetings to happen.
- ❖ I call this the Peace Room—do you see the big sign on the wall or over the fireplace?

Creating Peace Inside of Me

- Creating peace inside of me is a two step process:
  - One, I invite as many parts of myself to come forward and be seen, heard, and sensed.
  - Two, I practice living with all my parts on a day to day basis, acknowledging the existence of my parts, listening to their sometimes divergent voices, and loving and honoring all of them.
- I am now ready to meet as many parts of me as want to come forward and make peace with me and with each other.
- I send out invitations to all these parts to create peace between me and all the parts that are willing.
- Here is partial list of invitees. Feel free to add your own or drop from the list any parts you are not familiar with:
  - Critic
  - Monkey Mind or Chatterbox or Lower Self
  - Higher Self
  - Wuss
  - Scared Child
  - Warrior
  - Monster
  - Soul
  - Complainer
  - Add your own: _____
  - Add your own: _____
  - Add your own: _____
  - Add your own: _____
  - Anyone not named or known, who still wants to come to the Peace Room anonymously and reveal their identity later.
- My intentions for the Peace Room are:
  - Anyone showing up at the Peace Room is both open to be seen and to be heard, and willing to acknowledge and to listen.
  - We are all coming together to create peace inside of me.

- ➢ When peace has been created, my very own Ray of Creative Expression will appear inside my throat and radiate outward.
- ➢ It will shine its brilliant light out into some form of creative expression in my life.
- ❖ I rest in the knowing that the invitation to all the parts willing to create peace within me has been expressed. The results of that invitation will show up in the days to come.
- ❖ I am willing to acknowledge, listen, honor and love all parts of myself in the days to come.
- ❖ I now notice any changes in my body, in my sense of well being, in my breathing.

~~~~~~

- ❖ I once more focus my awareness into my chest cavity.
- ❖ I feel my upper lungs rise and my shoulders stretch with the inbreath, slowly counting to five, and fall with the outbreath, again slowly counting to five.
- ❖ I continue watching the rise and fall of my upper lungs for about four to six long slow breaths.
- ❖ Anytime now I can access my Peace Room and experience its effect on my life in the hours, days, and months to come.

Completion

- ❖ When I am complete, I bring my awareness back to the world outside of me.
- ❖ I wiggle my toes and fingers.
- ❖ I stretch my body like a cat with a few lazy, long, full body stretches.
- ❖ I am back in my waking reality.

Suggestions

This is a start. Now begins the art of actual peace making. Give yourself time, a month, a year, the rest of your life, to watch what happens with your different parts. Most likely you will be able to identify individual parts more easily, and a name might pop up, if naming is what you want to do. Watch your own reactions to different parts coming up. Applying some of the communication techniques described in the **More** section of Chapter 11: Feeling Fullness might help you improve your relationship with yourself.

You might want to re-read this exercise several times to invite more parts to come up and make peace. If you are working with one chapter a month, you may do this exercise daily. Keeping a journal might be a fun way to keep track of your process.

Two things can happen when we allow peace to happen between all the parts inside of us:

- ❖ Our external community might start showing up in new and more connected ways.
- ❖ Our creative expression may start flowing out of us, both as a wholly new experience, and/or on a different and more intense way so that the Ray of Creative Expression is able to come forth and shine outside of us.

If you want to make sure that you experience more Community Fullness in your life, try the Mandala Breathing described at the end of the Breathing Exercise: Color of Loving Fullness.

Pleasure Exercises

Solo: Wave Breath

The Wave Breath can help the body to remember a connection between the head and the pelvis through coordination of breath and movement, thus creating more of a community within our bodies. The Wave Breath is one of the most powerful exercises that can help us integrate seemingly opposite parts of our bodies. When we remember that connection, it will eventually result in very pleasurable involuntary movements of the pelvic musculature. These involuntary movements not only occur in sexual activity, but can also come on in moments of high emotional excitement.

For example, when my wasband Chris had signed the papers to sell his computer company in Berlin for a substantial sum, we went out dancing afterwards at our favorite disco called the "Far Out". It had been a long five years from the start of the company through years of intense uphill struggles, high personal debts, pure hanging in there, to the surprise offer of the purchase. And the sale of the company had actually been completed that day…

We both stood on the dance floor looking into each other's eyes and realizing that it was starting to sink in: the company had actually been sold. All of a sudden my body had a life of it's own. My pelvis started moving back and forth in its own rhythm and its own sense of release, bringing with it tears of joy and waves of pleasure.

The Wave Breath is also known as the "orgasm reflex", coined by Wilhelm Reich in the thirties.

Preparations

- ❖ Lie on a flat surface, either your bed (remove all pillows underneath your head) or the floor
- ❖ Wear comfortable and loose clothing or no clothes

Exercise

- ❖ I am taking a few deep breaths into my belly.
- ❖ I breathe through my open mouth throughout the whole exercise, keeping my jaw relaxed and soft.
- ❖ When I breathe in, I tilt my hips down towards my feet. My back arches up and there is room between my back and the surface I am lying on.
- ❖ When I breathe out, my hips roll back towards my head. My back lies flat on the surface I am lying on.
- ❖ I breathe in and out for ten slow breaths, just gently rocking my hips back and forth.
- ❖ Once I have my breath and my hips coordinated, I add the movement of the neck.
- ❖ My head and neck moves down towards my chest, when I breathe in and tilt my pelvis towards my feet while my back arches up.

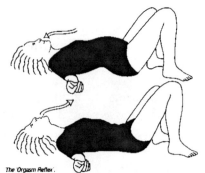

The 'Orgasm Reflex'.

- My head and neck moves down back, when I breathe out and tilt my pelvis towards my head, while my back flattens out.
- I breathe in and out for about ten slow breaths, moving both my head and my pelvis.

If you want a more intense experience, make sounds, especially an open mouthed one like a low "aowwww" sound. If doing this exercise feels uncomfortable, just know that you are doing the right thing…You might feel the urge to cry or scream or feel very frustrated. Just keep breathing through it. The emotions will move.

Suggestions

Do 20 breaths every evening just before you go to sleep, and 20 more every morning right after you wake up. It will relax your neck. It will help you move some feelings that are stuck. And it might eventually lead to the involuntary body contractions bringing about more release of emotions. Please do not underestimate the apparent simplicity of this exercise. It is a powerful tool to bring more feelings, and more pleasure into your body.

Partnered: Toning on Your Partner's Body

Vibration can be **very** pleasurable and is a way to connect various parts of our bodies. The idea here is to use both your voice and your lips together as tools to bring vibrational pleasure to different parts of your partner's body.

Preparations

- As the receiver, make yourself comfortable with the help of pillows.
- Both giver and receiver: close your eyes and connect with yourself.
- **Giver**: find your love for yourself and your partner inside of you.
- **Receiver**: sense how much pleasure you are willing to receive, to let in.
- This exercise feels best on a naked body.
- Have a silk scarf or a soft piece of animal fur handy!

Exercise

- As the **giver**, start by pursing your lips.
- Make low sounds that get your lips vibrating.

Fullness No Matter What

- ❖ Place your vibrating lips on your partner's body.
- ❖ It is a lot of fun to start on top of your partner's head and work your way down through all these body parts:
  - ➢ Forehead
  - ➢ Throat
  - ➢ Heart
  - ➢ Stomach
  - ➢ Lower ends of the rib cage
  - ➢ Belly
  - ➢ Palms of both hands
  - ➢ Hip bones
  - ➢ Pubic bone
  - ➢ Lingam or Pearl or Yoni
  - ➢ Perineum (between Lingam/Yoni and Rosebud)
  - ➢ Bottom of the feet
  - ➢ And the whole back, especially the lower back
- ❖ Play with these different effects:
  - ➢ High sounds
  - ➢ Low sounds
  - ➢ Loud sounds
  - ➢ Soft sounds
  - ➢ Pursed lips
  - ➢ Tightly stretched out lips
  - ➢ Open mouth
  - ➢ Wet lips
  - ➢ Dry lips

Suggestions

After you have toned on your partner's body, you might want to take the silk scarf or the animal fur (or both!) and softly and very slowly start stroking your partner's skin. **Giver**, enjoy your partner's reactions! **Receiver**, you might want to keep your eyes closed to be able to just focus on your sensations. After a while, switch roles and have the giver be the receiver.

Mind

Finding Community within Us

I found out the hard way that community starts within me. All my adult life I have wanted to live in community with like minded others. I especially wanted to raise my two children Felix and Emily in a communal context. It made so much more sense to me than the two-parent-nuclear-family that is the norm these days.

My ideal was a small village of like-minded and like-hearted people raising children together, pooling their resources, and sharing their lives. I wanted to be able to walk over to a neighbor, knock on their door, although I knew it would always be open, and have some tea and simply chat. I wanted to be able to connect face to face instead of picking up the phone and having long conversations on the phone, or making an appointment to see each other in a week or so. I wanted that very tangible, very physical, very direct connection.

I tried twice to make this kind of intentional community happen, but for various reasons it did not come together. So I had to find community within myself. I realized (with some help from friends and my Spirit Guides) that I needed to first create community within me, so **need** was not the driving force underneath my desire to live in community.

What did finding community inside myself mean? Over the years I got to know several members of my internal community or family better. I actually got to know them so well that a few of them acquired their own names. Let me introduce you to the ones I have identified so far:

- ❖ Laaala, my Body (**she** wanted the four "A"s in her name!)
- ❖ Frieda, my Monkey Mind (or the earthbound Lower Self)
- ❖ Betty, my Worry Mind, especially active when I am trying to fall sleep (named after the beta brain frequencies that she loves to spike up!)
- ❖ THE Critic

- ❖ Raminani, my Higher Self
- ❖ And my Soul

I have learned that giving these parts names helps to identify them as separate identities. For example, I do no have to take the chattering of Frieda, my Monkey Mind, personal and it helps to quiet her down, if I say to myself: "Oh, here goes Frieda again, worrying about money. Haven't we been there before?" Once I realize that worrying is Frieda's job, I usually can move on to more constructive activities.

Raminani was a name I had come up with, when I was 15 or 16 years old, and wanted to convert to the Hindu religion. After I had been told that that was not possible, the name stuck. I used to write letters to Raminani in difficult times in my journal. I later realized that Raminani was the name of my higher self and am now using it to communicate with that part of myself.

I am not sharing my Soul name here, as to me soul names are very private and not to be shared in public. But my relationship to my soul is deep and direct and full of joy and awe.

Naming the different parts within myself also helped to accept them. When I discovered therapy in my thirties, I went for it. I was hoping that if I could just get myself fixed, get rid of all these unwanted, wounded, dysfunctional, shameful parts within me, then, and only then, would I finally feel lovable. So I tried out every form of therapeutic fix-it approach I could lay my psyche bare to. I have to say I learned a lot about all my childhood wounding, I got to know myself and my dysfunctions very well, but I did not become more loveable in the eyes of others or myself.

As fixing them did not work, I began to create relationships with these dysfunctional and disowned parts of myself. I learned to accept them as a part of me, not to be tossed out into the garbage, but to be indulged in like a family member that is not your favorite aunt, but she is still family. That did help to create more peace within me. Acceptance instead of fixing was the key here.

The more I was able to accept all my diverse parts, the more they actually turned out to be assets. Especially in writing this book and watching the information pouring forth, I can see that all these so-called dysfunctional parts of me were absolutely necessary. They provided particular viewpoints into this life of fullness that I would otherwise not have had at my disposal. There is a cooperation happening here, that I would have never dreamed possible. Here are some examples:

- ❖ Frieda is the organizer here. Her "personality" needs order and structure. She is very good at keeping track of all the chapters and the overall structure of the book. For example, she makes sure that I save regularly on my computer while writing, and make back-up copies of my text files etc.
- ❖ Laaala, my body, lets me know exactly, what it is she needs to support all of us in the creative process of writing this book. "We" have had a craving for fresh coconuts as a treat, and "we" have gotten into juicing fresh vegetables to keep the energy up. Laaala also lets me know when it is time for a break, to do some stretching, yoga, or go for a walk. As a result I have so much energy available for this book that it is a joy to sit down and write every day for hours.
- ❖ Someone also makes sure that I always have the right information available to write the next part. All of a sudden I hear someone mention a book. I get it and in reading it find out that I needed to add that particular aspect into the structure of this book.
- ❖ Whenever I feel stuck in the writing process, or am not sure about a word or concept to use, I just close my eyes and listen. Someone, I often don't even know who, provides the perfect answer, and the next round pours out of me.

I now see all members of my internal family as a team working together, actually singing as one song through many different voices. I would not want to miss one single member, one single experience that has brought me to this place. All of us together now form a brilliant ray of light bringing forth its very own illumination for all to see like the beacon of a lighthouse on the edge between ocean and shore.

~~~ A deep belly breath in ~~~

Soul

Blessings on Your Journey Home

Today and forever more,
As you move farther along life's path,
May the dreams of your immortal soul
Find within your creative imagination
The energy required to manifest
The reality you so earnestly desire!
Here's to wishing that you find
Within contemporary society
A place to stop and rest a bit
To marvel at this merciful world
As you watch it go by
Knowing that all things eventually return
To the place where friends are welcome.
Until that time, good luck on your journey!

~~ Jim Santsaver ~~

~~~~~~~~

He moved in a way that suggested he was attempting the world speed record for the nonchalant walk.

~~ Terry Pratchett, The Light Fantastic ~~

~~~~~~~~

A COMMUNITY OF THE SPIRIT

There is a community of the spirit.
Join it, and feel the delight
of walking in the noisy street,
and being the noise.

Drink all your passion,
and be a disgrace.

Community Fullness

Close both eyes
to see with the other eye.

Open your hands
if you want to be held.

Sit down in this circle.

Quit acting like a wolf, and feel
the shepherd's love filling you.

At night, your beloved wanders.
Don't accept consolations.

Close your mouth against food.
Taste the lover's mouth in yours.

You moan, "She left me." "He left me."
Twenty more will come.

Be empty of worrying.
Think of who created thought.

Why do you stay in prison
when the door is so wide open.

Move outside the tangle of fear-thinking.
Live in silence.

Flow down and down in always
widening rings of being.

~~ Rumi (Coleman Barks translation) ~~

Fullness No Matter What

More

Review: The Music and Lyrics of Tori Amos

Here is a fullness of creativity that has been delighting me for many years. Tori Amos was raised as a minister's daughter with an education in classical piano music. At some point she seems to have exploded out of that structured environment into freeflow creativity, both in the lyrics and the melodies of "her girls", as she calls her songs. Tori Amos can pack several melodies into just one of her songs that would have made several separate beautiful songs in the hands of a less creative musician.

Her lyrics always surprise me in both their direct sensuousness and creative use of imagery. For example:

> Girls you've got to know
> When it's time to turn the page
> When you're only wet
> Because of the rain

~~ Northern Lad on "From the Choir Girl Hotel" ~~

~~~~~~~~~~

> I got lost on my wedding day typical the police came
> But virgins always get backstage no matter what they got to say

~~ Jackie's Strength on "From the Choir Girl Hotel" ~~

~~~~~~~~~~

> Muhammed my friend
> It's time to tell the world
> We both know it was a girl back in Bethlehem
> And on that fateful day
> When she was crucified
> She wore Shiseido Red and we drank tea
> By her side

~~ Muhammed My Friend 0n "Boys for Pele" ~~

~~~~~~~~~~

> You caught me lingering in another girl's paradise
> The way she paints the world—I want that in my life
> Emeralds, you should know, are renting in her meadows
> With a stroke beauty lives how could I resist
>
> ~~ Another Girl's Paradise on "Scarlet's Walk" ~~

In her always sold out concerts I have found her courageous enough to let her music stand on its own without a big show of overhead screens, a large band of musicians and dancers, and lighting and smoke effects. When I saw her a few years ago, it was just her, the piano, and a bass player. At the same time I felt entranced watching her sing and play her piano as she seemed in total ecstasy while performing her songs.

The occasional introductions to her songs have a dry sense of humor that is worth while listening to on some of the recordings of her live performances. I just love a woman who can play the piano like a goddess, sing songs to me that continuously stretch my imagination, and make me laugh at the same time. Yum!

http://www.toriamos.com

Herb Leonhard. *Tori Amos: Lyrics.*

And her own book coming out in February 2005:
Tori Amos & Ann Powers. *Tori Amos: Piece by Piece.*

3

Inspirational Fullness

What If

What if I could live from moment to moment
As if every moment is new right here in front of me
As if it never happened, never touched me
And never was experienced by me before

What if new eyes were my companion every single time
Like the eyes of my newborn children when they came to me
Fresh and precious as presents given to me
Under very special circumstances

What if that newness brings with it a remembering so deep
That yesterday and today vanish and it all blends
Into one great flow of experiences for the sake of experiencing
No rhyme, no reason necessary for that form of living

What if I decided to live like that
From now on and for every day now
Letting life take me from one moment
To another moment without past
And without judgements, right or wrong,
Of good or bad or else
All that is left is letting my life bring to me
That which I came here for
And then just go for it

~~ Ulla! ~~

Body

To live a life full of inspiration, or even to be an inspiration for others—what a gift, what a joy, what a blessing. Isn't that something worth living for? What do I mean by inspiration? The word inspiration comes from the Latin words "in" and "spirare", meaning to "breathe in", bring breath, that is, life into everything we do.

Breathing Exercise: Vessel of Inspirational Fullness

This exercise is an invitation to explore fullness in our third eye, the area of our forehead and the space behind the eyes. The third eye has traditionally been associated with mental clarity and the seeing of visions. For me it is the place I can instantly find peace and stillness when I bring my awareness there. A lover putting his hand on my forehead can bring ease and relaxation into a moment of stress, worrying, or being lost in thought and I come right back to the here and now.

Preparations

Have a pen and paper handy.

This Breathing Exercise is designed to be experienced while you are reading it, preferably out loud to yourself, if you are in a position to do so. If not, at least mouth the words; it will help you slow down and stay focused. If you are with a partner who is open to sharing this exercise, take turns reading it out loud to each other. Make sure you are in a position to relax while you are reading, without falling asleep too quickly.

If you want to intensify this exercise, invite your spirit guides and angels, known or unknown, seen or unseen, to join you in this experience.

Exercise

- ❖ I bring my awareness to my forehead above my eyes and below my hairline.
- ❖ I place my hands on or close to my forehead, as long as I feel relaxed in that position.

- ❖ I appreciate my forehead, just for being there as part of this wonderful creation called the human body.
- ❖ I focus my breath into my forehead, that is I imagine my breath reaching all the way into my forehead by breathing into the upper wings of my lungs and extending that breath through the middle of my head into my forehead.
- ❖ If I feel any discomfort or tightness in my upper chest area, my head, or my forehead, I notice it, and then totally accept it by directing my very own Loving Color into the tender or tight area. I bring that Loving Color of acceptance into every area of discomfort, one after another, until my upper chest area, my head, and my forehead are glowing with acceptance.
- ❖ I feel my upper lungs rise and my shoulders stretch with the inbreath, slowly counting to five, and fall with the outbreath, again slowly counting to five.
- ❖ I continue watching the rise and fall of my upper lungs for about four to six long slow breaths.

~~~~~~

- ❖ I focus my awareness into my forehead.
- ❖ I imagine a space behind the bones of my forehead reaching all the way to the top of my skull and the back of skull.
- ❖ This space has the outside dimensions of my brain cavity.
- ❖ Its inside dimensions are that of an imaginary Sacred Space.
- ❖ That Sacred Space could be:
  - ➢ A circular Greek temple with slender columns on a softly rounded hill,
  - ➢ A church full of stained glass windows brightly lit it up by the sun streaming through,
  - ➢ A gazebo with wooden posts full of blossoming jasmine vines in the midst of a park,
  - ➢ A rose bower in its fullest bloom of fragrant roses in the midst of a rose garden,
  - ➢ An open grotto overlooking the waves on a beach far below,
  - ➢ Deep inside the burial chamber of an ancient pyramid,

- ❖ Any Sacred Space I want to create that invites me to spend some time there.
- ❖ I now imagine a precious vessel made of gold, silver, crystal, blown glass, or wood in the center of the Sacred Space resting on some form of elevated platform.
- ❖ I imagine myself standing in front of the vessel which is at my chest level.
- ❖ My bare feet are resting on the floor. I am sensing the warm wood, or the cold rock, or the grainy sand of the floor.
- ❖ I lay both of my hands on the sides of the vessel and sense its texture of cool metal, or cold crystal, or warm wood.
- ❖ I now focus my eyes into the vessel. In it I see a clear liquid which half fills the vessel.
- ❖ Into the clear liquid I direct the following question three times out loud: "What inspires me to be all I came here to be in this, my current life?"
- ❖ I focus my eyes out beyond the vessel into the surroundings of ocean, or forest, or church, or temple, or a park full of large ancient trees, or vistas as from beyond a high mountain. I take in my surroundings.
- ❖ I then bring my eyes back to the vessel and its liquid inside.
- ❖ All of a sudden a ray of light from the setting sun, the rising sun, the full moon, or a magical source hits the liquid and lights it up:
  - ➢ I see a symbol.
  - ➢ I hear a word or a melody.
  - ➢ I feel a feeling.
  - ➢ I sense a response in my body.
  - ➢ I receive a message.
- ❖ I see myself sitting down in front of the vessel on the steps of the Sacred Space, or in its opening, enjoying the beautiful surroundings and resting in the knowing of a gift received.
- ❖ I thank the Vessel of Inspiration for this precious gift to me.
- ❖ I notice any changes in my body, in my sense of well being, in my breathing.

~~~~~~

- ❖ I once more focus my awareness into my upper lungs area.

- ❖ I breathe into my upper lung area, slowly counting to five on the inbreath, and again slowly counting to five on the outbreath.
- ❖ I sense the inbreath slowly raising up my upper lung area.
- ❖ I sense the outbreath slowly letting my upper lung area come down.
- ❖ I continue watching the raising of my upper lung area on the inbreath, and the falling of my upper lungs area on the outbreath for about four to six long slow breaths.
- ❖ Anytime now I can access my Vessel of Inspirational Fullness and experience its effect on my life in the hours, days, and months to come.

Completion

- ❖ When I am complete, I bring my awareness back to the world outside of me.
- ❖ I wiggle my toes and fingers.
- ❖ I stretch my body like a cat with a few lazy, long, full body stretches.
- ❖ I am back in my waking reality.
- ❖ I take a piece of paper and sketch the symbol, write down the word, find a way to transcribe the melody, describe the feeling or the response in my body.

Suggestions

Give yourself time, a month, a year, the rest of your life, to watch how and when and in what form inspiration is revealing itself in your life. You might want to reread this exercise a couple more times, if you don't sense a clear result, or want more pieces of the puzzle. The important part is to know you have taken the next step and it will show you the way into a different future. If you are feeling impatient and frustrated, be with the frustration and the impatience. Just accept yourself as feeling frustrated and being impatient. Just accept it for that moment. And the door will open into your next step.

If you want to make sure that you experience more Inspirational Fullness in your life, try the Mandala Breathing described at the end of the Breathing Exercise: Color of Loving Fullness.

Pleasure Exercises

Solo: Cobra Breath for One

Sexual energy in our western Culture is usually expressed genitally, downward, and outward. That is especially true for men, as it is more obvious through the ejaculation in orgasm. But most sexual orgasms for women, especially the clitoral ones have that same genital, downward, and outward flow of energy, just not quite as obvious.

There is another way to do this. Sexual energy can start in the Jewels, and flow inward and upward. This results in the separation of ejaculation from orgasm. Yes, men **can** experience orgasms without ejaculation! Those non-ejaculatory orgasms are usually not quite as sharp, defined, or intense as the ejaculatory ones. But they move like waves through your whole body and are immensely pleasurable (I have been told and also observed!). An important aspect of those non-ejaculatory orgasms is that men do not loose their energy after one or two or three or four or more orgasmic releases.

For women a whole new range of orgasmic experiences can open up when we discover these softer wavelike orgasms. We can keep coming and coming and coming in all kinds of intensities, feelings, sizes—you name it—you can have it!

These kinds of non-ejaculatory or wavelike orgasm can become gateways into more inspiration in our lives as they lead us into altered states of awareness. These altered states are one way to easily access various aspects of inspiration.

Anyway, the Cobra Breath is one way how to train your body to move sexual energy inward and upward instead of downward and outward. This exercise will give you an idea as to how it works. If you really want to pursue this technique in depth, look under the **More** Section of this chapter for specific information.

Preparations

The effects of the Cobra Breath can only be experienced in an upright upper body position. That means you need to find a way to comfortably sit or kneel while still being able to touch your Jewels. Pillows under your buttock (if you are sitting) or between your legs (if you are kneeling) help a lot. You might need to experiment a bit to find the most comfortable upright position for yourself.

Exercise

- Start getting aroused genitally in whatever way you are familiar and comfortable with while in an upright position.
- Use deep belly breathing with an open mouth to send as much turn on energy into your Jewels. Make moaning open mouthed sounds to increase intensity.
- Stop touching yourself just before you get to your "point of no return".
- Squeeze your PC muscles hard and hold them (the PC muscles are those that allow you to stop your flow of urine). This creates a genital energy lock.
- Press your chin down towards your chest, hold your breath, and lock your throat muscles. This creates a throat energy lock.
- Close your eyes and look up towards a point behind your forehead, called your Third Eye.
- Press your tongue against the roof of your mouth.
- Keep holding your breath, squeezing your PC muscles, pressing your chin down, looking up towards your Third Eye, pressing your tongue against the roof of your mouth, until you run out of breath.
- Relax the rest of your body while you are doing all the above…
- Then take one more quick sip of breath in.
- While you breathe out through your teeth with your mouth in a smile:
  - Relax the PC muscles and release the genital lock,
  - Move your chin up and release the throat lock,
  - Keep your eye focused upwards, and
  - Keep your tongue pressed against the roof of your mouth.
- Notice any effects. If your sexual energy is able to move upwards through you body, one of the effects you might experience is a sensation of exploding light in your Third Eye. Bingo!

Suggestions

By the way, if you are serious about meditating to quieting your mind, this is a great way to speed up your process. Studies have shown that two to three years of regular Cobra Breath practice have the same effect of quieting the mind and inducing altered states of consciousness as Buddhist monks are able to achieve after 20 plus years of non-sexual meditation.

This exercise can also be done with a partner. You need to find an upright position that works for both of you, like having him sit on the edge of the bed and her sitting on his lap (if you are both not very flexible). Or him in full lotus position with her in his lap (if you are really flexible). Or anything in between.

Build up as much sexual energy as possible through sexual union, but avoid having any orgasm. Then follow the steps outlined above, starting with the "genital energy lock". You can build energy and do the cobra breath several times, before you do decide to orgasm. Look for double special effects!

Partnered: Inspirational Lovemaking for Two

Inspirational lovemaking to me is when I cannot wait to be in my lover's arms. When I spill over with juicy sexy ideas to try out. When it does not matter how late at night or early in the morning it is, because I want to make love, no matter what. All of this is typically the case when the relationship is new. When we have been lovers with our partner for a while, inspirational lovemaking sometimes is hard to find. Here are a few suggestions how to bring back inspiration into the bedroom:

- ❖ **Go to Bed Early or make Love in the Morning or in the Afternoon**
  This one is crucial. Making love when we feel tired after a long day is not the easiest thing to do, especially when you have been lovers for a while. I have found that my pleasure life needs just as much planning and time as the rest of my life in these busy times we are living in.
- ❖ **Physical Exercise before Lovemaking**
  This one really helps. Go for a walk, or go to the gym to move your body, and feel invigorated. But don't push yourself too hard into exhaustion, as that is not a good basis for lovemaking either. Or just lay next to each other and breathe deeply and rapidly while looking into each other's eyes. Or put on some fast dance music and dance your pretty buns off till you feel out of breath!
- ❖ **Spend Some Time Away from Home**
  Go away for a night or two to a bed and breakfast, or a small hotel, or camping. Make lazy time for just the two of you. Pleasure and time are very friendly with each other. They each get better through the other…

- ❖ **No TV in the Bedroom**
  This is a must to me (and I do not have many "Musts" in my life). Television has the propensity to be a pleasure killer for various reasons in case you had not noticed it. Don't get me started…
- ❖ **Make a Date and Prepare for it**
  Inspirational lovemaking starts in the mind. Decide in the morning to go to bed early that night to have ample time to make love. Then tease each other all day to build excitement and turn-on. Call her up at work and ask her what she is wearing underneath her clothes. Tell her that you are feeling hard for her already and that you are touching yourself. Call him on his cell phone and leave a message reminding him in your sexiest voice of his very important date that night. Tell him that you can't wait to run your hands all over his body. Appreciate each other, and say how much you are looking forward to this special date.
- ❖ **Try any of the Partnered Pleasure Exercises in this Book**
  Any of the Partnered Pleasure Exercises will provide entry points into your lovemaking that are probably not part of your usual sex routine. Try something new, different, or unusual. Go for something other than what you are used to.

The important part to remember here is to have fun while making love. For so many of us lovemaking turns into something deadly serious, and no wonder something dies on the way…

Mind

Inspiration at its Best

Let me take you on a journey into one kind of magical inspiration. Imagine a four year old boy growing up on a large farm. There are lots of different animals, large meadows, a brook feeding a pond and running through the lands. There are large trees to climb on, other children of different ages growing up with him, and a number of adults around in different states of busyness.

Imagine you are his grandfather or grandmother and have time and patience on your hands to watch him, to let him show you his world, to be available. All day he comes running to you, and either brings you something he has discovered, like a blue bug with yellow feelers that is crawling on is skin, or a black rock that sparkles. Or he drags you off your comfortable bench in the shade of an old oak tree to show you the new baby piglets, or the geese that landed on the pond on their way north, or the new tractor plowing the fields. Or he snuggles up to you, and tells you about the big tree he tried climbing and nearly fell out of, or the hole in his socks from running without shoes, or the ripe raspberries he picked and brought to you all smooshed up in his hands.

To me this is inspiration at its best. Most four year olds have just enough vocabulary to tell you what they are seeing, experiencing, hearing, discovering in simple terms. But they are still in the thrall of seeing this world, their world, with fresh eyes. Everything is worth being explored, looked at, smelled, or tasted. The whole world is there to be discovered, no matter how small and ordinary. Everything is glorious.

Some of us are blessed and never loose that four year old way of relating to the world around us. Some of us are gifted with it after many years of painful absence and get to feel like a four years old at the age of 48.

~~~ *A deep sigh out* ~~~

To Be of Service

I believe we cannot force or demand inspiration into our lives, but we can invite it. We can even make the invitation so irresistible, that inspiration cannot help but follow that invitation and grace us with its radiant presence. One way to make this irresistible offer to the Muse of Inspiration is to become actively involved in a venture that is service oriented. By service oriented I mean an individual or a group of people coming together, whether highly structured or loosely gathered, in order to help those that need more help than we do. The important aspect I see here is to offer our help without getting paid to do so. There is absolutely nothing wrong with getting paid to do "good work", but I am offering a different quality here.

When we offer our skills, time, money, and/or energy out of our free choice to a cause that helps those that need it more than we do, there is another kind of exchange going on. One could argue that we actually are the ones benefiting most from that exchange in the following ways:

One, it often means that we are stepping outside our comfort zone, outside the usual group of people that we associate with. That in itself is often a healthy thing to do as that edge outside our comfort zone gets sharpened and we often feel more alive on that edge. Comfort is a tricky thing. It can easily move into complacency, or even narrow mindedness with an underlying boredom, that takes the spunk out of us.

Two, by experiencing first hand the challenges and misfortunes of others we often are able to appreciate our own situation much more. We get to find out how well we are actually doing compared to those less fortunate. It offers a balancing of our ego structures which very convincingly like to make us think that all that matters is only our very own personal welfare. Thus it can bring back inspiration into our lives for all the reasons mentioned.

~~~ *A deep belly breath in* ~~~

Soul

Life is a joy in all its experiences.
For there is nothing that comes your way
That you did not need.
There is nothing that comes your way
That you do not have a part of.

~~ Dr. Peebles ~~

~~~~~~~~~~

Birdsong brings relief
to my longing.

I am just as ecstatic as they are,
but with nothing to say!

Please, universal soul, practice
some song, or something through me.

~~ Rumi (Coleman Barks translation) ~~

~~~~~~~~~~

Inspirational Fullness

When it's all over, I want to say all my life
I was a bride married to amazement.

~~ Mary Oliver ~~

~~~~~~~~~~

He felt instinctive that if you were going to fondle a cat while discussing matters of intrigue, then it should be a long haired white one. It should not be an elderly street tom with irregular bouts of flatulence.

~~ Terry Pratchett, Night Watch ~~

More

More information on the practice of the Cobra Breath:

Sunyata Saraswati & Bodhi Avinasha. *Jewel In The Lotus: The Tantric Path To Higher Consciousness. Complete and Systematic Course in the Science of Tantric Kriya Yoga.*

Bodhi Avinasha. *The Ipsalu Formula: A Method for Tantra Bliss.* http://www.ipsalutantra.com

Book Review: Ellis Peters: The Brother Cadfael Series

Mary Pargeter, the author of 50plus novels, lived from 1914 till 1995 in England. She wrote 30 plus mystery novels under her penname Ellis Peters about Brother Cadfael, a Benedictine monk in England in the 12th century during the civil war between the two royal cousins, Empress Maud and King Steven, both contenders for the royal throne. She wrote these mystery novels in the tradition of a good "whodunit" though situated at a time before carriages, mail service, and before the inquisition.

The author has managed to evoke a microcosm in which life has a deeply satisfying internal order. There are murders, there are laws, there are heroes and villains, there is a world of both good and evil, but they are all balanced out into a deeply coherent and functional world. A "bad" deed, for example a cold blooded murder, gets revenged not by an act of law by the sheriff or the king, but by the murderer's own behavior. In "One Corpse Too Many" the murderer Adam Corsell dies in a "combat till death" with his opponent Hue Berringard by falling onto his own poignard, and not by his opponent's hand.

To me it is a very good example of a deeply spiritual world that is not pollyannaish, not just full of cheap happy endings. Ellis Peter's world and stories are full of challenges, depicting the whole range of human behavior from exemplary to despicable. But these challenges are being resolved in a very satisfactory way with all behaviors and acts balancing out at the end. You come away feeling full and rich, ready to trust the inherent goodness in life once again.

The interesting thing is that she manages to portray this balanced world in the midst of a world torn apart by civil war, where morals and laws are slowly but surely eroding into an inherently unstable political situation. She describes the ability to hold fast to integrity, love, and balanced out actions in the midst of a world falling apart. What wonderfully rich and satisfying morality plays, worth reading or listening to in depth to help us remember that kind of moral capacity at its best during our own challenging times.

I highly recommend reading these stories out loud to lovers, friends and family, or to listen to the books on tape. I especially recommend the narrator Patrick Tull on the Recorded Books series, as his voice has a deeply satisfying timbre, plus his reading has a wonderfully slow pace that lets you literally sink into the less hectic pace of these 12th century tales.

Here is a website providing a list to all of Ellis Peter's books in the Brother Cadfael series: http://user.chollian.net/~beringar/e-cad.htm

Recorded Books, LLC. http://www.recordedbooks.com

4
Gratitude Fullness

Fullness No Matter What

When I Say Thank You

When I whisper thank you
A door opens up
A soft breeze blows through me
And there is freshness
All inside me

When I sing thank you
The birds answer my call
The flowers brighten my day
And the grass caresses my bare feet
All around me

When I shout thank you
The heavens open up up and away
The earth holds me firmer
All above and below me

When I say thank you
To myself
And mean it
Then I am here
And all is well
Yes all is well inside of me

~~ Ulla! ~~

Body

Something so simple and yet so rich—living in gratitude for everything we have, for what we are receiving, and even for what we don't have. It is a daily practice that eventually proves the saying: "What comes around goes around."

Breathing Exercise: Fountain of Gratitude Fullness

Preparations

Specific instructions for this particular exercise:
For maximum effect, this particular breathing exercise is best done sitting up in a very relaxed position with your back leaning against something comfortable.

This Breathing Exercise is designed to be experienced while you are reading it, preferably out loud to yourself, if you are in a position to do so. If not, at least mouth the words; it will help you slow down and stay focused. If you are with a partner who is open to sharing this exercise, take turns reading it out loud to each other. Make sure you are in a position to relax while you are reading, without falling asleep too quickly.

If you want to intensify this exercise, invite your spirit guides and angels, known or unknown, seen or unseen, to join you in this experience.

Exercise

- ❖ I bring my awareness to the very top of my head, where my hair (or my skin) meets the air around me.
- ❖ I wiggle my forehead to make the very top of my head move (if I can) to fully anchor my awareness just barely inside my body.
- ❖ I focus my inbreath into the top of my head, that is I feel my upper lungs rise with the inbreath, and I imagine that I can gently push my breath all the way through my neck, through my head, and into the top of my head.
- ❖ This breath is like a wave on the ocean being watched from a boat looking onto a sandy shore. I watch the wave building up to a crest, breaking, and rolling down the beach all the way into the top of my head, slowly counting to five.

- I watch my outbreath recede like a wave from the beach. It recedes from the top of my head through my head, through my neck, and I watch my upper lungs fall with the outbreath, slowly counting to five.
- I continue watching the flow of the waves, my inbreath, and my outbreath for about four to six long slow breaths.

~~~~~~~

- I find something I am grateful for in my life. It can be something ordinary, everyday, normal, like: "Thank you, car, for transporting me safely to and from work every day." Or it can be something new and exciting like: "I am feeling so grateful for the new love that has come into my life."
- I really feel that gratitude.
- Get into the joy and delight and richness of being grateful.
- I imagine an opening on the very top of my head.
- I now sense that gratitude rising to the top of my head and shooting up and out into the space above my head in the shape of a blossom with six petals (see the art image at the beginning of the Gratitude chapter.).
- I now have my very own Fountain of Gratitude.
- The gratitude shooting up has its very own special texture.
- It feels like soft liquid light glittering in the sun. It is especially shimmering in moonlight.
- Its color is opalescent, that is it has the color of rich opals that have imbedded speck of all colors.
- When the Fountain of Gratitude looses its momentum above my head, it cascades back down around my head onto my shoulders and runs all the way down my body.
- I can feel the liquid light running smoothly and gently down my whole body like a blessing, like a caress, like a shower of delights.
- Every time I express, think, or feel gratitude in my life, it activates the Fountain of Gratitude, and I know myself blessed.
- I simply rest in that sense of grateful blessing.
- This sense of feeling blessed is always available to me. All I need to do is express, think, or feel gratitude for something in my life. And I can always find something to be grateful for. Thank you for that.
- I notice any changes in my body, in my sense of well being, in my breathing.

~~~~~~

- I once again focus my inbreath into the top of my head, that is I feel my upper lungs rise with the inbreath, and I imagine that I can gently push my breath all the way through my neck, through my head, and into the top of my head.
- This breath is like a wave on the ocean being watched from a boat looking onto a sandy shore. I watch the wave building up to a crest, breaking, and rolling down the beach all the way into the top of my head, slowly counting to five.
- I watch my outbreath recede like a wave from the beach. It recedes from the top of my head through my head, through my neck, and I watch my upper lungs fall with the outbreath, slowly counting to five.
- I continue watching the flow of the waves, my inbreath, and my outbreath for about four to six long slow breaths.
- Anytime now I can access my Fountain of Gratitude and experience its effect on my life in the hours, days, and months to come.

Completion

- When I am complete, I bring my awareness back to the world outside of me.
- I wiggle my toes and fingers.
- I stretch my body like a cat with a few lazy, long, full body stretches.
- I am back in my waking reality.

Suggestions

You now have your very own Fountain of Gratitude always available to you. As with so many imaginative exercises, the more you practice them, the better they work for you. Anytime you feel low on energy or unappreciated, invisible, or rejected, just activate your own Fountain of Gratitude, and know yourself blessed, accepted, appreciated, and welcomed—by yourself. So be it!

If you want to make sure that you experience more Gratitude Fullness in your life, try the Mandala Breathing described at the end of the Breathing Exercise: Color of Loving Fullness.

Pleasure Exercises

Solo: Touching My Own Body with Gratitude

This is a beautiful exercise to reconnect to all (or most) parts of our bodies and find a way to be grateful for them, no matter what shape, size, health, or age they are.

The idea here is to be comfortable, undisturbed, and by yourself in order to communicate with yourself through touch, words, and feelings how grateful you are for this wonderful perfect body. If you are visually oriented, you might want to have a mirror in front of you to look at yourself. If you are more kinesthetically oriented, use your hands. You might want to light some candles or use soft lighting. Easy and relaxing music in the background can help to set a gentle and sweet mood.

If expressing gratitude towards your own body is a difficult task for you, it might need some easing into. My suggestion is to start with the one part of your body that you definitely know you love. This could be your intensely blue eyes, your long slender hands, your thick Lingam, your soft breasts, your impish nose, your big toe, or any other part. It does not matter what part, as long as you can find that loving, accepting, soft, sweet feeling.

Once you have found that feeling or sense of gratitude, use it as a blue print for the rest of your body. The idea is to move through your whole body, part after part, from head to toes, or from toes to head, and as many parts in between as you care to gratefully address. Here is are a couple examples of what you might say out loud to yourself, or think about to yourself while you are lovingly caressing that particular body part:

"Hello thighs. I am so grateful that you are part of my body. I appreciate your strength and sturdiness, as you carry me so well on my morning hikes. I thank you for being part of me."

"Hey yummy little breasts! You rock me!"

Go through your whole body like this. Once you feel complete, just close your eyes and sense into your body. Notice the difference.

Partnered:
Touching Your Partner's Body with Gratitude

This is a beautiful exercise to express to your partner how grateful we are for your partner's body, no matter what shape, size, health, or age it is.

The idea here is to have some time set aside in order to tell your partner through touch, words, and feelings how grateful you are for your partner's wonderful and perfect body. Take turns doing this exercise. One of you expresses gratitude, one of you just receives. You might want to light some candles or use soft lighting. Easy and relaxing music in the background can help to set a gentle and sweet mood.

If expressing gratitude towards your partner's body is a difficult task for you, it might need some easing into. My suggestion is to start by identifying the one part of your partner's body that you know you love. This could be her intensely blue eyes, his long slender hands, his thick Lingam, her soft breasts, her impish nose, his big toe, or any other part. It does not matter what part, as long as you can find that loving, accepting, soft, sweet feeling.

Once you have found that feeling or sense of gratitude, use it as a blue print for the rest of your partner's body. The idea is to move through your partner's whole body, part after part, from head to toes, or from toes to head, and as many parts in between as you care to gratefully address. Here is an example of what you might say out loud to your partner while you are lovingly caressing that particular body part:

"Hello belly. I am so grateful that you are part of…'s body. I love your soft round fullness. I love the feel of that softness under my hands. I thank you for being there."

Go through your partner's whole body like this. Once you feel complete, just look into each other's eyes and hold each other. Each of you notice the difference. If you are able to, put your insights and feelings into words and take turns sharing them.

Guess what, making love after this exercise can feel very rich and full…

Mind

Surrender to Saying Yes

In our culture we are less familiar with the art of surrender than with personal achievement and goal orientation. Struggle is generally considered an integral part of mastery. I always felt that if something found its way into my life effortlessly and easy, there was something right about it. Struggle to me seemed such a waste of time.

Yet it wasn't until I was introduced to Eckhart Tolle and his book "The Power of Now" did that belief in effortlessness rather than in struggle make sense. One of his premises is that if we surrender to life, that is, say Yes to that which life brings to us, moment to moment, day to day, we will find out that we actually live in a benevolent universe full of joy, ease and loving kindness.

"Surrender is the simple but profound wisdom of *yielding to* rather than *opposing* the flow of life. The only place where you can experience the flow of life is in the Now, so to surrender is to accept the present moment unconditionally and without reservation."

Let me define saying Yes here a bit more in detail: most of our life is spent complaining about things that go wrong, things that overwhelm us, things that are not to our liking, etc. The list is endless. Complaining about life is a way of saying No to life. It is a way to put up resistance to life.

Saying Yes basically means to stop complaining or resisting that which life brings to us. It does not mean we do not say No anymore. Let me give an example: I am at a restaurant and have ordered some food. When the waiter brings the food, it turns out to be badly burnt. I have a couple of options to respond to this occurrence:

- ❖ One, I can take it personal that poorly cooked food has been brought to me, and complain about the fact that this has happened to me as in "I already had such a bad day", "Why does this always happen to me?" etc—we all know this scenario very well.
- ❖ Or two, I can just accept that I have been served poorly cooked food by simply saying Yes to that occurrence. "OK, I have been served badly burnt

food. So what." I then have an option to say No to the food by asking the waiter to take the food back and bringing me another dish.

Saying Yes to life does not mean we never say No. It only means that No becomes a second step after we have said Yes to the initial occurrence of something. That way we remove resistance yet maintain our ability to discern.

I decided to find out whether it was actually true that we live in a benevolent universe, once we stop resisting it. I decided to practice saying Yes to as much as I could muster the courage for. What followed that decision were difficult, challenging, uncertain times full of an inadvertent involvement in financial scams, the disillusionment of a most promising relationship, going into personal and credit card debt, legal worries etc. Boy, did I pick some challenges to practice saying Yes to! Every time when the gut wrenching fears, the worries, the drama started, my daily prayer was to focus inside my body, to relax into it, and to say to myself over and over again: "All I have to do here is say Yes." As a result I ended up moving from Marin, California to Ashland, Oregon with a chance to start over, and eventually finding my way into fullness and into writing this book.

Now I actually know that life for me is very benevolent and supportive, once my basic premise has become saying Yes to what life brings to me, no matter how challenging and difficult it might look. I am much more joyful, at ease and trusting in the "goodness" of my life, finding myself supported and held more than I ever thought possible.

~~~ A deep sigh out ~~~

The Attitude of Gratitude

One way of saying Yes to life is to be grateful for **whatever** shows up. When I feel empty, or depressed, all I need to do is start listing the things I am grateful for, saying to myself: "I am grateful for…" It helps to get very basic like being grateful for the car that is working, the house I am living in, the food I eat, my children in my life, the friends and family I am close to etc. There is literally no end to finding things to be grateful for, especially if we become aware of the many things we take for granted. Interestingly enough, when I don't feel good, it is quite a chore to find that "attitude of gratitude". But once I get started, it usually flows quite easily.

Being grateful brings out the fullness in us. By focusing our attention on the areas that are working, available, doing well, instead of looking at what we don't have, what is not working, and what we would like more of, we shift our perspective from scarcity to fullness. Saying thank you for everything in our lives is another way to move away from complaining into saying Yes. By being grateful I acknowledge the wealth in my life at any given moment.

The attitude of gratitude is a way to stay actively involved in situations where we feel very much out of control and helpless, whether due to physical or emotional constraints. Sometimes circumstances bring us to a point where any form of outward activity feels futile, useless, or even damaging. It is very hard to keep our spirits up and our energy moving when we are in one of life's lulls. Practicing the attitude of gratitude is **one** activity that is always available to us, no matter how challenging our life looks like physically, or no matter how stuck we feel emotionally. In other words, saying thank you is one thing we can always do, even if it feels like the hardest thing, or the last thing we would like to do. It works. Let me tell you, it works.

~~~ *A deep belly breath in* ~~~

Soul

Tripping over Joy

What is the difference
between your experience of Existence
and that of a saint?

The saint knows
that the spiritual path
is a sublime chess game with God

and that the Beloved
has made such a Fantastic Move

that the Saint is now continually
tripping over Joy
and bursting out in Laughter
and Saying "I surrender!"

Gratitude Fullness

Whereas my dear
I am afraid you still think

you have a thousand serious moves.

~~ Hazif (Landinsky Translation) ~~

~~~~~~

MEMO FROM GOD

To: YOU
Date: TODAY
From: THE BOSS
Subject: YOURSELF
Reference: LIFE

I am God.

Today I will be handling all of your problems.
Please remember that I do not need your help.
If life happens to deliver a situation to you
that you cannot handle, do not attempt to resolve it.
Kindly put it in the SFGTD (something for God to do) box.
It will be addressed in MY time, not yours.
Once the matter is placed into the box, do not hold on to it

~~ Unknown Source ~~

~~~~~~~~~~

The world is your friend if it reminds you of God,
And it is your enemy if it makes you forget God.

~~ Unknown Source ~~

~~~~~~~~~~

Among the worst words that can be heard by anyone high in the air, the pair known as "oh-oh" possibly combines the maximum of bowel-knotting terror with the minimum wastage of breath.

Fullness No Matter What

~~ Terry Pratchett, Thief of Time ~~

~~~~~~~~~~

Willst du immer weiter schweifen?
Sieh, das Gute liegt so nah.
Lerne nur das Glueck ergreifen,
Denn das Glueck ist immer da.

Do you want to keep on roaming?
Look, the goodness is so close.
Learn to grasp the joyful moment
Cause the joy is always there.

~~ Johann Wolfgang von Goethe ~~

~~~~~~~~~~

This is the crucible of awakening,
where we are opening to our higher potential,
while simultaneously having to consciously suffer
the humiliations born
of our continued unconsciousness.

~~ Unknown Source ~~

~~~~~~~~~~

My job is acceptance.
To keep an acceptant spirit.
To Accept.
Not to change the world.
Only to change the soul.
So that it can be in the world.
Be rightly in the world.

~~ Ursula K. Le Guin, Four Ways to Forgiveness ~~

~~~~~~~~~~

A craftsman pulled a reed from the reedbed,
cut holes in it, and called it a human being.

Gratitude Fullness

Since then, it's been wailing a tender agony
of parting, never mentioning the skill
that gave it life as a flute.

~~ Rumi (Coleman Barks Translation) ~~

~~~~~~~~~~

More

The Teachings of Eckhart Tolle

When Eckhart Tolle's book "The Power of Now" hit the best seller list, a friend of mine was so impressed by this gem, that he bought a number of copies and gave them away to friends. When I had received my copy, it took me several months to finally open this book. Once I did, I could not put it down. Finally there was someone who could help me make sense of the emotional roller coasters I had lived on for centuries, it seemed.

By calling our difficult emotional states "The Pain Body" my life got very simple all of sudden. I did not need to try to understand the origin of my feelings. I did not need to process them and dig deeply into their muck. I did not need to find fault with my upbringing, my parents, my grandparents, or the culture I grew up in. All I needed to do was notice that "The Pain Body" was active, do my best to stay with the pain just as a sensation, and let myself move through its force field to the other side.

It helped that I had already found a particular piece of wisdom at one of Gangaji's early meetings (Gangaji brings her own kind of fullness to the teachings she received in India) where I heard her say, "bearing the unbearable is bliss". It had stuck with me as something important and true, but I did not know how to apply it. Eckhart Tolle's concept of the pain body gave me the How.

When I went to one of his seminars in Esalen, California, I felt touched by the simplicity of his presence. I literally could follow him into the silence that is the container for everything. He led us into it, either through following the sound of his tinkshas, little flat bells, into the silence that could be found when there was no more sound. Or he asked us to listen to the sound of the crashing waves on the California coast that constantly could be heard coming through the canvass walls of the pavilion, and let that sound take us deeper into again the underlying silence that contains all and everything.

These practical examples helped me come to terms with my chatterbox monkey mind that has a very hard time staying silent when it is not engaged in some kind of activity. I found out that if I just accepted that constant irritation, just let go into its presence, I could always find the silence underneath it, no matter how much chatter was happening. I found acceptance in Eckhart Tolle's presence. That acceptance of myself and consequently of any given situation has made my life a lot more fluid, easy, and joyful than it used to be when I tried so hard to fight it. And it all started with Eckhart Tolle's particular fullness of silence.

Eckhart Tolle. *The Power of Now*.
Eckhart Tolle. *Stillness Speaks*.

Also, check out the tapes of his retreats. They are all worth while listening to, not for the content as he keeps saying the same thing over and over again, but for the place from which he speaks: a tangible presence of stillness.

www.eckharttolle.com

Gangaji: http://www.gangaji.org

Gangaji with Roslyn Moore. *Just Like You: An Autobiography*.

Gangaji. *Freedom and Resolve: The Living Edge of Surrender*.

5
Heavenly Fullness

Heaven on Earth

I sing it from my eyes
I call it with my belly
I shape it through my skin
I sense it round my ears
I taste it on my breast
I know it in my bones
I scratch it over my hips
I hear it under my breath

I like it in my life

~~ Ulla! ~~

Body

Let's breathe some heaven into our bodies and our lives right now, right here. Let's bring some of that deep sky blue energy from all the way up there to all the way down here, and let us be filled with it up to the rim.

Breathing Exercise: Inverted Tetrahedron of Heavenly Fullness

Preparations

Specific instructions for this particular exercise:
For maximum effect, this particular breathing exercise is best done sitting up in a very relaxed position with your back leaning against something comfortable.

This Breathing Exercise is designed to be experienced while you are reading it, preferably out loud to yourself, if you are in a position to do so. If not, at least mouth the words; it will help you slow down and stay focused. If you are with a partner who is open to sharing this exercise, take turns reading it out loud to each other. Make sure you are in a position to relax while you are reading, without falling asleep too quickly.

If you want to intensify this exercise, invite your spirit guides and angels, known or unknown, seen or unseen, to join you in this experience.

Exercise

- ❖ I bring my awareness to the top of my head, where my hair (or my skin) meets the air around me.
- ❖ I wiggle my forehead to make the top of my head move (if I can) in order to fully anchor my awareness just barely inside my body.
- ❖ I focus my inbreath into the top of my head, that is, I feel my upper lungs rise with the inbreath, and I imagine that I can gently push my breath all the way through my neck, through my head, and into the top of my head.
- ❖ This breath is like a wave on the ocean being watched from a boat looking onto a sandy shore. I watch the wave building up to a crest, breaking, and

rolling down the beach all the way into the top of my head, slowly counting to five.

- I watch my outbreath recede like a wave from the beach. It recedes from the top of my head through my head, through my neck, and I watch my upper lungs fall with the outbreath, slowly counting to five.
- I continue watching the flow of the waves, my inbreath, and my outbreath for about four to six long slow breaths.

~~~~~~

- I imagine projecting my awareness to a place about three feet above my head.
- I imagine an inverted tetrahedron all around my awareness above my head. A tetrahedron has four equilateral triangles, see image.
- I imagine the tip of the inverted tetrahedron resting very lightly on the top of my head. I cannot feel the physical pressure, but notice a gentle presence.
- The base of my imagined tetrahedron reaches all the way into the heavens above me into infinity.
- One of the corners of my inverted tetrahedron is in line with my nose. Its opposite flat side is in line with the back of my body.
- The color of this inverted tetrahedron is light blue.
- Its texture feels like cool liquid air.
- This upside down, light blue tetrahedron represents my connection to the heavens.
- I rest in the awareness that I am connected to heaven through an inverted tetrahedron reaching all the way into infinity.
- I am inviting heaven into my life.
- I notice any changes in my body, in my sense of well being, in my breathing.

~~~~~~

- I imagine the tip of the upside down, light blue tetrahedron reaching down into my heart.

- I notice any changes in my body, in my sense of well being, in my breathing.

~~~~~~

- I imagine the tip of the upside down, light blue tetrahedron reaching all the way down into my perineum. For women this is the area between the Yoni and the Rosebud. For men this is the area between the Twin Globes and the Rosebud.
- I notice any changes in my body, in my sense of well being, in my breathing.

~~~~~~

- I imagine the tip of the upside down, light blue tetrahedron reaching all the way down beyond my feet into an area about one foot below my physical feet. My whole body is now inside the upside down light blue tetrahedron.
- I notice any changes in my body, in my sense of well being, in my breathing.

~~~~~~

- I once again focus my inbreath into the top of my head, that is I feel my upper lungs rise with the inbreath, and I imagine that I can gently push my breath all the way through my neck, through my head, and into the top of my head.
- This breath is like a wave on the ocean being watched from a boat looking onto a sandy shore. I watch the wave building up to a crest, breaking, and rolling down the beach all the way into the top of my head, slowly counting to five.
- I watch my outbreath recede like a wave from the beach. It recedes from the top of my head through my head, through my neck, and I watch my upper lungs fall with the outbreath, slowly counting to five.
- I continue watching the flow of the waves, my inbreath, and my outbreath for about four to six long slow breaths.
- Anytime now I can access my light blue inverted tetrahedron of Heavenly Fullness and experience its effect on my life in the hours, days, and months to come.

Completion

- When I am complete, I bring my awareness back to the world outside of me.

- ❖ I wiggle my toes and fingers.
- ❖ I stretch my body like a cat with a few lazy, long, full body stretches.
- ❖ I am back in my waking reality.

Suggestions

Once the inverted light blue tetrahedron has been activated, we can practice seeing ourselves in it thus activating our own particular "heaven on earth". Here are some ideas for further exploration:

- ❖ I imagine the upside down light blue tetrahedron reaching all the way down beyond my feet, thus completely encasing my body.
- ❖ I imagine it spinning clockwise all around my body.
- ❖ Clockwise means the corner of the tetrahedron directly in front of me moves to the right, to the back of my body, and all the way around in that direction.
- ❖ The tip stays pointed downward and the tetrahedron spins clockwise around its central vertical axis.
- ❖ I notice what it feels like to stand or sit inside an inverted tetrahedron that spins all around my body.
- ❖ I simply rest in that experience.

Make sure to do the Completion part after practicing the spinning of your inverted light blue tetrahedron. You might feel a bit disoriented after the spinning.

If you want to make sure that you experience more Heavenly Fullness in your life, try the Mandala Breathing described at the end of the Breathing Exercise: Color of Loving Fullness.

Pleasure Exercises

One of my favorite movies is called "Firelight" with Sophie Marceau and Steven Dillane as the protagonists. It is a love story situated in England in the early 1800s exploring the power of desire. In one of the scenes the female protagonist sets up the parameters for magic time: "Do up know about firelight? It's a kind of magic. Firelight makes time stand still. When you put out the lamps and sit in the firelight's glow, there aren't any rules anymore. You can do what you want, say what you want, be what you want. And when the lamps are lit again, time starts again and everything that was said or done is forgotten. More than forgotten. It never happened." Firelight time is a time between times.

On the edge pleasuring is such a time between times. Here are some differentiations so that you can find your way around. In a typical sexual situation we like to build and build sexual arousal until we experience orgasmic release. The following four states are characteristic of most sexual arousal scenarios:

- ❖ **Low arousal state**: we experience some sexual and pleasure energy running though our Jewels and possibly through our body.
- ❖ **High arousal state**: we experience strong sexual and pleasure energies in our Jewels and normally are focusing that energy by contracting our muscles to reach for orgasmic release.
- ❖ **Point of no return**: the highest point of sexual arousal energy which has been building up to the point where the orgasmic release is inevitable, and cannot be stopped.
- ❖ **Orgasmic release**: the letting go into orgasmic release involving involuntary muscle spasms followed by a relaxing of all muscles.

On the edge pleasuring is most effective in the "high arousal state" just before the "point of no return". What we are looking for is the highest sexual arousal state without going over the edge into orgasm. Not only are we looking for it to just pass through it, but the idea is to literally hang out there for longer and longer periods of time. That high sexual arousal state is where we can experience maximum pleasure without having an orgasm. It is also a way into timeless pleasure experiences and a gateway into transcendent pleasure, that is, pleasure outside our bodies.

How do we get there? Normal sexual arousal activities that lead into high sexual arousal followed by orgasmic release are based on muscle contractions. We try to build up enough of a sexual charge to get us over the edge into orgasm. In "on the edge" pleasuring the idea is to build sexual arousal through a combination of sexual stimulation and contraction, and then to start **relaxing** when we get close to the point of no return. It is the relaxation in the high arousal state that opens the door to transcendent pleasure experiences. It opens the door into time between times, time without rules, without restrictions, with all normal activities suspended. What an adventure!

Solo: On the Edge Pleasuring

Preparations

Create some time alone and undisturbed, preferably not just before you go to sleep.

Exercise

- ❖ Start by pleasuring yourself to build sexual arousal.
- ❖ Notice at what point you start contracting your muscles to reach for orgasm. The contraction usually happens in the thighs, the belly, the Rosebud, and the pelvic floor.
- ❖ Notice your breathing. Is it short, fast, more in your chest, which is an indicator for contracted muscles.
- ❖ When you get close to orgasm, slow down your stimulation and relax all your muscles, especially your legs, the pelvic floor, your belly, and the muscles around your Rosebud.
- ❖ Start stroking your body moving the arousal energy from the Jewels to your belly, your heart, your neck and head, your arms and hands, and your legs and feet.
- ❖ Take slow deep breaths into you belly with your mouth open.
- ❖ Make some soft moaning sounds to play with the pleasure in your body.
- ❖ When you feel your arousal lessening, start stimulating again, but stop just before orgasm. Again spread the arousal energy through your whole body by stroking your body in an upward motion.
- ❖ Repeat that process until you either feel just satisfied and full of whole body pleasure, or until you are ready to have an orgasm. That orgasm most likely will feel more intense and much stronger than the orgasms you are more familiar with.

Suggestions

If you want to explore a variation on the same theme, try to relax already at the beginning of your sexual stimulation. Just keep noticing where you are wanting to contract in order to build more arousal. Just play with that edge between more arousal through contraction and more relaxation in the arousal.

Partnered: Taking Your Partner for a Pleasure Ride

Preparation

- Create some time to explore the Pleasure Ride other than late at night just before going to sleep.
- Decide who will be the giver and who will be the receiver.
- **Receiver:** Lie on your back.
- **Giver:** Sit next to your partner in a position that allows you to both comfortably look in your partner's eyes and touch your partner's Jewels.
- **Both Giver and Receiver:** Close your eyes and connect with yourself.
- **Receiver:** Ask yourself how much pleasure you are willing to receive.
- **Giver:** Find your love for yourself and your partner inside of you.

Man Pleasuring Woman

- Start by connecting with your partner's heart. You might want to place a hand on her heart and look into her eyes for a minute or two. Keep your eyes soft and unfocused.
- While you are looking into her eyes, tell her how much you love her, how much you appreciate her in your life, and how much you love giving her pleasure right now.
- Assure her that there is nothing she needs to be doing but to feel her pleasure and to keep opening up to it.
- Start stimulating her sexually by honoring her manually (orally can be too intense and not precise enough for this kind of exercise, but ask her).
- Touch her with both passion and love.
- Tell her how beautiful she looks.
- Keep telling her that you love her. (For most women pleasure and emotions are very closely connected.)
- Tell her how much you enjoy watching her Jewels get engorged when she gets turned on.
- Tell her how beautiful she looks in her arousal.
- When you notice her starting to tighten or contract her muscles, or when her breathing pattern changes in order to go for the Big O, slow down in honoring her.

- Ask her to relax into the pleasure, to open up to feeling more pleasure, to enlarge the pleasure container.
- Ask her to especially relax her buttocks, her thigh muscles, her PC muscles, the muscles around her Rosebud, her belly.
- Notice her feet and hands. Are they relaxed? How about her neck? Is her mouth open and relaxed?
- Keep pleasuring her slowly and deliberately, while asking her to relax even more.
- Watch her face closely if you are honoring her manually (there is so much beauty to be seen in that relaxed arousal).
- Keep reminding her that this is not about having an orgasm. This is about just being pleasured.
- Ever so often take your hands and stroke her belly from the pubic bone in an upward motion, spreading her turn-on into the rest of her body, into her stomach, her heart, and her throat.
- Try out different kinds of sexual and arousing touch and keep asking her to relax into it.
- Ask her if there is a particular place where she would like to be touched.
- Keep moving her turn-on energy into her body.
- This can go on for quite a while as there is no goal to be achieved, no clear ending point.
- When you both feel complete, take her in your arms, hold her, and gently stroke her skin. Remember, she is still flying out there in her pleasure land. It might take her a while to come down. Some good hard pressure with the heel of your hand on her Pearl might help her to come back to this world more easily.
- She might also be shedding some tears, tears of gratitude, tears of releasing old emotions, who knows. Just stay with her until she has completely returned from this journey.

Woman Pleasuring Man

- Start by placing one hand on his heart and one hand cupped around his Jewels.
- Look into his eyes for a minute or two. Keep your eyes soft and unfocused.

- While you are looking into his eyes, tell him how much you love him, how much you appreciate him in your life, and how much you love giving him pleasure right now.
- Assure him that there is nothing he needs to be doing but to feel his pleasure and to keep opening up to it.
- Start stimulating him sexually, either by honoring him manually or orally.
- Touch him with both passion and love.
- Tell him (when your mouth is empty!) how much you enjoy his Lingam. How great it feels in your hands and/or in your mouth.
- Gently play with his Twin Globes while stroking and/or licking his Lingam.
- When you notice him starting to tighten or contract his muscles, or when he changes his breathing pattern in order to go for the Big O, slow down.
- Ask him to relax into the pleasure, to open up to feeling more pleasure, to enlarge the pleasure container.
- Ask him to especially relax his buttocks, his thigh muscles, his PC muscles, the muscles around his Rosebud, his belly.
- Notice his feet and hands. Are they relaxed? How about his neck? Is his mouth open and relaxed?
- Keep pleasuring him slowly, while asking him to relax even more.
- Watch his face closely if you are honoring him manually.
- Keep reminding him that this is not about having an orgasm. This is about just being pleasured.
- Ever so often take your hands and stroke his belly from the pubic bone in an upward motion spreading his turn-on into the rest of his body like into his stomach, his heart, and his throat.
- Try out different kinds of sexual and arousing touch and keep asking him to relax into it.
- Ask him if there is a particular place he would like to be touched at.
- Keep moving his turn-on energy into his body.
- This can go on for quite a while as there is no goal to be achieved, no clear ending point.
- When you both feel complete, take him in your arms, hold him, and gently stroke his skin. Just be with him.

Suggestions

This is a whole new way of exploring pleasure. It is about relaxing into a high energy state, in this case high sexual arousal. The tendency will be to rush up the steep pleasure mountain, and shoot down as fast and hard as possible. The pleasure ride described above explores high country with shallow dips and small peaks, but no great heights and deep valleys. This pleasure exercise is a start. If you enjoy it, there is a whole new world waiting for you.

Mind

Heaven on Earth

So many of the established religions on this Earth, past and present, have the exploration of one concept in common: the concept of a life after the body has died, called heaven, paradise, Kingdom Come, Eden, afterlife, etc. Life after death either promised everything that life here on Earth could not provide, like peace, virgins, bliss, eternal joy, to name just a few. Or it served as punishment for wrongdoings in life here on Earth and was called hell, purgatory, Hades, netherworld, eternal damnation, again to name just a few. I guess the Grand Experiment allowed for many different ways to explore the mystery of what happens after we physically die. As very few have ever returned to tell the tale of after death, there has been a lot of room for many different interpretations.

Interestingly enough, there is another correlation common to most religions. The less emphasis was placed on experiencing pleasure in and through the body during life on Earth, the more emphasis was put on life after death, the promise of a heaven full of delights once life in the body was over. Or put differently, most pleasures of the body, except for the pure act of conception, were considered sinful and were punishable by some form of damnation in hell after death.

There also has been a lot of room to explore what it feels like to give our power away to outside authorities, who used the concept of life after death both as a reward for "good", that is acceptable behavior, and as a threat for "bad", that is unacceptable behavior. Giving our power away has kept a number of us busy over the last 2000 years as there were so many different variations to play with.

My hunch is that there is new game in town called Heaven on Earth. The strong hold of the established religions is falling apart, at least in the Western world. There is more room for personal explorations of areas that were, so far, off limits like sexuality, physical pleasure, or personal freedom. At the same time these explorations are ripe with the usual pitfalls of going too far into the other extreme. It is amazing how many excesses can be explored in today's materially oriented culture.

But what does Heaven on Earth mean in terms of fullness? I believe that by exploring and integrating all the different aspects of fullness into our lives here on earth we have the chance to live a life that can rightfully be called Heaven on Earth. And to be really clear, everybody has the opportunity to experience this Heaven, as to me that Heaven on Earth is totally independent from material wealth. It is an internal reality that, once it fills us up to the brim, spills over into the material world around us. But only then. What I am suggesting here is Fullness No Matter What, Fullness independently from the world of matter.

Here is an interesting question to ponder: What will we have to look forward to after death, when life on earth becomes a Heaven on Earth? Who will we as human beings turn out to be when Heaven on Earth is within reach for anyone of us?

~~~ A deep sigh out ~~~

High Energy States

If I let my imagination wonder into a possible Heaven on Earth in the (hopefully) near future, one way I find is living in sustained high energy states. And I see whole communities being able to live and work and play in the context of sustained high energy.

In my opinion we live in a culture where most of our waking time is spent in fairly stable low energy. As children, when we have more energy than we know what to do with and are happy to express all that energy without holding back, we are repeatedly being told: "Sit still! Don't be so boisterous! Do you always have to make so much noise? Stop running around—it drives me crazy!" So early on we learn to bring our energy levels down to that of our environment.

Culturally we create excitement through energy peaks, that is we look for an experience that ideally will bring our energy up fast and strong, and then come down just as fast. This is nowhere reflected better than in our typical sexual encounters—fast and hard sexual turn-on, climactic release, followed by coming back down to the original low energy state. Thus we experience over and over again that high energy is only tolerable and desirable as a short-term peak experience.

That kind of low energy living in my opinion is the opposite from living in fullness. One of my definitions for fullness is a sustained high energy state, one where we are steeped in high energy which lets us live in high altitude landscapes of soft ups and downs like sweet green rolling hills, instead of jagged, rugged mountain peaks and steep valleys. And I am not saying there is anything wrong with rugged mountain terrain—I just don't equate fullness with that kind of energetic landscape.

~~~ *A deep belly breath in* ~~~

Characteristics of High Energy States

High energy states are accompanied by a number of phenomena that can bring up a sense of discomfort. Initially it feels really good to be in a sustained high energy state. Remember when you last fell in love, and all that sweet loving energy kept you awake late at night, woke you up early in the morning, and let you breeze through your day? Life can be like that most of the time, even without a new lover/partner. But it might take getting used to, if it happens all the time.

High energy states let us feel our feelings more easily, as we are more permeable and flexible energetically in a high energy state. Thus we are more aware of feelings that in a low energy state we normally would be able to ignore. Living with more awareness of our feelings takes some getting used to. It especially requires practicing communication techniques (see chapter on Communication in the Mind Section of Pleasure Fullness) to learn how to safely express and discharge our emotions. Btw, emotions do come up more easily, but they also move on more easily.

We are usually more tuned in with our environment and our partner, thus more sensitive. That sensitivity brings with it a heightened sense of awareness and increased aliveness. At the same time it takes some getting used to as we are processing more information and can easily have a sense of overload, or of feeling overwhelmed.

High energy states are easily accompanied by a sense of being out of control. Our defense mechanisms do not work as well; we experience ourselves as more vulnerable, open, and/or defenseless. That state feels scary to many of us, especially in the beginning. The flip side to that sense of being out of control is that we feel more alive, juicier, and more present. Joy is so much more easily available. **And** it does take getting used to.

One of the mechanisms at work in a low energy but high peak culture is that when we get to a place where we feel sustainable high energy, it is like air that is too thin high in the mountains. We unconsciously start looking for ways to slide down that mountain again, if not rapidly crash down. There are a number of ways to bring down our energy and make sure that we are back in that "safe" low energy space. They are called "Upper Limits".

~~~ A deep belly breath in ~~~

Upper Limits

Gaye and Katie Hendricks originally came up with six different strategies how we bring high energy down, usually in an unconscious way. I added a few, based on my own experiences:

- ❖ **Worrying:**
  God, what would we do if we had nothing to worry about! We would surely make it up. When we escape into our heads, and start worrying about whatever offers itself most conveniently, we stop being connected to our selves and live in our heads. Worrying easily dissipates high energy. I personally would not know anything about that strategy…☺
- ❖ **Eating Food:**
  A typical example of how eating food can bring us down energetically is making love while feeling really connected and afterwards having the urge to raid the whole refrigerator. Any food after intense experiences, and especially sugar or junk food helps us unconsciously to come down again, to not feel so good anymore.

❖ **Arguing:**
Starting a fight over virtually nothing is very effective to bring ourselves and others down. Is creates distance, and believe it or not, a safe, that is familiar sense of separateness.

❖ **Talking a Lot:**
The German word is "zerreden", meaning you talk about something until it is broken, dissipated, gone. The kind of talking that cheapens experiences is a sure way to come down.

❖ **Going Unconscious:**
Some examples of "Going Unconscious" are channel flipping on TV and getting lost in a book or magazine, especially when others are present. It is a form of withdrawing into unconsciousness, or to avoid feeling too good.

❖ **Concealing Feelings:**
Another good one. When we do not share with those close to us what we are really feeling, it creates distance between us and others. Distance is a low energy state.

❖ **Deflecting Positive Energy:**
We have all been in that situation: someone is paying us a compliment, and we go: "Oh, that is nothing! I just did that to…" We just won't let the positive energy in. We somehow have closed ourselves up against feeling a natural high.

❖ **Lying and Breaking Agreements:**
Another form of unconsciously creating distance is not telling the truth. It keeps us separate. The same goes for breaking agreements, that is, changing agreements without renegotiating first. It breaks trust and creates large amounts of separation through hurt feelings and a sense of betrayal.

❖ **Becoming Emotionally Needy Without Making Clean Requests:**
"If you really love me, you should know what I need." This is an effective way of making the other wrong and thus creating distance through these kinds of protective expectations. By protective expectations I mean expectations that are not cleanly and openly expressed. A partner has no way of responding correctly if expectations are not expressed openly.

A typical example of upper limits that most of us recognize easily is the following: we have spent a wonderfully connected and juicy time with our lover or partner and are basking in that sweet intimate space. Next thing we know, a fight has started out of the blue, usually over some silly trifle. And bang…we are back to feeling separate and disconnected, and as strange as it sounds—safe again.

Here is another example that my good friend Robert Fry, who recently died, kept pointing out a number of times. He taught and wrote the melodies and words for both Dances of Universal Peace and Sufi Dancing. They are forms of circular line dancing with very simple melodies, repetitive words, and simple gestures. You can get very high through this simple method of structured group movement. And Robert kept reminding us over and over again not to start talking right away, after one dance was over. Talking in that context was a sure way to dissipate the energy that we all together had generated. He suggested to contain it, let it build, let it carry all of us together into a different realm.

~~~ *A deep sigh out* ~~~

Safe Ways to Integrate High Energy

What can we do about these unconscious patterns that keep us from feeling good over longer stretches of time? First of all, recognize the pattern for the pattern that it is, by realizing that we do not have to blame our past marriages/relationships, our parents, or our childhood. We do not need to analyze and understand the various possible reasons for the disruption of feeling well. That makes it fairly uncomplicated to get **back** into feeling well. By just having one reason for the disruption, namely having reached our "upper limits", it keeps life simple. I like simple things.

I believe that once we recognize the upper limits pattern, it is the only pattern we need to really look at, as it is the only one that can be dealt with right now, right here. If we focus on our past, childhood wounding, or old family dynamics, all it does is bring us out of the present and into a mental state. And most importantly, once the origins of a pattern are in the past, there is nothing we can do. **But** if we use the upper limit definition, then we get to both stay and affect a change in the present.

Once we have reached our upper limits and are trying, successfully or not, to bring ourselves down, one way to do so safely and consciously is to take some space to reconnect to ourselves. It's just me and me, babe. If the upper limit is the result of having spent some intimate time with a partner, the best thing to do is to spend some time apart. Reaching upper limits with a partner is usually a sign that we have spent all the time together that we can stand at that moment. We just need some time apart to integrate all the intensity of being in a high energy state.

Another way is to just be silent, stop talking, and get busy with every day activities like doing your laundry, or washing the dishes. A friend of mine just came back from Burning Man, an experiment in creative living in the middle of the Nevada desert around Labor Day weekend. For a week 30,000 plus people create a whole city, bring their particular creative expressions to be seen, and watch others express themselves. When the "Man Burns" on Saturday night, and the Temple the following night, the show is over, and literally **everything** is taken away down to the last piece of glitter, so nothing is left except the empty desert.

She came back so full of intense impressions and deep insights and unusual experiences, that all she could do was stay with all that she had brought home without even sharing much through words. I encouraged her to expand her container for intensity, that is, to hold more energy without having to release it through words. Sometimes we jump into words too fast, and miss the real impact an intense experience has had on us. What I am suggesting here is to not look for easy words to describe something that impacted us, but to contain it, hold it inside, and watch for shifts in perception or behavior in the days to come. Here is a quote that describes the above in a different way:

~~~~~~~~~~

But sometimes the mind of the most sensible person
encountered something so big, so complex, so alien to all understanding,
that it told itself little stories about it instead.
Then, when it felt it understood the story,
it felt it understood the huge incomprehensible thing.

Pratchett, Thief of Time

~~~~~~~~~~

When I grew up in Germany, one thing my parents loved to do was to hear Bach Oratorios sung in church. Germany has these beautiful and large Baroque churches built with great acoustics. We would go to these musical feasts, often sitting on fairly hard benches, but inspired by the music and the church interior. When the music was over, no one clapped. We would all sit in silence for a few minutes, until we would get up and just walk out, again silently. I had been told early on, that this kind of music had been written and performed in honor of God and thus needed no acknowledgement though clapping. I remember feeling very impressed after these kinds of church concerts, very full in the sense of filled up.

Unfortunately, that custom is no more. To me the effect of all music, whether secular or sacred, is now dissipated through clapping. I do not mean to begrudge the performers their rightful acknowledgement, but I feel that something got lost here.

About ten years ago, my fairy friends Fairoh and Cheeah on Maui helped me regain that silent integration of an intense experience, though in a different context. They introduced me to the "art of integrating high energy states". We all three went to play with a blowhole on the North Shore of Maui in a deserted part of the island. A blowhole is a hole in the shore rocks with a cave underneath that is open towards the ocean. At high tide the waves literally crash into the cave and shoot up a spray of water through the blowhole high into the air.

The three of us took turns standing naked above the blowhole, delighting in the impact of the water spraying up onto our bodies. The mixture of cold water shooting up from below, warm sunshine from above, and a cool wind on our skin was exhilarating! We played like children with the water spout, running and screaming and just letting it all out!

On the way back Cheeah and Fairoh showed me how important it was to bring that kind of intense experience safely home. It was not enough to just go and have the experience and be done with it. It was just as important to contain it, to hold the space for it, and to stay connected to ourselves after the joyride. After a two hour drive with barely any talking we arrived home, and I felt I had truly received the gift of the blowhole, never to be forgotten, and still available to me today, in all its glory.

~~~ *A deep sigh out* ~~~

Soul

The mystery does not get clearer by repeating the question,
nor is it bought with going to amazing places.

Until you've kept your eyes
and your wanting still for fifty years
you don't begin to cross over from confusion.

~~ Rumi (Coleman Barks Translation) ~~

~~~~~~~~~~

"I'm not going to ride on a magic carpet!" he hissed. "I'm afraid of grounds." "You mean heights," said Conina. "And stop being silly." "I know what I mean! It's the grounds that kills you!"

~~ Terry Pratchett, Sourcery ~~

~~~~~~~~~~

MERMAN

Go to bed. The priests are dead
Now no one can call you bad
Go to bed. The priests are dead
Finally you're in Peppermint Land

(Baby…) And let it out
Who could ever say you're not simply wonderful?
(Simply wonderful, yes…)
Who could ever harm you?

~~ Tori Amos, Merman ~~

~~~~~~~~~~

More

If you are interested in exploring more about the uses of the tetrahedron, especially the star tetrahedron, here are a few sources:

Drunvalo Melchizedek. *The Ancient Secret of the Flower of Life, Vol I and II.*

Drunvalo Melchizedek. *Living in the Heart.*

http://www.floweroflife.org and http://www.drunvalo.net

Gaye & Katie Hendricks. *Conscious Loving: The Journey to Co-Commitment.* www.hendricks.com

Sufi Dancing and Dances of Universal Peace: http://www.dancesofuniversalpeace.org

Burning Man Event www.burningman.com

6

Guidance Fullness

The Door is always Open

Do we really know the door is always open?
All we have to do is go stepping through
No holding back or onto anything
The magic garden has been waiting
Has always known and loved us
And it has called to us
Since we have left
Whenever

It's true
We can know
The door is always open

~~ Ulla! ~~

Guidance Fullness

Body

In this chapter there is an opportunity to meet and connect with any Fourth dimensional beings like spirit guides, angels, nature sprites, ascendant masters, etc, who are gathered around us, but on the invisible planes. All of them ready, willing, and able to be of service to us, to human kind, to all of creation. By the way, if you are just dying to find out why it's called "The Sofa", go directly to the Mind Section of Guidance Fullness.

Breathing Exercise: Sofa for Guidance Fullness

Preparations

Specific instructions for this particular exercise:
For maximum effect, this particular breathing exercise is best done sitting up in a very relaxed position with your back leaning against something comfortable.

This Breathing Exercise is designed to be experienced while you are reading it, preferably out loud to yourself, if you are in a position to do so. If not, at least mouth the words; it will help you slow down and stay focused. If you are with a partner who is open to sharing this exercise, take turns reading it out loud to each other. Make sure you are in a position to relax while you are reading, without falling asleep too quickly.

If you want to intensify this exercise, invite your spirit guides and angels, known or unknown, seen or unseen, to join you in this experience.

Exercise

- ❖ I bring my awareness to my neck, this amazingly complex construction, which connects my head and the rest of my body.
- ❖ I place my hands around my neck in a comfortable position.
- ❖ I appreciate my physical neck for doing such a wonderful job of holding up my head while still allowing for quite a range of motion, even though some of us might feel more restricted in that aspect.

- ❖ I lovingly accept any restrictions on range of motion in my neck. I bring a breath of acceptance into every area of discomfort, one after another, until my neck is glowing with acceptance.
- ❖ I focus my breath into my neck, that is I imagine my breath reaching all the way into my neck by breathing into the upper wings of my lungs and extending that breath through the collarbones into my neck.
- ❖ I feel my upper lungs rise and my shoulders stretch with the inbreath, slowly counting to five, and fall with the outbreath, again slowly counting to five.
- ❖ I continue watching the rise and fall of my upper lungs for about four to six long slow breaths.

~~~~~~

- ❖ I focus my awareness into my neck and the area around it.
- ❖ I imagine a very comfortable sofa curving around my physical neck. (For those of you who consider my sofa just a bit too silly, you can imagine a rainbow curved around your neck. Just substitute the word "rainbow" whenever you read the word "sofa".)
- ❖ I imagine the color, the texture, the shape, the feel, the look of the sofa in as much detail as I can. I want it to be just right for my new and/or old friends to feel comfortable to meet with me.

The Invitation

- ❖ I am now ready, willing and able to experience whoever of the spirit realm is around me.
- ❖ I am sending out invitations to all those who are ready, willing, and able to be recognized, seen, felt, and/or heard by me. Only those beings are invited that are willing to totally and absolutely support me. All others, thank you very much, and please stay away.
- ❖ The invitation has been sent when I look at my guidance sofa with my inner eyes and see it charged with sprinkly, glittery, sparkly lights.
- ❖ I keep breathing into the neck/sofa area, sensing it expand, seeing it settle in, feeling its comfort, for about four to six long slow breaths.
- ❖ During the next hours, days, and months I am staying open to meeting my new/old friends in a variety of ways.

❖ I notice any changes in my body, in my sense of well being, in my breathing.

~~~~~~~

❖ I once again focus my breath into my neck, that is I imagine my breath reaching all the way into my neck by breathing into the upper wings of my lungs and extending that breath through the collarbones into my neck.
❖ I feel my upper lungs rise and my shoulders stretch with the inbreath, slowly counting to five, and fall with the outbreath, again slowly counting to five.
❖ I continue watching the rise and fall of my upper lungs for about four to six long slow breaths.
❖ Anytime now I can access my Sofa of Guidance Fullness and experience its effect on my life in the hours, days, and months to come.

Completion

❖ When I am complete, I bring my awareness back to the world outside of me.
❖ I wiggle my toes and fingers.
❖ I stretch my body like a cat with a few lazy, long, full body stretches.
❖ I am back in my waking reality.

Suggestions

A personal connection to the spirit realm is always available to us. I found though, that the better I feel, the easier I sense the connection and receive the answers I am looking for. When I am in a rut, desperate for answers, or needy for connection, it becomes very difficult for me to sense the presence of spirit beings. It becomes even more difficult to experience them sitting on my sofa. It becomes even more impossible to hear or sense any answers to my questions.

I learned that if I touch in with my sofa on a regular basis, especially in times of relaxation and ease, I could learn to "find" them. For example I touch base every morning on my morning hike, during an evening meditation, just after I wake up or before I go to bed. The best way to describe that finding is I learned to identify their energetic signature, and could then more easily recognize that signature even in difficult times.

The Practice

Whenever I have a minute and am in need of a larger perspective, or when I just feel like connecting into the spirit realm, here are some words that work for me:

> I am ready willing and able
> To connect with those in the spirit world
> That are of like energy and intent
> Seen or unseen, known or unknown
> I bless your presence in my life.

Here are a number of ways how a response from the spirit realm to a question of mine might look like:

- When I am need of answer to a question or a solution to a problem, I just ask the question as clearly in my head as possible. (Careful though: If I am too attached to a particular outcome, or nervous about a particular answer, it might be difficult to receive the answer. The less I care what the answer looks or sounds like, the easier it is to receive it.)
- I might hear a voice in my head accompanied by tears;
- I might take a deep breath while sensing a surprisingly clear thought;
- I might have a sense of having literally been **hit** by an insight—it takes my breath away.
- Sometimes their presence feels like a breath of fresh clean cool air.
- Sometimes I feel myself relax into my body when I sense their presence.

If you want to make sure that you experience more Guidance Fullness in your life, try the Mandala Breathing described at the end of the Breathing Exercise: Color of Loving Fullness.

Pleasure Exercises

Solo: Inviting the Spirit Realm

Any experience on this earthly plane can be intensifies by inviting spirit guides and/or angels into the experience. For example: I love receiving an "under water massage" (also called "Water Dancing") in warm water pools. Whenever

I remember, I invite my spirit guides to be part of that experience as to me it is just heavenly. I get to float in warm water at body temperature. I get to be held and massaged in that weightless atmosphere. I get taken under water and twirled and moved about while breathing out very slowly. I get brought back to the surface to take another deep breath, before I am pulled back into the warmth of the water. If I open my eyes just a fraction, just enough to perceive light and shadows, but because of the eyelashes not enough to let water through, I even get to add the perspective of light seen through layers of clear water. All of that is very sensuous and delightful, and it gets even more so when I invite my invisible friends to join me in that experience.

My invitation here is for you to invite your unseen friends into any physical activity that you feel comfortable enough sharing with that kind of company. The spirit guides are never there to interfere. They are only there to help and support when asked to, and to intensify any experience just because it becomes a shared experience. How often do we have this sense as a single of wanting to share a beautiful sunset with someone! Any beautiful and intense experience seems to be more real if it is shared with some one, seen through four eyes, and felt through two bodies. Spirit guides are no substitute for a loving companion, but they do fulfill that witness function that we so often long for in those special moments.

So just ask them to be your companion when you are:

- Going for a walk in the woods with the blazing colors of fall all around you,
- Sitting on the beach watching a tropical sunset over the ocean,
- Swimming under a waterfall of a cold fresh mountain lake in the heat of summer,
- Eating a delicious home cooked meal by candle light,
- Touching yourself to get aroused or into orgasm,
- Laying on a blanket under the silvery light of a full moon on a warm summer night,
- And enjoying many, many more delights of this so rich earthly life!

The spirit guides are here to let us know that we never ever have to be alone when we do not want to be. I know, because I felt so intensely alone most of my life, until I became aware of the possibilities that these unseen friends offer.

Partnered: Left Eye Pleasuring

Many years ago a psychic and friend on Maui, Triana Hill, taught me how to "see" spirit guides. When we sit facing someone looking left eye into left eye with soft vision for a period of time, the face in front of us will take on distinct features of one or several of the spirit guides around us, if we ask for it. It is as if there is a soft transparent fabric in front the physical face, onto which the features of a spirit guide are being projected. This process gets intensified when we add sensuous contact into the exercise.

The first step is to find a way to sit facing each other comfortably. You then move your faces so that each left eye is able to look directly into the other left eye. Keep your eyes and your vision soft, that is let the image you are looking at become blurry. You will notice that not only does the eye of your partner become soft and blurry but the whole face will look soft and blurry. One way to keep your vision soft is to imagine that you are actually looking at a point three feet behind your partner's eye while looking into the eye.

Keep breathing slowly into your belly and keep letting your left eye stay soft. You will notice that your shoulders might drop down, your neck might release, or you might start to yawn. The longer you keep your vision soft, the more likely is the chance that you will "see" the face of one of your spirit guides projected onto your partner's face. It will not be the clear image of a photograph, but more like a face seen at dusk with light and shadows playing in and out of your vision.

You can each "see" a different spirit guide in the face across from you at the same time. Or you might have a sense of them taking turns showing up. When I did this exercise, I "saw" an older male face look at me with so much love and sweetness, that even right now I can still see and sense that love.

Once you feel relaxed enough to "see" a face, and comfortable with this process, you can add another level by softly touching each other while keeping your vision soft. The touching of your bodies is like an invitation for the spirit guides to play with us on this earthly plane. They love being included in our earthly activities, especially the pleasurable ones. If you don't feel too shy about it, you can literally invite them to be part of your lovemaking. It will add another dimension of experience to your pleasure as you are sharing it with someone inside of you who has no physical senses…it is quite trip.

Mind

Both in my experience and my understanding there is a whole "other" realm out there that is accessible to us with senses other than the five senses based on bodily functions such as: touch, sight, sound, taste, and smell. Part of that "other" realm is the world of inner voices, guidance, angels, spirit guides, nature sprites, etc. I have found such joy, a sense of connection, and a whole other aspect of fullness by opening myself up to that "other" realm.

May I Introduce to You…?

My direct experience with this "other" realm comes through spirit guides in all kinds of forms and shapes. They have been a part of my daily life for more than a decade. I found my connection to them through various means:

- ❖ I had been told of the presence of different guides in a number of readings by psychics and channels;
- ❖ I experienced them directly under the influence of psycho-active and hallucinogenic substances;
- ❖ Several times the awareness of someone new being present around me just popped into my awareness;
- ❖ And one found me and became my teacher, friend, and invaluable guide into this present state of fullness. This last one is called Dr. Peebles, and is channeled by William Rainen.

William used to travel up and down the West Coast of the USA and about every six months or so I would have a personal reading with both William Rainen and Dr. Peebles, which would be taped. Through these readings Dr. Peebles has become a friend and partner and over the years I learned to hear him inside my own head. I have learned to able to have conversations with him about my daily life, my relationships, my work, and this book.

I do have a quirky mind as you might have noticed by now. When I am in need of help from the spirit realm, I always picture a circular, very comfortable sofa around the back and the sides of my neck. I imagine all my spirit guides and angels and whoever considers themselves part of my team sitting on that sofa. I see them dangling their legs and saying: "Let's see, what is Ulla up to today?

What trouble has she gotten herself in again? And now she wants help to get her out of it?" They all meet on that sofa and discuss my affairs and me.

Over the last 15 years my invisible friends have changed like the changing of the guard. I would be aware of them for a period of time, and then they would fade away, only for a new one to show up in my awareness. Each one would bring a particular gift that would stay with me, even after they left. While living on Maui I had a dragon as a companion for a while. He was a **big** dragon. I always sensed him sitting on the roof of my car while I was driving around the island. I could "see" his wings and tail flapping in the wind, while I was having conversations with him. He brought to me a particular kind of courage that I very much needed at that time.

Then there was the imp, all dressed in green, who would show up when I was walking in the woods. I always found him kind of set back to my right, just at the edge of my physical viewing range. He made me laugh easily just by his presence and brought a particular kind of delight and impish joy into my life.

While I was dealing with the effects of a health crisis, Marian, a healer spirit guide came to me. She carries a light blue healing rose, which emits a shower of light blue sprinkles. She would shower me with these light blue sprinkles, which I then could watch sink into my body and into my blood stream, brightening up my blood and bringing health and wellbeing to me.

For a while Mother Mary came to me. She showed up during a meditation one day. In my imagination she was wearing a wide, floor length coat of dark, dark blue velvet that she would wrap around me when I felt in need of comforting. I shared that image with my seven-year-old daughter, when we were separated for while, and to my knowledge it helped her find comfort when she missed me.

But seriously, the sofa is just an easy place for me to locate my support team and have some fun doing it. I feel very connected to that sofa and its occupants, as I would not be who I am today, doing what I am doing, and enjoying my life as much as I do, without my invisible friends.

~~~ A deep belly breath in ~~~

Understanding

In my understanding of this realm we humans on earth live in what is called the third dimension (the dimensions I am mentioning here are based on energetic frequencies and are not the same as physic's dimensions). In this third dimension our human experience is primarily defined through our human bodies with the five senses acting as filters. It is also characterized, among other attributes, by the ability to act through the combined use of our minds and bodies, specifically through the use of our hands. But we cannot easily pierce the veils created by our filters, that is, see into the future or into other dimensions. In other words we experience past, present and future as sequential events because we are bound by the rules of space and time.

Another attribute is that manifestations based on thoughts are not instant, but subject to space and time. When we think something into creation, it is not automatically created. It usually takes time and action to physically create here on earth what we have thought up.

The spirit guides, angels etc. inhabit the fourth dimension, a dimension that is not defined by the shape and construct of a material body, but by energy. It is further characterized by magic, instant manifestation of thoughts, and the absence of space and time limitations. That means every thought manifests instantly and simultaneously. But spirit guides and others of that realm do not have the ability to physically impact their environment, especially here on earth. Because they exist outside of time and space they can see far into the past, far into the future, and can also see various futures as simultaneously happening (something that is even hard for us to imagine and harder still to experience).

Both humans in the third dimension and spirit guides in the fourth inhabit the same space, believe it or not. And we both are on the same path of exploration and discovery, each in our own dimension, but together as inhabitants of this earth.

In short: we humans can act but not see—the spirit guides can see but not act. That makes us good candidates for working together as a team comprised of sovereign but interdependent partners. As humans and spirit guides we each have our very own strengths and weaknesses that compliment each other without the need for competition based on separation. We also can assist and further each other in the path of exploration and discovery.

~~~ A deep sigh out ~~~

The Bigger Picture

Some of the most valuable assistance in my life originally came from what another spirit guide, Alcazar (channeled by Prageet) used to call the "Bigger Picture." He taught and showed me that in almost all instances when I feel stuck, overwhelmed, frustrated, or out of sorts, it is because I am not able to see the "Bigger Picture" in a given situation. My focus is too small and my perspective on a given subject or situation too narrow, usually because I have limited my perspective to the personal aspect of a given situation. That is, I take things too personal instead of opening up the lens of my viewing capacity to include a larger perspective, like my family, my community, my town, etc. Every time I open up in a seemingly stuck situation to invite the "Bigger Picture", the dam breaks and I am able to move on with a clear head and outlook.

In dealing and conversing with my spirit guides, my most frequent question is "Can you help me see the Bigger Picture here?" or "What is the Bigger Picture here that I do not see?" Because the spirit guides exist outside time and space and per definition thus have access to a much larger perspective, that larger perspective is what they can offer. It is then up to us to receive, hear, see that offer, and make a decision as to its value.

Just because the advice originated in that "other" realm, does not always mean it is the best advice in town for a given situation. I learned that over many years of interactions. But, whether the advice or suggestion of a spirit guide is true or not, is not the issue here. What matters is that the asking in itself opens up the lens of perception so that other solutions and/or options become accessible. It creates an abundance of options instead of a dearth, and from that abundance ease flows. Every time I sense ease in my life, I know that I am on the right path. It does not mean that everything comes easy, because sometimes I have to work hard for a given situation, but the overall sense is one of ease instead of struggle.

~~~ A deep belly breath in ~~~

Soul

We in the spirit world come and visit you frequently.
We are never there to interrupt your busy schedule.
But we are there to remind you that you have everything deep within,
that you need to accomplish the rewards and the goals that your soul

Guidance Fullness

has set for this, your current life.
We are there to remind you that by following your intuition, your path,
you are always coming into the right time,
the right place to give yourself and every one else around you
the opportunity to have the experiences
that they need to accomplish their growth.

~~ Dr. Peebles ~~

~~~~~~~~~~

Daylight, full of small dancing particles
and the one great turning, our souls
are dancing with you, without feet, they dance.
Can you see them when I whisper in your ear?

~~ Rumi (Coleman Barks Translation) ~~

~~~~~~~~~~

Just because it's not nice doesn't mean it's not miraculous.

~~ Terry Pratchett, Interesting Times ~~

~~~~~~~~~~

I asked Spirit for strength
That I might achieve
I was made weak
That I might learn to surrender

I asked for health
That I might do great things
I was given infirmity
That I might do better things

I asked for riches
That I might be happy
I was given poverty
That I might be wise

Fullness No Matter What

I asked for power
That I might have the praise of humankind
I was given obscurity
That I might enjoy life

I was given life
That I might enjoy all things

I received nothing that I had asked for
But everything I had hoped for
Despite myself
My unspoken prayers were answered
I am among the ones most richly blessed

~~ Unknown Source ~~

~~~~~~~~~~

More

I found the following good website with lots of good information on Spirit Guides: http://www.awomansjourney.com/spiritguides.html

Paradoxing

Stretching

Come draw me out on widespread wings
As far and fast as I can stretch
Come pull on me in all directions
I want to be expanded to the fullest
Into an arch so high and far
It reaches all the way into oblivion

And when there is just no more reaching
When every nerve and sinew says no no
When arching stretches further than I dare
When pain and pleasure become one
Then split me open all the way into infinity

~~ Ulla! ~~

Paradoxing

Body

Just as a refresher: In the context of this book as a journey through fullness Paradoxing is both the carriage and you the passenger in the carriage, as outlined in the Introduction.

Breathing Exercise: Paradoxing Stretch in a Sphere

This breathing exercise is an invitation to explore the concept of Paradoxing inside our bodies. In a culture in love with linear thinking and doing, situations that involve paradoxes, that is the idea that something can be both true and false at the same time, or both good and bad, literally gets us out of our minds.

Preparations

Specific instructions for this particular exercise:

- ❖ Think of an issue in your life that has you split two ways. Damn if you do, damn if you don't. I sure want to have my cake and eat it too.
- ❖ Or think of some aspect in your life that you would consider your shadow or your dark side. Find its opposite and use those two aspects in the following Breathing exercise.

This Breathing Exercise is designed to be experienced while you are reading it, preferably out loud to yourself, if you are in a position to do so. If not, at least mouth the words; it will help you slow down and stay focused. If you are with a partner who is open to sharing this exercise, take turns reading it out loud to each other. Make sure you are in a position to relax while you are reading, without falling asleep too quickly.

If you want to intensify this exercise, invite your spirit guides and angels, known or unknown, seen or unseen, to join you in this experience.

Exercise

- ❖ I bring my awareness to the center of my upper chest area just below the collarbones, the crossroads between the horizontal line of my arms and the vertical line of my head and torso.

- I am appreciating the center of my upper chest area for doing such a wonderful job of being the crossroads between the horizontal and the vertical lines of my body.
- I focus my breath into the center of my upper chest area and place my hands on my chest in a comfortable position.
- If I feel any discomfort or tightness in my upper chest area, I notice it.
- I totally accept the pain or discomfort by sending my very own Breath of Ease and Acceptance into the tender or tight area. I bring that Breath of Ease and Acceptance into every area of discomfort, one after another, until my upper chest area, my neck, and my shoulders are glowing with acceptance.
- I feel my chest rise with the inbreath, slowly counting to five, and fall with the outbreath, again slowly counting to five.
- I continue watching the rise and fall of my chest for about four to six long slow breaths.

The Pentagram

- I remember the two issues, or opposite ends that I want to explore.
- I notice my thoughts, feelings or sensations first about one issue.
  - I notice my thoughts, feelings or sensations then about the other issue.
  - I bring my awareness to the center of my upper chest area into my very own **Peace Room**.
  - I imagine activating my very own **Ray of Creative Expression**.
  - I imagine sending that Ray of Creative Expression in a straight line through my right shoulder, my right arm, squeezing through my right elbow and wrist and lighting up the **Jewel of Integrity** in the center of the palm of my right hand.
- I imagine placing one side, the opposite end of my issue, or my dark aspect directly inside the Jewel of Integrity in my right hand.
- I imagine sending that Ray of Creative Expression in a straight line from the Jewel of Integrity in the center of the palm of my right hand directly into my left foot, activating the **Bubbles of Laughter** in the sole of my left foot.

- ❖ I imagine sending that Ray of Creative Expression in a straight line from the Bubbles of Laughter in the sole of my left foot all the way up into the top of my head, activating the **Fountain of Gratitude**.
- ❖ I imagine sending that Ray of Creative Expression in a straight line from the Fountain of Gratitude on the top of my head directly into my right foot, activating the **Bubbles of Laughter** in the sole of my right foot.
- ❖ I imagine sending that Ray of Creative Expression in a straight line from the Bubbles of Laughter in the sole of my right foot all the way up into my left palm, lighting up the **Jewel of Integrity** in my left hand.
- ❖ I imagine placing the other side of my issue, or opposite end directly inside the Jewel of Integrity in my left hand.
- ❖ I imagine sending that Ray of Creative Expression in a straight line from the Jewel of Integrity in the center of the palm of my right hand through my right wrist and elbow, through my right shoulder directly into the center of my upper chest area into my very own **Peace Room**.
- ❖ I have now imagined the outlines of a Pentagram using my hands, feet, and head as anchor points.
- ❖ I have placed the two sides of my issue into my hands, and am holding it in my body.
- ❖ I feel or sense into my body, now all connected through the Ray of Creative Expression.
- ❖ I notice any sensations, feelings, or agitation.
- ❖ I just rest with them.

The Sphere

- ❖ I bring my awareness into the center of my chest area into my heart by placing a hand on my chest.
- ❖ I connect with my very own Color of Loving.
- ❖ I imagine it glowing inside my heart.
- ❖ I imagine the glow growing into a sphere of light that keeps expanding and expanding until it reaches all the way around my physical body.
- ❖ I imagine stretching out my arms and spreading my legs to touch the edged of the sphere just as the Da Vinci Man in the drawing at the beginning of this exercise.

- ❖ I imagine my whole body being contained by the sphere of my own Color of Loving.
- ❖ I bathe in that sense of being completely surrounded in my own loving.
- ❖ I notice any feelings, sensations, or thoughts coming up.
- ❖ I just rest with them.
- ❖ I remember the two sides or opposite ends of an issue I imagined placing in the palms of my two hands.
- ❖ I notice my sensations, thoughts, or feelings about the issue.

~~~~~~

- ❖ I notice any changes in my body, in my sense of well being, in my breathing.
- ❖ I once again feel my chest rise with the inbreath, slowly counting to five, and fall with the outbreath, again slowly counting to five.
- ❖ I continue watching the rise and fall of my chest for about four to six long slow breaths.
- ❖ Anytime now I can access my Pentagram and my Sphere and experience their effect on my life in the hours, days, and months to come.

Completion

- ❖ When I am complete, I bring my awareness back to the world outside of me.
- ❖ I wiggle my toes and fingers.
- ❖ I stretch my body like a cat with a few lazy, long, full body stretches.
- ❖ I am back in my waking reality.

Suggestions

You can use this particular breathing exercise anytime you are dealing with some darker aspects of your personality, or with two seemingly opposing issues. By holding their polarity inside your body, you are inviting the universe to help you find a way to solve that particular issue or balance out your darker aspect. This is a powerful invocation for change in your life.

Paradoxing

Pleasure Exercises
Solo: Breathing the Bow and Arrow
Preparations

- Have some time alone and undisturbed available, preferably not just before you go to sleep.
- Think about two opposing ideas, concepts, choices in your life, that are both important to you. For example: commitment in a relationship and personal freedom, or a career and a deeply connected relationship, or a lot of money to go traveling the world and a simple land based life.
- Write the two ideas, concepts, wishes etc down on two separate pieces of paper.
- Have two different objects handy that somehow could represent these two opposing ideas. For example, a pinecone and a rock, or a piece of jewelry and a flower, or a piece of string and a bird's feather.

Creating the Bow and Arrow

- Decide which object represents which idea. Connect the appropriate piece of paper with the appropriate object of your choosing.
- Place one object plus paper in your left hand, and the other object plus paper in your right hand.
- Lay on your back either on your bed or the floor. Spread out both arms with the objects in each hand.
- Place the objects on the bed where your hands are, so that your hands are free to move without the objects.
- Reach up with both your hands and touch your head. You have just created the Bow part of your Bow and Arrow. It reaches from the left hand over your head down to your right hand.
- Place your hands back on top or close to the two objects.

Fullness No Matter What

- Imagine a string strung from you left hand through your shoulders into your right hand, that is, imagine tracing the string from one hand through your arm, your torso, the other arm and into the other hand.
- Imagine your head, torso, and legs as the arrow just being fit into the bow.
- Once more imagine all the parts of the Bow and arrow: the **String** strung between your hands across your upper chest, the **Bow** reaching from one outstretched arm and hand above your head over to the other outstretched arm and hand, your torso and your head as the **Arrow** with your head being the arrow head.
- Now your Bow is complete.

Pulling the String

- Take your hands and lay your hands in the nook between your collarbones.
- Imagine hooking your thumbs into your string.
- Pull your string by tracing a line with your thumbs all the way down your body until you touch your Pearl or your Lingam.
- Start playing with your Pearl or Lingam to physically hook in the bowstring.
- Get really aroused but don't have an orgasm to create the tension of the bowstring.
- Stop just before the "point of no return" and (if you can) remember the two opposing ideas, concepts, choices in your life.
- Now your Bow is strung, that is your bow is loaded.

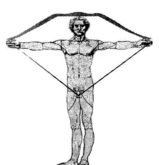

- If you don't release that tension into an orgasm, and just be with that tension, there is good chance the universe will. Something's gotta give. And change might just be the answer.

Suggestions

Once again, even though I am running the risk of sounding repetitive, have fun with this! If it works, great! If it doesn't, you had some good pleasure, hopefully, and tried something different. You can also use the image of the Bow and Arrow without the sexual component to help you balance two opposing ideas, concepts, choices in your life.

Partnered: The Crowning of the Jewels

This is a beautiful partner exercise to bring opposites together in a sensuous way, in this case your head and your Jewels, and we are not talking oral honoring here! This is a good exercise to do after orgasms, when you want to still feel connected to your partner, but not in an arousing way, and you are not too sleepy yet!

This exercise needs a place to lean against and enough room for one of you to lie on the back with stretched out legs. By the way, this is most enjoyable when you are both naked!

The idea here is for one of you to sit comfortably having your back lean against the headboard of your bed or the wall and supported by pillows. Spread your legs wide enough for your partner to slide in, while lying on her or his back. Slide in until the crown of your head touches your partners Jewels.

Woman sitting Upright, Man on his Back

As a man lying on your back, reach up with your hands to grab hold of both of your partner's hands. Gently and slowly slide into your partner's Jewels. Have your eyes closed while your head slowly gets closer and closer to your partner's Yoni and Pearl. Can you feel her heat on your scalp (or do her pubic hairs just tickle your skin)? Gently wiggle yourself into the right spot, one that exerts just enough pressure to feel good. Let her tell you what feels good to him.

Once you have both found a comfortable position, try to synchronize your breathing. As a woman sitting upright slowly breathe in and out with deep belly breaths, bearing down into your Yoni and squeezing your PC muscles. When you breathe out, relax your Jewels. As a man getting crowned, follow her breathing pattern. You will feel her breath through the contractions of his Yoni on the top of your head. Do about 15 slow breaths in and out or until you feel complete.

Man sitting Upright, Woman on her Back

As a woman lying on your back, reach up with your hands to grab hold of both of his hands. Gently and slowly slide into your partner's Jewels. Have your eyes closed while your head slowly gets closer and closer to your partner's Lingam and Twin Globes. Can you feel his heat on your scalp? Gently wiggle yourself into the right spot, one that exerts just enough pressure to feel good. Let him tell you what feels good to her. It helps for the man to adjust "his package" so that it feels comfortable, especially the sensitive Twin Globes. You can even lay your Lingam on her forehead if anatomy and state of arousal allow for that.

Once you have both found a comfortable position, try to synchronize your breathing. As a man sitting upright slowly breathe in and out with deep belly breaths, bearing down into your Lingam and squeezing your PC muscles. When you breathe out, relax your Jewels. As a woman getting crowned, follow his breathing pattern. You will feel his breath through the contractions of her Jewels on the top of your head. Do about 15 slow breaths in and out or until you feel complete.

For Both

Giver: explore sending your own Color of Loving (Chapter 1) with your breath through your Jewels into your partner's head and body.

Receiver: explore the synchronizing of your own breath with your partner's breath. There is nothing you need to do, just feel the connection between your hands, between your head and your partner's Jewels, and between your breathing. Can you feel the love pouring out of your partner's Jewels into your head and body? Have you ever felt loved through your partner's Jewels like that, which is not through sexual union or other forms of love making?

When you both feel complete, either switch roles, or just cuddle and switch roles another time. Just know yourself fully loved through your partner's Jewels in this unique way of being crowned through your partner's Jewels. Wear this crown proudly. It's a special one!

Mind

Left Foot versus Right Foot

As part of the Grand Experiment we in the Western world live very much in a problem oriented world with numerous "fix-it" approaches to all those problems. Wherever you look, there seem to be problems and more problems (and we do have some major problems facing us). But I realized that we have options here. We have numerous opportunities every day to shift our focus from problem orientation to fullness orientation and thereby actually be part of the solutions rather than the problems. Einstein said many years ago that "The significant problems we have cannot be solved at the same level of thinking with which we created them."

Let me tell you a story: A few years while visiting the Hawaiian island of Maui I was invited by a friend to participate in a fire walk. There were about 20 feet of very hot Kiawe wood coals (Kiawe is the Hawaiian version of Mesquite wood, which burns very hot!) available for anyone to walk across barefooted. I felt nervous. I had heard about this experience, had seen videos about it, but had never participated in one. At some point I had gathered enough courage to take my turn.

The minute I put my left foot down, I felt like I had made a mistake. I felt a searing pain and tried to walk across the 20 feet of scorching hot coals as fast as I could (interestingly, the thought to just step to the side and be done with the walk never occurred to me). When I got to the other side, I had a badly burned left foot. All my attention went to that burned left foot and the next three weeks on Maui were pretty miserable. I could not even go near a beach as sand aggravated the sore sole of my blistered foot. My mind berated me with all kinds of judgments, criticism, and reasons for having ended up getting my foot injured. In short, it was not the kind of uplifting and inspiring experience I had expected from fire walking.

Three or four years later I remembered this experience. In retelling it to a friend I realized that I had focused all my attention on the burnt left foot and its considerable pain. At the same time I had totally neglected to appreciate the fact that my right foot had managed the fire walk without getting burned at all. While all my focus had been on the problem of the burnt foot, I had missed the miracle of the "unburnt" foot. Remember, I had walked across 20 feet of red hot Kiawe coals and my right foot had stayed untouched by that scorching heat.

This realization that the fire walk had provided me with two entirely different but simultaneous realities and that I had chosen to focus on the problem instead on the miracle, allowed for a shift in my life. I began to see that at any given point I had a choice to focus my attention on my burnt foot or on my "unburnt" foot, that is, on the problematic aspects of my life, or the easy, effortless aspects. I had always heard and even used the common saying, "Is the glass half full or half empty?" but not until I had lived through and years later reevaluated the fire walk experience did that saying hit home.

I know now without a doubt that I have a choice in any given situation. Do I focus on that part in me (or in others or in the world) that is hurt and wounded and dysfunctional, or do I focus on that part in me (or in others or in the world) that is whole, has always been whole, and will always be whole. Each one of us always has both of these outlooks available at the same time. And we are always at choice as to whether we focus on the wounded part or the whole part, the problem or the solution.

~~~ *A deep sigh out* ~~~

Contrary Medicine Man

The world we live in today has extensively been exploring how to live on only one side of the fence. Said in a different way, it likes to see issues in black and white, and usually considers it obligatory to choose either one or the other. If we feel morally propelled to do so and take consequences into consideration, we tend to choose the white one. If we want to have some fun and don't care about consequences, or are just incurably curious, the black side is the one for us. Either way, a choice for one of two options seems the way to go.

Other cultures are exploring similar concepts. My friend Saha Johnson, who traveled in South America to study native medicine, told me the following story: He had spent time in a village that had several medicine men. One of them had been assigned the job of holding the opposite end of the spectrum for the whole village. When the whole village was celebrating a wedding by feasting, singing, and dancing, he would be found sitting in front of his hut and in earshot of the celebrants crying, lamenting, and sobbing. When the whole village was wailing and sobbing in deep grief over the death of a villager, he, again in earshot of the grievers, would be dancing, rejoicing, and singing loudly. His job was to always do, within earshot, the opposite of what the village was doing. His medicine was to always remind the whole village that whatever they were experiencing, it was only one side of the whole. This "contrary" medicine man held a much-honored position in and for the village, because he provided the "other half" in order for the whole to be balanced.

Paradoxing

One way to be catapulted into fullness involves being both the village and the contrary medicine man, that is, not making a choice if we can avoid it. That sets into motion a very interesting mechanism. When we refuse to make a choice in situations that demand it due to seemingly opposite concepts or ideas (or plain habit), and instead consciously decide to hold both opposite ideas or concepts in our awareness, we step into a creative force. Balancing two opposite ideas or concepts in our awareness, that is refusing to choose one or the other, sets up a tension between those two opposing ideas and concepts. That tension wants to be released, needs to be released, even has to be released. The Universe, God, Source will step in and resolve that tension by moving our awareness to the next level.

Going back to the fire walk experience, I realized not only that I have a choice on what to focus my attention on. But I also realized that I am simultaneously both aspects all the time. I am both burnt and whole at the same time. If I extend the experience with my feet to my whole being, this is what it looks like: I am at the same time a dysfunctional, sometimes neurotic, limited, fear based, contracted, imperfect being, and a whole, unlimited, expansive, absolutely perfect being.

I noticed that whenever I feel myself caught in the grips of contracting worry and fear thoughts, all I need to remember is to put my awareness into both of my feet. All of a sudden I relax, expand and let go of all the worrisome thoughts. Putting my awareness into both of my feet reminds me that I am always both: contracted and expanded, wounded and whole, imperfect and perfect. And guess what? Then it really does not matter anymore, what you feel like at any given moment. If we are everything anyway, why worry?

~~~ *A deep belly breath in* ~~~

My Story

Interestingly, I found that exact principle at work for much of my life. It is as if some part of me unconsciously knew how to create change in my life by letting me experience seeming opposites at the same time. That dynamic always propelled me into the next level of exploration.

I have a Masters Degree in American Literature and aspired to be a poet, while going to graduate school. As a student I happened to stumble across a class in computer word processing on a mainframe computer (this was before personal computers). The funny thing was that before I took that class I had been dead set against computers in general, and found them a nuisance and not at all conducive to writing poetry, my main passion then. Despite my original attitude, I actually ended up having a student job doing word processing for a whole book on the computer. I also found out that I liked working with computers. It opened up a whole new range of "career" options for an American Literature student aspiring to be a poet.

These original computer classes helped me to be ready when the first high tech incubator park in Germany, called the Gruenderzentrum, was opened in Berlin in 1983. A woman friend and I co-created a company called "tech-writers" to write computer handbooks for computer novices. I once again entered the world of business more on a lark. I was someone who had no idea how business worked, never had even worked in a major company, nor did I believe in the business model. Ideologically I was more of a hippie, ready to fight the "establishment" instead of joining it. But so what. As my great uncle Vollrath von Krosigk had taught me: "Was kuemmert mich mein Geschwaetz von gestern?" meaning, "what do I care what I babbled yesterday?"

My company "tech-writers" turned into a German media hit featured by most major German magazines, newspapers, television programs, radio stations, even the Wall Street Journal, for several reasons: One, for novelty reasons as "tech-writers" was the only women run company in Germany's first high tech incubator. Two, I fit the bill when I became pregnant a week after "tech-writers" had been founded, decided to have the child while still co-running "tech-writers", and in the eyes of the media became "the woman who can do it all, both career and motherhood". And three, I already then was very vocal in my opinions and ideas and most willing and able to express them in front of cameras, microphones, reporters and both small and large audiences.

Those are just two examples of how Paradoxing can be seen at work in my own life. By allowing myself to experience and explore seeming opposites at the same time, I was propelled into a much larger life than I had ever dreamed of.

Here is another way of saying the same thing: how can we create an irresistible invitation for change to enter our lives? By accepting both our present undesirable situation and the longing for change, we become the arrow and get literally catapulted into the change we sometimes so ardently desire. See Solo

Pleasure Exercise in this chapter to explore the Bow and Arrow principle from a different angle.

~~~ A deep sigh out ~~~

The Shadow

To me paradoxing is also a useful tool in relating to the Shadow, that is the darker aspects of our personality. It does not matter whether we encounter these darker aspects individually in various forms of therapy including Jungian analysis, or collectively in dictatorial regimes as Hitler's Nazi Germany.

So often those aspects are deeply buried and prefer to stay hidden in the dark until we finally find ourselves face to face with those darker aspects of our personality. That experience can easily immobilize us through feelings of guilt, fear, shame and even horror concerning those least desirable aspects of our personality. It is important to remember that, though least desirable, they are at the same time quite powerful and potent, and an integral part of our personality. So much of our deepest core strength lies hidden inside of us as long as our shadow remains unseen and unacknowledged.

One way to coax the shadow into being seen is to literally bring more light into our lives. When we invite the forces of love, joy, and especially sensuous pleasure into our lives, we can expect the shadow to put in more appearances, and to enrich our lives in the process. It's what makes us so richly human, those darker aspects, the ones we would rather die than share with anyone. It brings out true compassion with the rest of humanity, when we have to come terms with our own dark, devious, or despicable behavior, instead of hiding behind a "holier than Thou" facade.

I personally am able to commit deeply to a new relationship, only when both shadows have come out to dance. I really feel safe only when I have allowed myself to be seen in my less desirable aspects, and have seen and experienced my partner's shadow. There is a deep beauty in relationship that only unfolds when those darker aspects know themselves to be part of the relationship dance.

One way how to dance with our own shadow is to invite it into the paradoxing paradigm. Instead of blaming myself for the existence and visitation of those darker aspects of my personality, I offer them a proper placement using the bow and arrow image. Living in the awareness of the Paradoxing Pentagram (see Breathing Exercise: Paradoxing Stretch in a Sphere) allows me to remember that no matter what I experience, whether it is the highest bliss and joy and pleasure, the opposite experience is part of the whole. The same goes for the darker experiences like pain, jealousy, envy or rage: the opposite force is built in, and thus healing balance is always available.

~~~ *A deep belly breath in* ~~~

Soul

We are the mirror as well as the face in it.
We are tasting the taste this minute
of eternity. We are pain
and what cures pain, both. We are
the sweet cold water and the jar that pours.

~~ Rumi (Coleman Barks Translation) ~~

~~~~~~~~~~

Wonderful! Thought Vimes.
Sometimes it's like watching a wasp land on a
stinging nettle; someone's going to get stung and you don't care.

~~ Terry Pratchett, Night Watch ~~

~~~~~~~~~~

Each problem has hidden in it
An opportunity so powerful
That it literally dwarfs the problem—
If we just look for the hidden opportunities
Instead of dwelling on the problem.

~~ Unknown Source ~~

7

Connecting Fullness

I Am Reaching Out

I am reaching out
To all of me
So loving has a place

I am reaching out
To all of you
So laughing has a time

I am reaching out
To all of us
So heaven is just here

~~ Ulla! ~~

Body

Connection is something we so often look for in the world around us, that is, in our partners, children, family, friends and animals amongst many possibilities. We want them to include us in their worlds and often don't know how to ask for it. Here is an invitation to create connection by including ourselves, by connecting ourselves to the world around us. We are in charge here of the connection.

Breathing Exercise:
Web and Jewel of Connecting Fullness

Preparations

This Breathing Exercise is designed to be experienced while you are reading it, preferably out loud to yourself, if you are in a position to do so. If not, at least mouth the words; it will help you slow down and stay focused. If you are with a partner who is open to sharing this exercise, take turns reading it out loud to each other. Make sure you are in a position to relax while you are reading, without falling asleep too quickly.

If you want to intensify this exercise, invite your spirit guides and angels, known or unknown, seen or unseen, to join you in this experience.

Exercise

- ❖ I bring my awareness to my shoulders, my upper arms, my elbows, my lower arms, my wrists, the palms of my hands, my thumbs, and all the way into the tips of my fingers.
- ❖ I place my hands on top of each other on my chest in a comfortable position.
- ❖ I appreciate my arms and hands for doing such a wonderful job of giving me the chance to do so many things in my life.
- ❖ If I am remembering that my arms and hands can't do all I would like them to do, I completely accept any restrictions of movement just for the duration of this exercise.
- ❖ If I feel any discomfort or tightness in my arms and hands, I notice it.

- I totally accept it by directing my very own Loving Color into the tender or tight area. I bring that Loving Color of acceptance into every area of discomfort, one after another, until my arms and hands are glowing with acceptance.

~~~~~~

- I focus my inbreath into my arms and hands, that is I feel my chest area rise with the inbreath, and I imagine that I can gently push my breath all the way into my shoulders, into my arms, into my hands, and into my fingers.
- This breath is like a wave on the ocean being watched from a boat looking onto a sandy shore. I watch the wave building up to a crest, breaking, and rolling down the beach all the way into my fingertips, slowly counting to five.
- I watch my outbreath recede like a wave from the beach. It recedes from my fingertips through my hands, through my arms, through my shoulders, and I watch my chest fall with the outbreath, slowly counting to five.
- I continue watching the flow of the waves, my inbreath, and my outbreath for about four to six long slow breaths.

The Web of Connecting

- I imagine looking at my hands with my inner eyes.
- I imagine bringing my hands together palm touching palm.
- I feel a warmth between my palms, a soft glowing warmth. It spreads all over my palms, my fingers, and my thumbs
- I imagine my hands slowly spreading apart, very slowly. And when they do a web of many threads and connecting points is being formed between my palms.
- It looks like a cat's cradle, a game we might have played as children involving a looped string being woven between our ten fingers, creating a variety of patterns.
- This web is very flexible. When I move my palms closer together, it shrinks. When I move them farther apart, it expands. It does not break or rip except if I want it to.
- Its texture is both soft and light.
- It has a color, or a smell, or a temperature that is all my own.

- This is my connecting web.
- Anytime is feel disconnected from anything (a person, a place, a plant, or whatever), I imagine that thing or person between my hands inside my Web of Connecting.
- I am creating that connection by imagining the object or person in between my hands.
- I can imagine placing my whole body between my hands.
- I can even imagine placing a whole town, a country, between my hands. Size is no limitation, just my own imagination and creativity, and my wanting to feel and be connected.
- I can place anything or anybody into the web between my hands that I want to be connecting to.
- Once I have placed an objector a person into my web, I just rest with that image between my hands.
- I notice any changes and just be with them.

The Jewel of Integrity

- Once I have created a connecting web with an object or a person, and that connection settles in, the Jewel of Integrity lights up inside my palms.
- This Jewel of Integrity helps me stay connected in integrity. In integrity to myself and in integrity to all my connections within me and around me.
- It helps me to create and receive in right action to all living things on the planet, in the planet, and throughout the universe.
- When I am in doubt about my integrity all I need to do is weave my web of connecting and the Jewel of Integrity will light my way. Even if sometimes it feels like the harder and more complicated way to go.
- The Jewel of Integrity will help me smooth the way.
- The following words repeated three times will help when I am in doubt: "I am ready, willing, and able to create and receive in right action to all living things on the planet, in the planet, and throughout the universe."
- I simply rest in the knowing that I can weave the web and let the Jewel of Integrity light my way.
- I notice any changes in my body, in my sense of well being, in my breathing.

~~~~~~

- I once again focus my inbreath into my arms and hands, that is I feel my chest area rise with the inbreath, and I imagine that I can gently push my breath all the way into my shoulders, into my arms, into my hands, and into my fingers.
- This breath is like a wave on the ocean being watched from a boat looking onto a sandy shore. I watch the wave building up to a crest, breaking, and rolling down the beach all the way into my fingertips, slowly counting to five.
- I watch my outbreath recede like a wave from the beach. It recedes from my fingertips through my hands, through my arms, through my shoulders and I watch my chest fall with the outbreath, slowly counting to five.
- I continue watching the flow of the waves, my inbreath, and my outbreath for about four to six long slow breaths.
- Anytime now I can access my Web of Connection and the Jewel of Integrity and experience their effect on my life in the hours, days, and months to come.

Completion

- When I am complete, I bring my awareness back to the world outside of me.
- I wiggle my toes and fingers.
- I stretch my body like a cat with a few lazy, long, full body stretches.
- I am back in my waking reality.

Suggestions

If you want to make sure that you experience more Connecting Fullness in your life, try the Mandala Breathing described at the end of the Breathing Exercise: Color of Loving Fullness.

Pleasure Exercises

Solo: Pleasurable Connections in Nature

The beauty of being single is that we get to reach out and find alternative ways of being in pleasure rather than just constantly looking for pleasure with a partner. When we are in a love relationship we can enjoy the fact that we can more easily feel connected to pleasure, but we tend to limit our pleasure to only that one partner. When we are single, the initiative is ours by necessity and choice, and so we find ourselves sometimes more adventuresome…Did you think I was going to extol the advantages of multiple partners? Fooled ya. This is much better!

Here is an invitation to deepen your connection to nature with the help of imagination. This is about thinking outside the box. This is about opening up new and entirely different channels of pleasurable explorations. And this is about finding pleasure in everyday experiences. Here are a few suggestions:

- **Go swimming in a lake or a rock quarry on a hot summer day,** with or without bathing suit. Imagine the water being a lover, maybe a transparent green water nymph with long hair tresses, emerald green eyes, and long silky webbed fingers. Imagine the soft and cool water flowing across your skin being loving caresses by this green water nymph. Totally surrender to the caresses while you are swimming or wading in the cool water, maybe even close your eyes to stay really focused on every sensation the flowing water will bring to you.

- **The hot sand on an ocean beach could be a lizard lover,** moving very, very slowly across your skin, especially when you are lying on your back. Your lizard lover is making sure that his sun drenched touch penetrates you to your core. Feel the passionate wet and foamy embraces of the surf by kneeling in the wet sand while ocean waves break on a sandy beach. One minute the waves will pull you into the wide ocean, the next they will push you up the shore, back and forth, back and forth. Your ocean lover even leaves you with traces of the lovemaking in your bathing suit. Lots of wet sand…

- **If you happen to live near a field of sunflowers,** or pass one on the way to somewhere, take the time to visit the caressing hands of these tall golden giants. Wear as little clothes as seems proper or comfortable, close your eyes, and very slowly find your way through the rows of slightly scratchy rustling leaves. Stay in the sensations on your skin, on your face, on your hands, and on your legs. Open your ears to the sounds and your nose to the smells.

- **Hot springs in snow country offer some delightful sensations,** if you feel daring enough. First get thoroughly heated up in the embraces of your steaming hot mineral water lover. Then let yourself fall into the freezing cold embraces of your snow lover. Rub yourself in the icy snow, back and front. Create a snow eagle in your bathing suit, or even naked. When you feel cooled off, get back into the hot water embrace. And out again into the arms of your snow lover, and back again into the steaming hot water, and into the freezing cold snow. And hot. And cold. If you have the energy, go back and forth seven times. After a while your nerves simply give up…They cannot distinguish anymore between hot and cold. All of it becomes pure, unadulterated, invigoratingly intense pleasure.

- **When there is a summer thunderstorm brewing**, don't hide in the house and wait till it's over. Run outside to welcome your thunder lover with open arms. Let the raindrop caresses wash you clean of all your sorrows and worries. Get thoroughly soaked in the rain storm. Slowly lick off the drops that fall on your lips. Imagine the thunder or the lightning being another form of caress. Revel in the sensations, the sounds, and the smells of your thunderstorm lover.

- **Piles of drying leaves in the fall are another kind of sensation rich lover.** Who cares about dirty and wet clothes on a sunny fall day when there is still enough warmth left to dare to play with so many colors and textures and smells.

- **I nearly forgot about the icy cold and invigorating creek lover in the mountains.** Slide over and around the rocks into the rushing, bubbling embrace of that creek lover you always wanted to feel completely enveloped by.

- **Oh, and the soft, gentle, blossom nymphs of the fruit trees!** They love to just shower you with their treasure, especially when you have your eyes closed while embracing the tree trunk, ready to drink in the pink and white fruit blossom fragrances.

By the way, these pleasurable nature experiences are not only good for singles!

Partnered: Loving Touch of Your Partner's Jewels

I enjoy touching my partner's Jewels a lot, just for the sake of feeling connected on the physical level through touch. When I am lazing around in bed with my partner talking, hanging out, maybe after lovemaking, or in between, I really enjoy having my hands on his Jewels. I might be playing with his pubic hair, or just cupping my hands over his whole package. I also deeply enjoy being touched in that same loving and connected way.

Interestingly though, we usually do not touch each other's Jewels in a non-arousing way. When we touch Jewels, we tend to do it to elicit a sexual response from them. The following exercises are best enjoyed in a relaxed situation, with enough time and space to just play.

Women

It is a real treat for a woman to receive a loving massage on and around her Jewels. Start by touching her belly, her hips, and her upper legs. Then try gently pulling on her pubic hair all the way down to the Rosebud. When touching her Jewels directly, use lots of water soluble lubricant. You can spread her labias and gently stroke her Pearl, around the entrance to her Yoni, on the perineum between her Yoni and her Rosebud, and around the Rosebud, all of it with well lubricated fingers.

It feels really good to be touched lovingly inside the Yoni, again with a lot of lubricant. Try touching not so much with in and out motions, but from side to side across her Sacred Spot, the walls of her Yoni, and all the way around her cervix. If you want to see her really relax, take the heel of one hand and press it fairly hard onto her Pearl, and press the other one onto the entrance of her Yoni. Just hold both hands in that position for a few minutes.

Be prepared for some tears when you first put that kind of loving attention on a woman. She might have never been touched that lovingly and undemanding on her Jewels before.

Men

Men just love being touched on and around their Jewels—so many men habitually have their hands on their own Jewels when they sense themselves unobserved or at ease. But most of them associate the touching of their Jewels with action. So if you are doing this for the first time, let them know that there is nothing for them to do but relax.

Start by stroking his pubic area, play with his pubic hair by lightly pulling on it, gently play with his Twin Globes, cup both of your hands all around his Lingam and Twin Globes, just holding them. Massage the area around his Lingam, down to the perineum (the fleshy area between the Lingam and the Rosebud) and the muscles around his Rosebud. Ask him if there is any other way he likes being touched just for the sake of being touched.

If you want to see him really relax, try holding the head of his Lingam in a strong grip with your fingers wrapped around his Lingam below the head.

Start pulling the Lingam up. Pull slowly but hard, much harder than you think you should, until you sense it is enough, or you get a stop signal from your man. This kind of pull can produce a deep whole body relaxation and is great for times of stress or just before lovemaking.

Mind

My Old Story

This is the chapter I have had the most difficulties with, and for a reason. Most of my life I experienced myself as cut off and disconnected from the world around me. In my early twenties I saw myself as spending part of my life inside a high round glass tower. This glass tower was open to the sky, but totally cut me off from direct human connection. I could see people and the world around me, but neither one could touch me, and I could not touch them.

I started to keep a daily journal when I was 13 years old. I have 15 journals, and their main theme repeated over and over again is longing and loneliness. I always felt very disconnected, not only from the world around me, but also from myself. I must have spent most of my life outside my body living in imaginary thought worlds. I loved reading novels, especially science fiction, as those were the worlds I could safely participate in inside my glass tower. These worlds were based on imagination which came naturally to me, rather than on a reality I could not relate to.

When I shared my personal reality of the glass tower with a lover a few years back, he suggested that he would help me decorate my glass tower. We spent many hours imagining furniture and curtains and appliances for my glass tower. That made it easier to accept this part of me even though it was still painful.

~~~ *A deep sigh out* ~~~

A Friend's Story

While working on this chapter, a very good friend shared with me the following insights about himself. He is in his late fifties, a very successful businessman in several ventures both in the past and right now. He has been able to create a very comfortable life for himself, where he can run his business via a cell phone and computer access. He owns a nice house, is in the process of getting divorced, is healthy and is looking forward to the possibility of successfully selling his business within a few years. In short, a good, comfortable life with enviable circumstances.

But there is a big BUT here. He says of himself, that there is nothing in his life he really feels excited about. Nothing. Not love, nor any ideas, nor his business. Not even the fantasy of owning a Lear Jet (yes, maybe he'd feel for two minutes!). He has been missing excitement in his life since he has been in his thirties. His best friend, same age and gifted with even more financial wealth, shares the same sense: nothing to feel excited about even in a life full of material wealth and ease.

~~~ A deep belly breath in ~~~

My New Story

In the last year or so for me excitement has a new dimension and I can access it most of the time. Now I can break out in joyful tears over a full moon coming up big and round over the horizon. I feel touched by these little bright purple flowers blossoming on long frail stems by the side of my hiking path. I look at an old tall gnarly pine tree on my way into town and feel awed by that presence. I can sense a dog's love for me and want to roll in the grass with it, sharing its joy and exuberance. I can get excited about fresh ripe blueberries and eat them one by one letting their tart sweetness burst in my mouth. I feel caressed by the warm summer wind blowing through my hair, my clothes, and over my skin.

What changed? A good question. I am not quite sure, to tell you the truth. Somewhere in the last year my glass tower seems to have shattered and I now "know" myself to be connected. Connected to people around me, connected to myself, connected to nature in all its aspects. When fullness found me, it brought with it the gift of a never ending excitement about everything, both big and small.

What amazes me in the context of this book is how my painful personal reality of the glass tower is now serving me so well in effortlessly and easily visualizing and creating all these Breathing Exercises for this book. I am delighted how easily the invitations to find all these aspects of fullness accessible to each one of us have come to me. It was as if the images and ideas stood in line "to come out" and the book wrote me rather than me writing the book. My childhood wounding that had created the glass tower reality has turned into the gift of a vast and rich internal world. Here is a poem by Rumi describing how I feel now:

~~~~~~~~~~

RUMI, PAY HOMAGE

If God said:
"Rumi, pay homage to everything
that helped you
enter my arms."

There would not be one experience
of my life, not one thought, not
one feeling, not any act, I
would not bow to.

~~ Rumi (Landinsky Translation) ~~

~~~~~~~~~~

Separation

On my hike along the creek one morning the contents of this chapter finally became clear. First of all, my story is not unique. Hearing my friend's story and the stories of others around me allowed me to see that I am not alone in having lived part of my life disconnected from the world and the people around me. Further inquiry led me to examine the history of Western culture during the last 2000 years. In our Western civilization we are wearing historical and cultural blinders that predispose us to viewpoints leaning more towards separation than towards connection. (Please keep in mind that all these observations are to be understood in the positive context of the Grand Experiment and not as a critique—see Grand Experiment in the Introduction).

In my opinion, anytime we express a preference combined with a value judgment we are creating separation, for example: "I prefer the Green Party and it is the best party." This becomes especially effective when a preference combined with a value judgment turns into underlying assumptions of institutionalized thinking like in religions, churches, ruling classes, or governments. Here are some examples of preferential judgments in the last 2000 years:

- **Dominator Culture:** A preference for human beings as "crowning of God's creation" compared to animals, plants, minerals, the earth etc;
- **Rationalism:** A preference for the faculty of the mind over faculties of emotion or of the body;
- **Patriarchy:** A preference of men and male expression in the world over women and female expression;
- **Divide and Conquer:** A political preference and tactic of the British empire.

Dominator Culture

The Dominator Culture lives and acts by the tenet that mankind (and I use the word "man" here intentionally—see Patriarchy further down in this chapter) is "The Crowning of God's Creation", to use a Christian term. Implicit in that tenet is the assumption of a hierarchy in God's creation, and in that hierarchy human beings inhabit the top position. All other aspects like plants, animals, minerals, elements, the Earth etc, are seen as subjugated to human beings.

Also implicit in this tenet is that human beings have "dominion" over the rest of "God's Creation". We human beings are to rule over the other aspects and have the right to use them to our liking. Riane Eisler in her book "The Chalice and the Blade" presents an insightful description and analysis of what she calls our "dominator culture". She offers as an alternative to the dominator model a culture based on shared participation of all aspects on this planet Earth and calls it the "partnership culture".

In my opinion, one of the reasons we are finding ourselves at this point in such a precarious worldwide crisis in terms of ecology, financial disparity, terrorism, and weapons buildup (to name just a few) is this dominator model. Interestingly this crisis is masked by a thin veneer of affluence and functionality especially in the industrialized countries. Treating the world around us "as ours to use and do with whatever we please" has definitely contributed to the ecological crisis we are facing worldwide today. The dominator model creates separation between the dominators and the to-be-dominated.

Any form of "ruling over" creates separation. How else could you put yourself "over" someone. Separation, by definition, is the opposite of connection. In a dominator model the "ruling over" (another word is "controlling") becomes a substitute for "connected with". Being connected with the world around us has not been a high priority in our Western culture.

~~~ A deep sigh out ~~~

Rationalism

When we separate ourselves from aspects of the world around us, that separation is always mirrored on the inside. When mankind decided that the animal kingdom was below us and not as valuable, we also disconnected from the so called animal aspects inside of us, like sexuality, instinctual knowing, feelings, and pleasure. We decided and lived by the tenet that functions like the rational logical mind were more valuable than feelings or pleasure. That way we separated ourselves internally from what the animal world represented externally. And as a result most forms of physical pleasure (except maybe the pleasure of eating good food) have been declared undesirable, if not downright "bad".

~~~ A deep belly breath in ~~~

Patriarchy

Another Grand Experiment in separation through hierarchical evaluation was the domination of the male sex over the female sex. What an interesting precept: to declare more than half of the human population as inferior and thus subject to all kinds of dishonoring behaviors, disempowering treatments, and large scale restrictions of personal freedom.

It gets really complex when you look at the fact that it has been women, the mothers and educators of future male dominators who perpetuated this male dominator model to a large degree. They were the ones who raised their sons (and daughters) to fit the patriarchal mold. That feat could only be accomplished by separating women from women, turning them into competitors for those few proverbial crumbs falling off the table of male dominant power. Thus a double separating strategy has been at work here.

This also means that in this outwardly oriented world women have less to loose than men by turning their backs on the existing system. When you are jumping off a burning house, it is easier if you are not very high up. In other words, men still have more to gain by staying within this externally based system than women do, even with all accomplishments of the feminist and women's rights movement. That circumstance, curiously, is opening up more chances for women to find fullness inside than men.

~~~ *A deep sigh out* ~~~

Divide and Conquer

The British Empire actually named their expansion politics "divide and conquer". Whatever countries the British Empire expanded into, it determined two factions, played out one side against the other, and that way kept their home rule stable for about a century. Examples are Israelis and Palestinians in the Near East, Protestants and Catholics in Ireland, and Muslims and Hindus in India and Pakistan. Interestingly all these divisions outlasted the British Empire. They are still areas of major conflicts in today's political arena.

All these above mentioned examples of separation strategies are deeply embedded in our Western culture. That makes it very difficult to find our way back to a life based on connection rather that separation. My experience has been that a shift towards connection has the highest chance for success when we start inside of ourselves. When we create connection with all parts of ourselves inside our bodies for ourselves, we can let that internal sense of connection carry us into the world around us and into the changes that we can accomplish in our day to day interactions.

~~~ *A deep belly breath in* ~~~

Integrity

Interestingly, when we reconnect to all parts inside of our self and around us, there is a more or less automatic side effect: we find ourselves having an uncanny sense of what integrity means in our lives. Integrity comes from integer meaning "whole" and one of the meanings for integrity is actually "completeness". When we are in integrity, we are whole, we are complete. Decisions made in integrity are decisions made for the whole, not just for certain aspects.

For example, the Tibetans have a tradition to design and construct buildings in a way that they can still be useful, stable, and functioning seven generations later. If you use the conservative number of 40 years per generation, you are looking at 280 years! Those building decisions are designed to be in integrity with the needs and concerns of the inhabitants 280 years into the future. What a sense of connection!

When we realign ourselves with the needs of the whole planet Earth, as suggested in a partnership culture, we are being asked to make decisions based on concerns larger than just our very personal ones. Interestingly, being and deciding in partnership with a larger entity like the Earth in mind, can lead to a slowing down of activity and a simplification of our lives. It becomes harder to just charge into action as fast as possible when a whole cluster of aspects have to be included in the decision making process, especially if we are talking consensus here and not top down decisions. (There is a whole new discipline among botanists and horticulturists called "systems thinking" that teaches that kind of complex problem solving management. See More at the end of the chapter)

Here is a quote concerning this subject from one of the protagonists in Ursula Le Guin's book "The Farthest Shore":

> "An act is not...like a rock that one picks up and throws, and it hits or misses, and that is the end of it. When that rock is lifted, the earth is lighter, the hand that bears it heavier. When it is thrown, the circuits of the stars respond, and where it strikes or falls, the universe is changed. On every act the balance of the whole depends.
>
> The winds and the seas, the powers of water, earth, and light, all that these do, and all that the beasts and green things do, is well done, and rightly done. All these act within the equilibrium: from the hurricane and the great whales sounding to the fall of the dried leaf and a gnat's flight, all they do is done within the balance of the whole.
>
> But we (as humans) insofar as we have power over the world and over one another, we must learn to do what the leaf and the whale and the wind do of their own nature. We must learn to keep the balance. Having intelligence, we must not act in ignorance. Having choice, we must not act without responsibility."

This slowing down in order to assess what balance looks like is the total opposite of what we are experiencing in the technological realm. The ever faster spiral of technological inventions in my eyes can only be as fast because it is not in integrity with the rest of the world. The technological advances are produced in near slave labor like conditions (often prison labor as in China) in the third world. These advances are only affordable by the mass market in the Western World because of low third world wages. Looks like another Grand Experiment, this time in the mechanics of separation.

Here is another aspect of integrity in action: feelings and thoughts on the inside become congruent with actions and words on the outside. So often in our modern world it feels as if we have to choose between paying the rent or buying shoes for our children and meaningful work. As a result of making a choice, let's say for shoes for our children, we might end up not living or speaking our truth. We might hate our job, the work we do, or the boss we are working for. But because we "need the money" (and it is not always shoes for our kids, but also the new car, the trip to Hawaii, etc), we keep working in circumstances that are not conducive to speaking and living our truth.

The minute that discrepancy shows up in our lives, the discrepancy between what we think about our boss and how we act towards her or him, we are out of integrity with ourselves. Thus we are creating separation both with the working environment and within ourselves. Interestingly, that separation has a tendency to keep us from tapping into our fullest potential.

Here is a question the above scenario raises: what values are we teaching to our kids when a pair of shoes becomes more important than telling the truth, or even living in truth?

~~~ *A deep sigh out* ~~~

Right Action for All Living Things

Here is an invitation into a parallel universe. It looks pretty much the same as this one, that is there is the same solar system with the earth as part of it. There are people living on the earth. There are plants, animals, and minerals etc. But the dynamics are different. In this parallel universe the people have found out (due to being able to tune into our universe and watch our mistakes) that action follows different laws. The main law is the following one: I am ready, willing, and able to create and receive in right action concerning all living things on the planet, in the planet, and throughout the universe.

This needs a bit of a context. Part of the Grand Experiment in the 20th century has been a belief (and resulting practices) that there is a direct link between the clarity of our vision and intention and the fulfillment of all personal wishes, needs, and wants. This belief has promoted all kinds of more or less successful proponents (Napoleon Hill, Tony Robbins, to name just a few) that invite us to try their particular method of manifesting our dreams through a world of total abundance. That particular Experiment has always been a challenge for me, especially as I tried many of the methods and found out that none of them consistently worked for me.

If my main goal is to make my personal dreams come true, just because they are my dreams and if I even have the power to do so, what happens if the fulfillment of my dreams is in conflict with the dreams of the people around me? And let's go a step further, what if the fulfillment of my dreams creates a conflict with the rights and dreams of animals, plants, the living and breathing Earth? We have learned to reevaluate a shopping center being built on "useless land" like animal and plant rich wetlands. But what about the dreams of all those small house owners that together create a neighborhood with fenced in yards and asphalt streets? Now there is no more room for deer, wolves, coyotes, raccoons, skunks, birds, insects, grasses, and butterflies. What about creek and river rights to flood in spring? What about forest fires' rights to periodically renew the land and the forests?

Here is a whole other way of experiencing ourselves connected on an equal basis with the world around us. If we know ourselves connected to the earth and all living beings on the earth, where do we fit in? And where do our personal dreams fit in? Dr. Peebles, my Spirit Guide and teacher over the last nine years offered me a helpful formula to use. When I am asking spirit to help me manifest a dream or wish or need I say: "I am ready, willing, and able to create and receive (fill in the blank) in right action to all living things on the planet, in the planet, and throughout the universe." If I send my personal wish, dream, or need out to be manifested in this way, I at least can make sure that I am not taking away somebody else's needs. What if I am asking for a free parking space directly in front of the concert hall I am going to, and by me getting it, another person who has a hard time walking, needs to take a taxi to get from the parking space to the concert hall?

~~~ A deep belly breath in ~~~

Connecting Fullness

Soul

The truth may be out there, but lies are inside your head.

~~ Terry Pratchett, Hogfather ~~

~~~~~~~~~~

Out beyond ideas of wrongdoing and rightdoing,
there is field, I'll meet you there.

When the soul lies down in that grass,
the world is too full to talk about.
Ideas, language, even the phrase each other
doesn't make any sense.

~~ Rumi (Coleman Barks Translation) ~~

~~~~~~~~~~

Do nothing because it is righteous,
praiseworthy or noble to do so.
Do nothing because it seems good to do so.
Do only that, which you must do,
and which you cannot do in any other way.

~~ Ursula K. Le Guin, The Farthest Shore ~~

~~~~~~~~~~

God said,
"I am made whole by your life. Each soul,
each soul completes
me."

~~ Hafiz (Landinsky Translation) ~~

~~~~~~~~~~

More

Cleve Backster. *Primary Perception: Biocommunication with Plants, Living Foods and Human Cells.* "Cleve Backster used straightforward electronics that a student or garage-level scientist can replicate, to prove to humans that their thoughts and emotions affect the behavior of their own and other living cells." Interview by Paul Von Ward

Peter Russel. *The Global Brain Awakens: Our Next Evolutionary Leap.* Building on Lovelock's Gaia hypothesis, it shows how our global linking may be leading us toward an evolutionary breakthrough as significant as the emergence of life some three and a half million years ago.

Riane Eisler. The Chalice and the Blade.

Daniel Landinsky. *Love Poems for God.* I just love these translations...

Gay Hendricks, Ph.D. & Kate Ludeman, Ph.D. *The Corporate Mystic: A Guidebook for Visionaries with their Feet on the Ground.* An good guide to bringing a sense of connection to the corporate world.

Gerald M. Weinberg. *An Introduction to General Systems Thinking.*

Joseph O'Connor & Ian McDermott. *The Art of Systems Thinking: Essential Skills for Creativity and Problem Solving.*

Dennis Meadows & Linda Booth Sweeney. *The Systems Thinking Playbook.*

http://www.systems-thinking.de

http://www.thinking.net/Systems_Thinking/systems_thinking.html

Ursula K. Le Guin. *The Farthest Shore.*

8

Earthly Fullness

Fullness No Matter What

What if

What if I was able to be here at this time
And deal with whatever shows up
Under the overall premise that everything
That each and every thing, person, and occurrence
Is of my own choosing and creation
No matter what its appearance looked like
No matter how convincing my resistance was

What if all I needed to do was to sit still and say YES
To each and everything, person, and occurrence
Every storm, hurricane, and thunderstorm
Stretch out my human heart as far as possible and more
And let it all go by me, through me, around me
And most importantly of all, not do anything
Until the winds have quieted down
To that soft stillness again

What if out of that stillness of not reacting to the storm
Of not letting any winds disturb myself, my body, and my mind
Simple answers would show up both unexpected and familiar
Carrying the element of letting go within themselves
Not bound by all the storminess unleashed so easily
In human interactions everywhere and every day

What if I already know deeply inside of me
Exactly what to do and how to do it all
So that the eye of the hurricane
Becomes my home
And the resistance fades
And the suffering stops
And the joy pervades
Every moment

~~ Ulla! ~~

Body

As human beings in a human body we come from the Earth as all our food is based on earthly substances. And into the Earth we do return when our journey, this time around, here is complete.

Breathing Exercise: Tetrahedron of Earthly Fullness

Preparations

Specific instructions for this particular exercise:
For maximum effect, this particular breathing exercise is best done sitting up in a very relaxed position with your back leaning against something comfortable.

This Breathing Exercise is designed to be experienced while you are reading it, preferably out loud to yourself, if you are in a position to do so. If not, at least mouth the words; it will help you slow down and stay focused. If you are with a partner who is open to sharing this exercise, take turns reading it out loud to each other. Make sure you are in a position to relax while you are reading, without falling asleep too quickly.

If you want to intensify this exercise, invite your spirit guides and angels, known or unknown, seen or unseen, to join you in this experience.

Exercise

- ❖ I bring my awareness to the bottom of my feet, where the soles of my feet meet the air (or the ground or the blanket) around my feet.
- ❖ I wiggle my feet to make the soles of my feet move to fully anchor my awareness just barely inside my body.
- ❖ I focus my inbreath into the soles of my feet, that is I feel my belly rise with the inbreath, and I imagine that I can gently push my breath all the way through my legs, through my ankles, and into the soles of my feet.
- ❖ This breath is like a wave on the ocean being watched from a boat looking onto a sandy shore. I watch the wave building up to a crest, breaking, and rolling down the beach all the way into the soles of my feet, slowly counting to five.

- ❖ I watch my outbreath recede like a wave from the beach. It recedes from the soles of my feet through my ankles, through my legs, and I watch my belly fall with the outbreath, slowly counting to five.
- ❖ I continue watching the flow of the waves, my inbreath, and my outbreath for about four to six long slow breaths.

~~~~~~

- ❖ I imagine projecting my awareness to a place about one foot below my feet.
- ❖ I imagine a tetrahedron all around my awareness two feet below my feet. A tetrahedron is a pyramid with four triangular sides.
- ❖ I imagine the tip of the tetrahedron resting very lightly between the two arches of my feet. I cannot feel the physical pressure, but notice a gentle presence.
- ❖ The base of the tetrahedron reaches all the way into the core of the earth below me.
- ❖ One of the faces of the tetrahedron is in line with the front of my body. Its opposite corner is in line with the spine of my body.
- ❖ The color of this inverted tetrahedron is honey colored.
- ❖ Its texture feels like thickly flowing, slightly warm, richly tasting honey (if that is too far fetched, just stay with the color of honey).
- ❖ This honey colored tetrahedron represents my connection to the earth.
- ❖ I rest in the awareness that I am connected to the earth through a tetrahedron reaching all the way into the core of the earth.
- ❖ I notice any changes in my body, in my sense of well being, in my breathing.

~~~~~~

- ❖ I imagine the tip of the upright honey colored tetrahedron reaches up directly into my heart.
- ❖ I notice any changes in my body, in my sense of well being, in my breathing.

Earthly Fullness

~~~~~~

- I imagine the tip of the upright honey colored tetrahedron reaches all the way up into the center of my forehead.
- I notice any changes in my body, in my sense of well being, in my breathing.

~~~~~~

- I imagine the tip of the upright honey colored tetrahedron reaches all the way up beyond my head into an area about three feet above my head.
- I notice any changes in my body, in my sense of well being, in my breathing.

~~~~~~

- I once again focus my inbreath into the soles of my feet, that is I feel my belly rise with the inbreath, and I imagine that I can gently push my breath all the way through my legs, through my ankles, and into the soles of my feet.
- This breath is like a wave on the ocean being watched from a boat looking onto a sandy shore. I watch the wave building up to a crest, breaking, and rolling down the beach all the way into the soles of my feet, slowly counting to five.
- I watch my outbreath recede like a wave from the beach. It recedes from the soles of my feet through my ankles, through my legs, and I watch my belly fall with the outbreath, slowly counting to five.
- I continue watching the flow of the waves, my inbreath, and my outbreath for about four to six long slow breaths.
- Anytime now I can access my honey colored Tetrahedron of Earthly Fullness and experience its effect on my life in the hours, days, and months to come.

Completion

- When I am complete, I bring my awareness back to the world outside of me.
- I wiggle my toes and fingers.
- I stretch my body like a cat with a few lazy, long, full body stretches.
- I am back in my waking reality.

Fullness No Matter What

Suggestions

Once the honey colored tetrahedron has been activated, we can practice seeing ourselves in it with our imagination to activate our own direct "connection to the earth". Here are some ideas for further exploration:

- I imagine the honey colored tetrahedron reaching all the way up beyond my head, thus completely encasing my body.
- I imagine it spinning counter clockwise all around my body.
- Counter clockwise means the flat side of the tetrahedron directly in front of me moves left to the back of my body and all the way around in that direction.
- The tip stays pointed upward and the tetrahedron spins around its central vertical axis in a counter clockwise motion.
- I notice what it feels like to stand or sit inside a tetrahedron that spins all around my body.
- I simply rest in that experience.

Make sure to do the Completion part after practicing the spinning of your tetrahedron. You might feel a bit disoriented after the spinning.

If you want to make sure that you experience more Earthly Fullness in your life, try the Mandala exercise described in the Breathing Exercise:
Color of Loving Fullness under Mandala Breathing.

Pleasure Exercises

Isn't food something wonderful? I at least experience it as such. I **love** preparing food and cooking food. Cooking for myself, cooking with my friends, cooking as a family, cooking for my Beloved. I **love** preparing food and cooking food because food is such a wonderful way of feeling full, nourished, loved, cared for, caring. In one word: rich.

Solo: How to Enjoy Eating Delicious Food by Yourself

To me one of the most difficult things is to eat by myself **and** enjoy it. I prefer to eat with someone. When I eat alone, I always feel tempted to read a book or distract myself somehow from tasting my food. If you can relate, here are a few suggestions on how I stay present while eating food alone at home:

First I set the table nicely for myself. I like lighting a candle or two. For company I invite my spirit guides to eat with and through me. I take a bite, close my eyes and imagine them sharing the taste through my mouth. The more I experience and taste and the more I stay aware of my experiencing and tasting, the more they get to experience and taste and be aware off. Sharing my food in that way has definitely made my food taste better and richer.

Another way to stay conscious while eating food alone is to chew the food very…slowly, one…bite…after…another. To really savor every bite, to be aware of the different textures, to let the different tastes blend and mix through the chewing. This way of eating definitely can turn food into a very pleasurable affair.

In order to enjoy food like that, it helps to eat food made from fresh ingredients, lots of raw food, and healthy choices. I find it much harder to eat "junk food" slowly. It just does not cut it…

Partnered: Playing with your Food!

Remember how as kids we were taught not to "play with your food"? This is your chance to catch up on all those lost opportunities. Maybe even find many more ways that you did not know existed as a kid!

To me sharing food while making love is just really delicious. Mixing the taste of juicy food with the pleasure in other parts of my body makes something already good even better. I like having a bowl of bite sized fruit pieces next to my bed, or some fruit juices, so that I can add the taste stimulus into lovemaking when I feel like upping the pleasure ante.

My favorite food sensation is to fill my mouth with green or red seedless grapes. While I am kissing my partner face down, I pop open one grape after another with my teeth, so that the juices just **flood** his mouth while he is being kissed. Yummmy. If I have my hands on his Lingam at the same time, he is likely to hit the roof in terms of pleasure. This kind of fruit sharing while kissing invariably creates a special taste explosion!

Another way to add taste explosions to pleasure is to just have your favorite food handy in all kinds of lovemaking situations:

- **Drop some dripping mango slices into your lover's** mouth while pleasuring him or her manually.
- **Feed each other ripe strawberries** while in the afterglow of an orgasm.
- **Turn your lover's body into a fruit salad** by decorating it with different kinds of fruit pieces. Then very s l o w l y start eating them off your lover's body, while caressing the skin around the individual pieces, and licking off the juices.
- **Gently pop some grapes into your lover's Yoni** and then eat them covered in her juices when she tries to push them out by deep belly breathing. You might have to go fishing for the lost ones! Oh what a chore!
- **Cover your lover's Lingam in chocolate sauce** and lick it off in long slow licks starting at the base and moving all the way to the head. And again. And again.
- **Try whipped cream on her breasts** and very, very slowly work your way around to her nipples.
- I could go on and on…

The important part is to have fun exploring playing with your food, and if you end up laughing a lot, that's even better.

Mind

A Day in the Arms of the Earth

I enjoy a very personal relationship with the Earth. Maybe I can convey my connection to her by inviting you to take a peek at what a day looks like while I am writing this book.

Most mornings I go out on my morning walk in Lithia Park in Ashland, Oregon. I like to be out early in summer, before the heat spreads itself out and makes everything lazy and slow. I breathe in the cool morning air full of rich smells after the sprinkler systems have watered most of the park. I revel in the sounds of the rushing creek, the green of the trees and bushes, the colors of the different plants and trees and bushes in bloom, always changing, always different ones. After about an hour out in Mother Nature's garden, I invariably feel joyful and clean, and ready to do my day.

Earthly Fullness

On my way home I stop by my friend Pamela's garage to see what food surprises the Blessings Group has brought this time. For the past ten years Pamela Joy and her Food for People organization have been picking up produce (and some dairy and breads) that are no longer considered fresh by store standards. All of that food from three supermarkets and the farmers market in town normally would end up in the dumpster. The quality of the produce ranges anywhere from having some blemishes to being ready for the compost pile.

Most of the food eventually ends up in a couple food kitchens for the homeless, a senior center, and a food distribution center for immigrant workers. As a member of the Blessings Group I put in three to four hours a month doing pick-ups. In exchange for this help I can stop by Pamela's garage any time and take home as much free food as I need. I love giving dinner parties for friends and cooking scrumptious dishes for everyone as I always have an abundance of food available to me and I love sharing that abundance.

After I have loaded up my box with all the summer fruits and greens for a few days, I go home and prepare a large bowl of fruit salad. I marvel at the variety of fruits I get to taste every day keeping in mind they were all grown in the soil of this Earth somewhere. I then sit down to work on my book for most of the day, only interrupted by more free food in the form of summer salads, cooked vegetables, and fresh vegetable juices.

When I need a short break from my writing, I look up and give my eyes a rest by enjoying the view from my room. My eyes can roam across the valley full of light green vineyards, dark green fruit trees, and golden brown hills. When I need a longer break, I walk in the garden or rest in my hammock held up by two large cherry trees that in early summer gifted me (and all my friends) with the ripest, darkest, juiciest cherries I have had in a long time. I can hear and feel the wind blowing in the leaves, caressing my body with its warmth. Or I play with Heidi and Amy, my two black Labrador charges, and watch them run across the dry hay fields to catch some toys.

When my body feels too tight and stressed from sitting at the computer all day, I go to the outdoor hot springs in town at night. The Earth has provided hot mineral water with a slight sulfur smell for a hot pool, which draws the tightness right out of my muscles. It works especially well taking turns going from the hot pool to the cool pool (in winter the contrast is stronger and more invigorating) and back to the hot pool. Usually there are rich summer sunsets to see, changing every day, depending on whether there are clouds reflecting the rays into brilliant fiery colors, or just a soft range of pastel hues fading into dark blue darkness full of a myriad of stars. Sometimes the moon graces us with her presence, and makes all the bodies look radiant in her silvery light.

I am usually quite tired after a full day. When it gets dark outside I go to sleep in my tent that I have set up outside the house on a patio. I love sleeping outside in summer, especially in these dry summers with hardly any rains from June till late in October. I lie in my tent, letting the wind's rustling of the leaves sing me to sleep, and the smell of roses, freshly cut grass, and just plain greenness accompany me into my dreams. Usually a cricket or two is busy chirping through the night. I sleep much deeper outside than inside even though I-5's freeway traffic can be heard all over the valley. The blue jays wake me up just when the colors of a new dawn appear on the horizon.

There is a common thread in all these experiences that enrich and fill my day: all of it originates in this Earth somehow somewhere. I would not live in the kind of fullness I am describing in this book, if I were not living of the Earth and on the Earth. I am overflowing with gratitude and joy that I get to live my whole life on this magnificent planet called Earth.

~~~ *A deep sigh out* ~~~

The Sorcerer's Apprentice

One of my day jobs in the last seven years has been to help people get their belongings organized. I lend a helping hand in making decisions about what belonging is a keeper and what has overstayed its welcome or use. I usually get called in when these belongings seem to take over and develop a life of their own, which is fascinating to watch. First all these things seem to multiply and fill up any available space in the house like closets, cupboards, and drawers, no matter how much space is available initially. They tend to spill over into any available storage space like the attic, underneath the staircase, or the garage, even displacing cars. They even spill over into separate storage spaces that have to be paid for with monthly rent. That means not only do we pay money for things when we buy them, we pay money to keep them, often without really using them.

I myself have moved so many times in the last 14 years and I have learned that unless something is absolutely essential and easy to carry, I don't own it. It is an

Earthly Fullness

amazing phenomenon, our relationship with things, and it gives rise to another facet of the Grand Experiment: from my particular vantage point it seems like I am watching the Sorcerer's Apprentice in action.

Johann Wolfgang von Goethe wrote a poem in German called "Der Zauberlehrling". In the USA it is better known as the "Sorcerer's Apprentice" in the Walt Disney movie "Fantasia". Mickey Mouse as the apprentice, after having been taught the first rudimentary steps in magic, gleefully explores his newly found power. Too late he realizes that he has not yet learned how to put an end to this experiment and has to helplessly watch the ensuing mayhem. Luckily the sorcerer shows up just in time to prevent total mayhem.

To me it looks like humanity in the early part of the 20th century found out how to invent, build, and run machines, which allowed for an increase in productivity over manual labor. By the end of the 20th century the Western world has turned into a consumer goods culture and the rest of the world is both involved in the production of those goods and trying very hard to play catch up. For many of us life today is centered on consumer goods, whether it is as part of the invention, the production, the selling, the advertising, the purchasing, the repairing, or the disposal of them. Many lives today are solely based on things.

It looks like we in the Western World have become just like the Sorcerer's Apprentice. We have found out that we have the ability to create things, many, many things, useful and not so useful. This creation of things appears like magic because with the help of machines we are able to produce possessions that our hands plus hand-operated tools alone could never accomplish. We have gone to town exploring this ability and it is starting to take over every aspect of our lives. Some would say it already has taken over.

Now we do not really know how to stop this mayhem. It feels just like in the movie Fantasia: the things we created are running the show and we are desperately trying to contain them without much success. And many people are wondering why their lives have become empty and devoid of meaning, not realizing that a mayor chunk of their waking time is spent managing their things.

My big question here is: who or what in this present day scenario will step in as the sorcerer to stop this mayhem?

~~~ A deep belly breath in ~~~

Fullness No Matter What

Soul

THE SEED MARKET

Can you find another market like this?

Where,
with your one rose
you can buy hundreds of rose gardens?

Where,
for one seed
you get a whole wilderness?

For one weak wind
the divine breath?

You have been fearful
of being absorbed in the ground,
or drawn up by the air.

Now, your waterbead lets go
and drops into the ocean,
where it came from.

It no longer has the form it had,
but it's still water.
The essence is the same.

This giving up is not a repenting.
It's a deep honoring of yourself.

When the ocean comes to you as a lover,
marry, at once, quickly,
for God's sake.

Don't postpone it!
Existence has no better gift.

Earthly Fullness

No amount of searching will find this.

A perfect falcon, for no reason,
has landed on your shoulder,
and become yours.

~~ Rumi (Coleman Barks Translation) ~~

~~~~~~~~~~

For animals, the entire universe has been neatly divided into things to (a)
mate with, (b) eat, (c) run away from, and (d) rocks.

~~ Terry Pratchett, Equal Rites ~~

~~~~~~~~~~

MOTHERLAND

Motherland, cradle me,
Close my eyes, lullaby me to sleep
Keep me safe, lie with me
Stay beside me, don't go
Don't you go

~~ Natalie Merchant, Motherland ~~

~~~~~~~~~~

Happiness, thought Cadfael,…
consists in small things, not in great.
It is the small things we remember, when time and mortality close in,
and by small landmarks we may make our way at last
humbly into another world.

~~ Ellis Peters, An Excellent Mystery ~~

~~~~~~~~~~

More

Cecile Andrews. The Circle of Simplicity: Return to the Good Life.

Tetrahedron: If you are interested to explore more about the uses of the tetrahedron, especially the star tetrahedron, please take a look in the **More** section of the Heavenly Fullness.

Fantasia. Video by Disney

Book Review: All of Ursula Le Guin's Books

I have been reading Ursula Le Guin's every novel and short story since I first found her Earth Sea trilogy in a used bookstore in college in 1979. I moved many times since then, even back and forth across oceans, and her books were part of my ever smaller box of treasured (and frequently to be reread) books up until a few years ago. I only gave up schlepping my treasures around yet another time when I found out what a blessing public libraries are these days.

I just recently read out loud some of her short stories to my 91 year old friend Audrey and even though I have read these stories at least three times, I still found myself choked with tears at the end of every story. That is when I realized why I love Ursula Le Guin's writing so much. She has a way into and under my skin that will invariably touch me at a very deep and vulnerable place, as if her books were written just for me (she only has millions of other readers worldwide besides me, but who cares). I can read some of her books for the sixth time (as I have done with "Four Ways to Forgiveness") and still cry my heart out every single time.

Her writings are classified as "science fiction", but I call it "mind fiction". To me she not so much deals with the science of future worlds, as with the exploration of ancient mythological themes projected into a different landscape or a different time or a different planet system all together. For example, in her book "Left Hand of Darkness" I feel both her open curiosity and her choice of words leading me safely through a planet on which the human shaped inhabitants have no assigned gender. They instead go through a ten day Kemmering Period every 30 days, in which they find a temporary gender depending on the partner they match up with. And we get to watch what happens…

To me Ursula Le Guin writings embody fullness in the words, themes, and creative scenarios she uses to take her readers into journeys both deeply into the human psyche and far out beyond anything humanly familiar. That fullness, which she so masterfully evokes, has called me every time and time again to venture more fully into mine long before I actually embodied it.

The Author's Official Website: www.ursulaleguin.com

A website with all the information you ever need on Ursula K. Le Guin: http://www.arcadiabooks.org/leguin/index.html

9
Laughter Fullness

I Am Receiving It All

I am receiving it all
And loving it
Moment by moment
Giggle by giggle
Laughter by laughter
Yes

~~ Ulla! ~~

Body

Oh my God, what would my life be like without laughter! I would not have an ounce of sanity left, if I did not have the ability to laugh, especially to laugh about myself and my funny antics, habits, and ideas.

Breathing Exercise: Bubbles of Laughter Fullness

Preparations

Specific instructions for this particular exercise:
For this particular breathing exercise you need time and a space where you can make some noises, everything from slight chuckling noises to soft giggling to raucous laughter!

This Breathing Exercise is designed to be experienced while you are reading it, preferably out loud to yourself, if you are in a position to do so. If not, at least mouth the words; it will help you slow down and stay focused. If you are with a partner who is open to sharing this exercise, take turns reading it out loud to each other. Make sure you are in a position to relax while you are reading, without falling asleep too quickly.

If you want to intensify this exercise, invite your spirit guides and angels, known or unknown, seen or unseen, to join you in this experience.

Exercise

- ❖ I bring my awareness to my thighs, my knees, my calves, my ankles, my heels, the bottoms of my feet, and all the way into all of my toes.
- ❖ I wiggle my feet to make the soles of my feet move to fully anchor my awareness inside my feet.
- ❖ I appreciate my legs and feet for doing such a wonderful job of giving me the chance to walk, to run, to dance, to hike, in short, to move me from one place to another.
- ❖ If I am remembering that my legs and feet can't do all I would like them to do, I completely accept any restrictions of movement just for the duration of this exercise.

- ❖ If I feel any discomfort or tightness in my legs and feet, I notice it.
- ❖ I totally accept it by directing my very own Loving Color into the tender or tight area. I bring that Loving Color of acceptance into every area of discomfort, one after another, until my legs and feet are glowing with acceptance.

~~~~~~

- ❖ I focus my inbreath into my legs and feet, that is I feel my belly area rise with the inbreath, and I imagine that I can gently push my breath all the way through my legs, through my feet, and into my toes.
- ❖ This breath is like a wave on the ocean being watched from a boat looking onto a sandy shore. I watch the wave building up to a crest, breaking, and rolling down the beach all the way into my toes, slowly counting to five.
- ❖ I watch my outbreath recede like a wave from the beach. It recedes from my toes through my feet, through my legs, and I watch my belly fall with the outbreath, slowly counting to five.
- ❖ I continue watching the flow of the waves, my inbreath, and my outbreath for about four to six long slow breaths.

~~~~~~

- ❖ I wiggle my toes and contract my feet to get a sense of the soles of my feet.
- ❖ I imagine little opalescent (many colored like opals) bubbles inside the soles of my heel, my arch, my balls, and my toes. There are hundreds and hundreds of these small opalescent bubbles inside the soles of my feet.
- ❖ When I move my feet, they come loose from the inside of my sole and start traveling upwards through my legs.
- ❖ I imagine them bumping into each other and forming larger bubbles while they are traveling up through my legs.
- ❖ I imagine the bubbles bumping more into each other on the way up and becoming larger and larger.
- ❖ When they enter my torso I imagine some of them **bursting**!
- ❖ When the opalescent bubbles are bursting, it feels like being tickled on the inside with these light bubbly sensations.
- ❖ The bubbles are rising all through my body. Wherever they bump into an organ, they burst into tickling sensations.

- The more I wiggle my feet, the more bubbles rise, the more giggles burst in my body, the more I feel like laughing out loud.
- I let the laughter bubble up in me, and if I feel like it, start laughing out loud.
- I really let myself laugh as heartily as as full as I can. There might even be tears of laughter and joy.
- If cannot quite get into the spirit of laughter, I try giggles.
- Once the laughter has run its course, and I am all laughed out for right now, I notice any changes in my body, in my sense of well being, in my breathing.

~~~~~~

- I again focus my breath into my legs and feet, that is I feel my belly area rise with the inbreath, and I imagine that I can gently push my inbreath all the way through my legs, through my feet, and into my toes.
- This inbreath is like a wave on the ocean being watched from a boat looking onto a sandy shore. I watch the wave building up to a crest, breaking, and rolling down the beach all the way into my toes.
- I watch my outbreath recede like a wave from the beach. It recedes from my toes through my feet, through my legs, and I watch my belly fall with the outbreath.
- I continue watching the flow of the waves, my inbreath, and my outbreath for about four to six long slow breaths.
- Anytime now I can access my Bubbles of Laughter and experience its effect on my life in the hours, days, and months to come.

Completion

- When I am complete, I bring my awareness back to the world outside of me.
- I wiggle my toes and fingers.
- I stretch my body like a cat with a few lazy, long, full body stretches.
- I am back in my waking reality.

Fullness No Matter What

Suggestions

These laughter bubbles are always available to us. Any time we walk, or hike, or just only wiggle our toes, we can imagine the laughter bubbles forming, traveling up our legs, and bringing us at least a smile, if not joy and giggles and laughter. Any time we feel in need for some lightness, it's all there at a wiggle of our toes and the power of our imagination.

If you need a stronger reminder, just read the Breathing Exercise out loud to yourself, and I bet the laughter bubbles will just reappear and softly tickle your insides. You might need a few repetitions of that laughter exercise to fully let it sink in that laughter is available to us any time, just by focusing inward and inside our body.

If you want to make sure that you experience more Laughter Fullness in your life, try the Mandala exercise described in the Breathing Exercise:
Color of Loving Fullness under Mandala Breathing.

Pleasure Exercises

Sexual energy is about building energy and creating a release. That release typically is achieved through orgasm. Laughter has that same release quality that an orgasm has, that is, it has a relaxing and "deflating" effect on any energetic charge, particularly on sexual energy.

Solo: The Effects of Laughter on Turn-on

This one is a hard one for me…To me laughter and sex go together really well, as I adore the intimacy both lovemaking and funny stupid stuff brings with it. But I tend to associate that kind of intimate laughter, the one that is situational and not comedic, always with a partner.

Here is what I did come up with: a Scientific Research Projects on the Effects of Laughter on Turn-on. Let's say that you are single and you are feeling really horny, turned on, and longing for sex, lovemaking and/or intimacy. You have not had any good sex or lovemaking (besides Mr. or Mrs. Palm and their five fingers) for a while. You are feeling really charged up and ready to grab the next guy or gal off the street.

Laughter Fullness

Try reading a really funny book, or watching a really funny video or DVD. One that has you in stitches most of the time. One that gives you side aches because it is so funny. One that you can watch over and over again and still it makes you laugh.

Afterwards, and here you have to be thoroughly scientific, check your level of turn-on. I bet that you will be able to measure very scientifically that it has gone down (even if that only lasts 23 1/2 minutes…). And even if it did not go down, at least you had a good laugh or two.

Partnered: Stunny Fuff!

When you are exploring sensuous whole body pleasure, you want to stay away from activities that build too much energy too quickly. That quick build up brings the focus automatically into genital pleasure and into the "build energy and release energy" pattern. In sensuous explorations the focus is on slower building of energy and frequent deflating in order to build again. Laughter is one of the best (and funniest) ways to accomplish the deflation of energy.

Here is a list of funny suggestions to try out (at least I think they are funny):

- ❖ **Strange Positions:** Get or borrow a Yogic or Kamasutra book to see what position makes you laugh the most. Pick the strangest, most complex positions and try making love in them. Find out which tickles your funny bone the most.

- ❖ **Play with Fruit,** especially juicy ones like red and green grapes, strawberries, peeled and sliced pieces of mango or oranges. Fill up your mouth and kiss each other with all the juices running down your body. But—you cannot wipe the juices off. You can only lick them off wherever they land. Here is a hint: have lots of old towels and sheets handy.

- ❖ **Play Doctor,** that is remember how you felt when you were five or six years old, and explored for the sake of exploring. Have fun exploring. Be curious. Try things out just for the sake of trying them out, not for getting an effect.

- ❖ **Play with Oil** while making love and see how slippery you can get and still hold on to each other.

- ❖ **The Not Quite Tickle Game:** if you and/or your partner are ticklish, gently tickle each other, finding just that edge where stroking or touching becomes tickling, that middle line. Stay on that edge. As receiver breathe through it, relaxing into it, playing with that edge of tension and release.

- **Pretend to be cartoon characters in bed making love:** What do you imagine Goofy or Donald Duck would be as a lover? Or Daisy? Or Minnie Mouse? Talk like them, move like them. Just pretend that you are these cartoon characters, and see what happens (apparently Roger Rabbit was quite a lover).
- **The Naming Game.** Give silly names to your body parts. Call your Lingam a dinosaur, a cucumber, a rattlesnake, or an elephant. Call your Yoni a pillowcase, Disneyland, a fuzzy wuzzy, or a swimming pool. See what happens when the dinosaur crawls into the pillowcase, or the rattlesnake meets the fuzzy wuzzy…
- **Allow yourself to be goofy**, to do stupid things, to look silly, and to act outrageously. All of it creates room for laughter and silliness and joy. And sometimes that kind of laughter is just as good as making love.

Mind

I Love to Laugh

Laughter is a mystery to me, because I do not really know how it does so well what it does. And to tell you the truth, I don't even want to know. Mind you, I **love** laughing, big, open, deep, belly laughter. When I am laughing, because someone found my funny bone or because I found something funny, you know it. Everyone knows it!

I love people who can make me laugh. I love good jokes, even if I have heard them before. I love funny sexual jokes, as I love including sexuality in my life as a reminder that I am a sexual being even when I am not in bed making love. And I love laughing about myself. That to me is the best kind of laughter. Not because I am making fun of myself and putting myself down as so many comedians do on TV, but because I think sometimes I am just a riot in my egocentricities and my silly habits.

Sometime in my early twenties I found a children's toy figure of a Smurf (remember Smurfs, the little blue men and women in white pants and sleepy caps?). This particular one had one arm pointing at something in the distance, and the other hand was cupped over its mouth. To me it represented a reminder to let myself laugh more about myself. I imagined it pointing its finger at me. At that point I wanted to bring more laughter in my life, and I thought if I could just learn to laugh more about myself, life would be much better and easier. I carried that little Smurf everywhere in my handbag for many years until my kids discovered it and turned it into one of their toys. I guess I did not need it anymore.

I remember going to see an Italian clown called Dimitri in my twenties in Amherst, Massachusetts. He had this very gentle sweet humor, softly rising sometimes from just moving his little finger. All I remember is he made music on a tiny violin with these very slow small deliberate movements. The audience would be silent, watching spell bound. All of a sudden you would hear these little high voiced giggles of small children bubbling up, followed by the louder laughter of the adults. Such soft humor in ordinary situations. I don't understand how he did what he did, but I loved it and it allowed me to laugh from some very sweet place inside of me.

~~~ *A deep sigh out* ~~~

Soul

They may have been ugly.
They may have been evil.
But when it came to poetry in motion,
the Things had all the grace and coordination of a deck-chair.

~~ Terry Pratchett, Equal Rites ~~

~~~~~~~~~~

In every job that must be done there is an element of fun;
you find that fun and snap, the job's a game.

~~ Mary Poppins ~~

~~~~~~~~~~

You that come to birth and bring the mysteries,
your voice-thunder makes us very happy.

Fullness No Matter What

Roar, lion of the heart,
And tear me open!

~~ Rumi (Coleman Barks Translation) ~~

~~~~~~~~~~

The Ephebians made wine out of anything they could put in a bucket, and ate anything that couldn't climb out of one.

~~ Terry Pratchett, Pyramids ~~

~~~~~~~~~~

More

Patch Adams and his Gesundheit! Institute brings laughter and health together. http://www.patchadams.org/home.htm

"The Funny Times" is America's leading liberal monthly humor review. Now in its 19th year, they collect the best of the best in the cartoon and humor world. http://www.funnytimes.com

10

Security Fullness

Fullness No Matter What

Not Enough

Not enough said the Queen
When they brought her riches
From all over her world

Not enough said the Queen
When they offered her exotic tastes
From all the corners of her lands

Not enough said the Queen
When they celebrated her with magic
Miracles and silvery fairy dust

Not enough said the Queen
When they brought to her
The wisest teachers and masters

Not enough
Not enough
Not enough

Finally she looked out to sea and said
I'm not enough
And cried herself to sleep

~~ Ulla! ~~

Body

Security—what a multi-facetted concept in our materially oriented Western culture. Culturally we believe that we can buy security in form of personal ownership of land and houses, paying all kinds of insurance, and surrounding ourselves with more material goods than we really know what to do with. Or we believe we can fake security by acting "cool". At the same time we wonder why we are not really happy.

Breathing Exercise: Seat of Security Fullness

Preparations

Specific instructions for this particular exercise:
For maximum effect, this particular breathing exercise is best done sitting up in a very relaxed position with your back leaning against something comfortable.

This Breathing Exercise is designed to be experienced while you are reading it, preferably out loud to yourself, if you are in a position to do so. If not, at least mouth the words; it will help you slow down and stay focused. If you are with a partner who is open to sharing this exercise, take turns reading it out loud to each other. Make sure you are in a position to relax while you are reading, without falling asleep too quickly.

If you want to intensify this exercise, invite your spirit guides and angels, known or unknown, seen or unseen, to join you in this experience.

Exercise

- ❖ I bring my awareness to all the surfaces I am sitting on. I wiggle around a bit to become aware of the cheeks of my behind, the underside of my thighs, the bones of my pelvis, the outside of my hips, possibly either my scrotum, or the lips of my labia, the small of my back, and my whole backside, all the way up into the shoulder blades.
- ❖ I am becoming aware of how many body parts are involved in the act of sitting.

- ❖ I appreciate all these body parts for doing such a wonderful job of helping me to spend part of my daily life in a sitting position.

~~~~~~

- ❖ If I feel any discomfort or tightness in any of the body parts involved in sitting, I notice it.
- ❖ I then totally accept the pain or discomfort by directing my very own Loving Color into the tender or tight area. I bring that Loving Color of acceptance into every area of discomfort, one after another, until that whole area is glowing with acceptance.

~~~~~~

- ❖ I now focus a slow breath into my pelvic floor area, that is, I breathe deeply into my belly counting to five. While I am breathing in, I bear down as if I have to evacuate my bowels. That will tighten up the muscles of my belly.
- ❖ When I breathe out, again counting to five, I relax all the muscles of my belly and let them soften.
- ❖ In this particular exercise I notice my belly area contract with the inbreath and relax with the outbreath
- ❖ I continue breathing in and bearing down and breathing out and letting go for about four to six long slow breaths.

~~~~~~

- ❖ I move my awareness into my pelvic area.
- ❖ I sense an imaginary seat inside my pelvic area.
- ❖ I imagine this imaginary seat fitting just inside the soft layer of my skin, reaching from the underside of my thighs to both sides of my thighs, all around my hips, around my behind into my small back and up my whole back into my shoulder blades.
- ❖ This seat has the outer dimensions of my various body parts. Its inner dimensions operate by imaginary rules.
- ❖ It is made of a very unusual substance that at the same time is:
  - ➢ soft and touchable like the richest silk velvet,
  - ➢ flexible and adjustable like Play Dough,

- - stable and strong like old oak wood, and
  - protective like a roof over your head.
- It knows what temperature I like best and continuously adjusts that temperature to my liking.
- It feels like I am sitting on a warm, very big, very comfortable body that is holding me. Just holding me sweetly.
- I take a moment to revel in being held in such a safe and loving and comfortable embrace.
- This seat is my very own seat of security.
- When I am embraced and held in it and by it, I am safe.
- I can relax.
- I know that everything will be fine.
- I can let the world take care of itself and just be here right now.
- If any worry thoughts come up, I thank them and let them go.
- I am just allowing myself to feel held and embraced for this moment.
- I notice any changes in my body, in my sense of well being, in my breathing.

~~~~~~

- I once again focus a slow breath into my pelvic floor area, that is, I breathe deeply into my belly counting to five. While I am breathing in, I bear down as if I have to evacuate my bowels. That will tighten up the muscles of my belly.
- When I breathe out, again counting to five, I relax all the muscles of my belly and let them soften.
- In this particular exercise I notice my belly area contract with the inbreath and relax with the outbreath
- I continue breathing in and bearing down and breathing out and letting go for about four to six long slow breaths.
- Anytime now I can access my Seat of Security Room and experience its effect on my life in the hours, days, and months to come.

Completion

- When I am complete, I bring my awareness back to the world outside of me.

- ❖ I wiggle my toes and fingers.
- ❖ I stretch my body like a cat with a few lazy, long, full body stretches.
- ❖ I am back in my waking reality.

Suggestions

Now you have a space in your body, where you can feel safe just inside of you, whenever you need it, no matter what is going on around you. It might take some practice, that is, reading this particular exercise a few more times, but that sense of security is now yours just for the asking.

It works really well to drop into it when all these pesky money worries knock on your door, insisting that they are very urgent and real and extremely important. I am not saying, don't deal with money issues. But don't let money worries ruin your day.

If you want to make sure that you experience more Security Fullness in your life, try the Mandala exercise described in Breathing Exercise:
Color of Loving Fullness under Mandala Breathing.

Pleasure Exercises

In our Western culture the Rosebud of the human body is a body part typically better left in the dark of our underwear and the privacy of a bathroom behind locked doors. Other cultures know about the importance of including the Rosebud as part of a health regimen, especially for men. Some celibate monks in the Asian Daoist tradition have been known to practice a form of Male Sacred Spot massage on themselves, that has kept that part of their body healthy into old age and seems to have contributed to their longevity.

Excluding the Rosebud from our awareness except as "when we have to go" is a major omission. This much overlooked Rosebud plays such an important part in how secure we experience ourselves in our lives. And all of that independently from any form of insurance, title deeds, and full bank accounts.

Solo: Awakening the Rosebud

If you want to explore your Rosebud in a safe and comfortable way as a single, here are three suggestions for some breathing and yoga exercises.

Preparations

Wear loose and comfortable clothes.

Exercise

1) "Crouching Low"
    - ❖ Start on all fours on the floor or on your bed with spread legs.
    - ❖ Now sit back on your legs until your chin rests on the floor between your out stretched arms.
    - ❖ Breathe all the way into your belly in this position.
    - ❖ Notice how your breath seems to reach all the way into your Rosebud, especially if you bear down as if you are going to evacuate your bowels.
    - ❖ Notice your Rosebud opening up into a Rose. Feel the area around your Rosebud being stretched and gently massaged from the inside.
    - ❖ Breathe out in this position and contract your Rosebud muscles.
    - ❖ When breathing in, relax your Rosebud muscles.
    - ❖ Do about ten belly breaths in and out.
    - ❖ Add deep belly "aaaawww" sounds and see where they resonate in your body.
    - ❖ Can you sense the sounds all the way in your Rosebud?
    - ❖ Explore different levels of loudness, or different vowels like "eeeeee" or "oooooouuuuuu" etc.
    - ❖ Move out of this position and lay flat on your back.
    - ❖ Breathe normally.
    - ❖ Notice any changes.

2) "Sitting on your Heel"
    - ❖ Sit cross legged on the floor.
    - ❖ Take your right leg and place your right heel as close as you can get underneath your Rosebud, so you actually end up sitting on it.
    - ❖ Move your left leg across your left leg as far as you feel comfortable, and place the side of your foot on the floor, if you can.

Fullness No Matter What

- ❖ Place both hands to the left and the right of your hips on the ground. You should have a straight spine in that position. If not, adjust your hands and legs.
- ❖ Now breathe deeply into your belly two or three times staying in that position.
- ❖ Notice how your breath seems to reach all the way into your Rosebud, especially if you bear down as if you are going to evacuate your bowels.
- ❖ Feel the area around your Rosebud being stretched and gently massaged from the inside while pushing against the heel of our foot.
- ❖ Breathe out in this position and contract your Rosebud muscles.
- ❖ When breathing in, relax your Rosebud muscles.
- ❖ Do about ten belly breaths in and out while contracting your Rosebud muscles.
- ❖ Your know when it is time to change legs.
- ❖ Take your left leg this time and place your left heel as close as you can get to your Rosebud.
- ❖ Move your right leg across your right leg as far as you feel comfortable.
- ❖ Do the above breathing steps and Rosebud muscle contractions.
- ❖ When your left leg feels tired and cramped, move out of this position and lay flat on your back.
- ❖ Breathe normally.
- ❖ Notice any changes.

3) **Try the Breathing Exercise in the Partnered Exercise below.**

Suggestions

Try these positions and breathing exercises every day for a week and notice changes. Are you more aware of your Rosebud in general and not only as a useful prop to remind you to go to the bathroom? Do you notice when you start tightening up your Rosebud muscles? When you relax them? Play with these insights.

Partnered: Loving Attention for the Rosebud

Giving that much neglected yet vitally important body part some loving attention has helped me personally and my partners rest more easily in our day to day lives. It is amazing what the loving manipulation of my Rosebud by my partner will do to my worries, especially concerning not enough money.

If you want to familiarize yourself and your partner with your Rosebud as a pleasure spot, here is a breathing exercise to start with. You can do it together lying side by side and holding hands if you want to feel connected:

- Start by breathing into your belly. Do a few deep belly breaths.
- On your next inbreath into your belly bear down, as if you are constipated and have to press, while you are breathing in.
- Let go while you breathe out.
- Bear down on your next inbreath, this time notice how your whole Rosebud area opens up on that bearing down.
- When you breathe out, contract your Rosebud muscles.
- Take turns breathing in and bearing down and breathing out and contracting.
- Do this for about 20 breaths.
- Go back to normal belly breathing and relax the muscles of your Rosebud.
- Notice any changes.
- Share your feelings, sensations, and possible insights with each other.

For women Rosebud union can be very satisfying and open up whole new areas of pleasure besides the added benefit of experiencing yourself as more secure. The same benefits apply to Male Sacred Spot massage. In both cases my suggestion is to approach these areas with a healthy dose of openness and curiosity, and with care and some help though books, websites, and classes.

I am not going into details here concerning further pleasurable exercises like Rosebud sex and Male Sacred Spot massage as it exceeds the scope of this book. But in the **More** section of this chapter there are some suggestions for further explorations if you feel so inclined.

Mind

Breastfeeding Patterns and Social Implications

When my son Felix was born, my mother watched me breastfeed him on demand, that is, when he was hungry I responded by breastfeeding him. Sometimes he went through growth spurts and needed to drink every two hours for a couple days, until my breasts produced more milk, and he went back to drinking my milk roughly every three hours. She also observed me and Chris, the father of my son, with our son constantly close by. He slept in the same bed with us at night. During the day one of us always had him on our body somewhere, and if he was not on our body, he was in a carrying basket right next to us.

All of this brought up some intense feelings for her. She experienced remorse and sadness as she told me that I had been fed on a strict four hour schedule with no holding or touching in between. My mother literally said: "You must have been starving both physically and emotionally. You were definitely not getting enough food nor were you being touched enough. You also must have been crying yourself to sleep still hungry." When I was born in the fifties the prevailing thought had been not to "spoil" a child by feeding or touching a child too often. She told me that she always looked forward to the feeding and changing times as she then felt free to cuddle and touch and play with me. Watching me relate with my son brought up a sense that she had missed out on a closer connection with me starting in early childhood.

I tucked that information away, and did not think much about it until I did some intense therapeutic work in my forties. It brought up some of the preverbal feelings associated with the emotional and physical starvation of my early childhood (the simultaneous end of a relationship and a week of fasting did the trick). I accessed some deep feelings, scary feelings of not enough: not enough food, not enough touch, not enough love. And there were other occasions to tap into those feelings of starvation, of not "enoughness".

As a result of these personal experiences I have a hunch that the strong emphasis in our Western world on material possessions is at least partially the result of our baby feeding schedules. By the way, the four hour rule did not only apply to breast feeding but also to bottle feeding, which was very popular in the fifties and early sixties. A newborn's reality is totally based on matters of sleep and food, and everything connected to that. We experience the whole world around us through the food and touch we receive, whether there is an abundance so that we rest in wellbeingness, or whether there is scarcity, and we do not trust that whatever we need will be provided.

What message does a four hour feeding schedule give to a new born? For me it looks something like that:"I am not being fed when I feel hungry. I never know when food is being provided. Four hours mean nothing to me as I do not have sense of time yet. What I need is to be fed when I feel hungry. Then I can relax and know all is well."

The message here is: "My needs do not matter. I will be taken care of, but not on my terms, not when I need it the most. I cannot trust that I will be taken care of as I cannot sense a connection between me feeling hungry and me getting fed."

I believe that these very early conditions form some of the basis of our belief systems and determine our behavior as adults. Interestingly enough, our modern day culture shows a stronger emphasis on material security and less emphasis on knowing that no matter what, we will be taken care of as we always have been.

In my life that pattern has shown up in financial phases of either feast or famine. So far I either had a lot of money or very little money. I have been a millionaire, when my wasband and I successfully sold the first CD-ROM software house in Germany in 1987. And I have lived through times where I only had $40 for a whole month.

I never know what my next step financially will look like—will it be feast or famine? I can recognize that early childhood pattern of either having more than enough when the feeding time finally did come, or starving when I was hungry and no breast was available for hours.

The amount of gut wrenching fear that comes up every time I get close to my financial edge still amazes me, although I have gotten more used to it over the last years. (I have a hunch that we only have a certain amount of worry energy allotted to us. When our personal quota is used up, there is no worry left—sorry.)

I know that I am not the only one with that experience, as over the years I have talked to a number people of my generation, who when they asked their mothers, found out that they were raised in a similar pattern. I believe that this basic early childhood pattern has decisively influenced the sense or absence of security we each experience.

~~~ *A deep sigh out* ~~~

Security and Vulnerability

Security is not only an issue for us concerning material possessions. It is also about the image we project into the world around us. We as a society place value on the ability to dress smart, act secure, and look as if we know what we are doing, all the time. This stance has lead us to create an external persona, which originally was designed to help us fit in with the crowd we would like to hang out with, most usually as teenagers. Or it was designed to get us the "right" job, "the "right" connections, the "right" this or that. This persona of "being cool" can be more or less successful in achieving that particular goal, but I believe that later in life we pay for it by missing out on deeper experiences.

"Being cool" to me is a way to live a life based on external securities, like doing, saying, or wearing all the "right" things we think we are expected to do, say, or wear. And when we place a lot of emphasis on looking cool, we often find out that we are not having as much fun as we thought we'd have. I have a good friend, Markus, who moved to Hollywood to try to make it as an actor. He hung out there for three years, being cool, and got nowhere. When he gave up his dream of making it as an actor, he moved to Marin County and found out, after years of trial and error, that wedding photography was his passion, and that he was actually really good at it.

But he still kept telling me that he was not meeting the right women and that he was spending too much time alone. Interestingly, when I last saw him, he was in relationship with this beautifully brash, passionate, explosive French woman, and he was opening up deeper and deeper to loving her in all her complexities. And to me he was visibly glowing.

When I asked him what had changed he told me: "I stopped trying to be cool. I finally decided to accept myself the way I am and not try to be different, or act different or be who I think I ought to be." This is exactly what I mean. When we stop trying to be cool and allow ourselves to be vulnerable, life changes for the better.

Here is another example: Robert Bly tells this wonderful story about a boy who finds out that certain characteristics of his are not welcomed by his family, his friends, the world around him. So he puts all those unwanted characteristics in a big bag that he carries on his back. One unwelcome characteristic after another. By the time he is in his thirties, he is schlepping this **big** bag around with him, and is wondering where his energy and zest for life went. He feels unsatisfied, depressed, and bored with himself and the world around him.

Finally he decides that the bag is too heavy for him to keep carrying it around. He starts taking back all the things that in his youth he had stuffed into the bag. The more things he takes back as his own, no matter what everyone is telling him or might be thinking of him, the more alive and the happier he feels. When the bag is empty and he has taken back all the parts of himself, and thrown the bag away, he is finding himself full of energy, passion and joy.

My point being, the more vulnerable and real we allow ourselves to be, the richer life gets, as it is based on a real Me instead of a stripped down, partly rejected, shrunken image of myself. All parts are available to share my perceptions of reality and all of them are also available to celebrate the world around me.

~~~ A deep belly breath in ~~~

Added Benefits for Men

I see an added benefit especially for men, when they are willing to become less cool and more honest. Lovemaking becomes so much better for and with a vulnerable man. Our culture tells a man not to show feelings, to be strong all the time, to make it in the world. That persona makes for a one-dimensional man, and especially a fairly "wooden" lover, believe it or not. The more open and soft a man becomes, without loosing his maleness, the more juicy he becomes. All the technique a man is willing to learn means very little if he is not also willing to open up to his feelings and to accept more of who he really is. The less secure a man pretends to be, the more vulnerable he allows himself to feel and act, the more lovable and the sexier he becomes in my book.

Here is an example: when you are feeling nervous and don't really know what to do or how to do something in a sexual context, don't just brave it out and pretend. Be open and honest and say something like: "I am feeling really nervous right now, and am not quite sure what to do next." Don't just perform for her—it is a way of disconnecting from her and most importantly, from yourself. And let me tell you that if a woman looks down upon you for being honest like that, you don't want her as a lover or partner. By the way men, don't just take my word for it. Try it out. What do you have to lose except lookin' cool?

~~~ A deep sigh out ~~~

Soul

Ram Tzu knows this…
You are perfect.
Your every defects perfectly defined.
Your every blemish
is perfectly placed.
Your every absurd action
is perfectly timed.
Only God could make
something this ridiculous
work.

~~ Unknown Source ~~

~~~~~~~~~~

To live content with small means;
to seek elegance rather than luxury,
and refinement rather than fashion;
to be worthy, not respectable,
and wealthy, not rich;
to listen to stars and birds,
babes and sages, with an open heart;
to study hard;
to think quietly,
act frankly,
talk gently,
await occasions,
hurry never;
in a word, to let the spiritual,
unbidden and unconscious,
grow up through the common—
this is my symphony.

Security Fullness

~~ William Henry Channing ~~

~~~~~~~~~~

The following was written by Audrey Hepburn
who was asked to share her "beauty tips":

1. For attractive lips, speak words of kindness.
2. For lovely eyes, seek out the good in people.
3. For a slim figure, share your food with the hungry.
4. For beautiful hair, let a child run his or her fingers through it once a day.
5. For poise, walk with the knowledge that you never walk alone.
6. People, even more than things, have to be restored, revived, reclaimed and redeemed; never throw out anyone.
7. Remember, if you ever need a helping hand, you'll find one at the end of each of your arms. As you grow older, you will discover that you have two hands; one for helping yourself, the other for helping others.
8. The beauty of a woman is not in the clothes she wears, the figure that she carries, or the way she combs her hair. The beauty of a woman must be seen from inside her eyes, because that is the doorway to her heart, the place where love resides.
9. The beauty of a woman is not in a facial mode, but the true beauty in a woman is reflected in her soul. It is the caring that she lovingly gives, the passion that she shows.
10. The beauty of a woman grows with the passing years.

~~~~~~~~~~

Dissolver of sugar, dissolve me,
if this is the time.
Do it gently with a touch of a hand, or a look.
Every morning I wait at dawn. That's when
it's happened before. Or do it suddenly
like an execution. How else
can I get ready for death?

You breathe without a body like a spark.
You grieve, and I begin to feel lighter.
You keep me away with your arm,
but the keeping away is pulling me in.

Fullness No Matter What

~~ Rumi (Coleman Barks translation) ~~

~~~~~~~~~~

The fishes are confused
in searching for the sea.
Find what you can't lose.
Be free

~~ Kirtana, This Embrace ~~

~~~~~~~~~~

"What is it that a man may call the greatest things in life?"
"Hot water, good dentishtry and shoft lavatory paper."

~~ Terry Pratchett, The Light Fantastic ~~

More

Good Vibrations website for information and toys on about anything sexual: www.goodvibes.com

Jack Morin, PhD. *Anal Pleasure and Health*. A good book on the practical aspects of Rosebud pleasure.

Lynne Twist. *The Soul of Money: Transforming your Relationship with Money and Life*. What an insightful book by one of the leading fundraisers for charitable causes, who also happens to be a great inspiration herself. http://www.soulofmoney.com

Robert Bly. *A Little Book on the Human Shadow*. http://www.robertbly.com

Kirtana. *This Embrace*. Wild Dove Music. Kirtana put her experiences with Gangaji into some beautiful songs which Eckhart Tolle uses in his seminars as a way into his form of stillness.

Pleasure Fullness

The Joy That Wanting Brings

Now that I am all opened up again
A body's touch, a lover's energy
I am missing it

Now that my senses are awake again
My body calls for heat and smell
In loud and ample voices

Now that I'm raw and soft again
Where do I go with all this force
That I let out, out of this cage so quick

Now that I tasted juice again
I just want all of it
I want a lot of it

Now that I am all opened up again
I find the secret place inside of me
And laugh and moan and scream
And walk and dance and sing
Of all the joy that wanting brings
Of all the joy that wanting brings

~~ Ulla! ~~

Body

Pleasure is what keeps the wheel in motion. Pleasure is what keeps us wanting to stay here on Earth. All the chapters have Pleasure Exercises, as pleasure has a part in every one of the fullness aspects I am presenting here, just as we breathe in, just as we breathe out.

Breathing Exercise: Three Spheres of Pleasure Fullness

Preparations

This Breathing Exercise is designed to be experienced while you are reading it, preferably out loud to yourself, if you are in a position to do so. If not, at least mouth the words; it will help you slow down and stay focused. If you are with a partner who is open to sharing this exercise, take turns reading it out loud to each other. Make sure you are in a position to relax while you are reading, without falling asleep too quickly.

If you want to intensify this exercise, invite your spirit guides and angels, known or unknown, seen or unseen, to join you in this experience.

Exercise

- ❖ I bring my awareness into both my reproductive organs and my sexual organs by placing my hands on my pubic bone or my Jewels in a comfortable position.
- ❖ I squeeze my PC muscles a couple times very gently, just to become more aware of my Jewels.

~~~~~

- ❖ If I feel any discomfort or tightness in my Jewels, I notice it.
- ❖ I then totally accept the pain or discomfort by directing my very own Loving Color into the tender or tight area. I bring that Loving Color of acceptance into every area of discomfort, one after another, until my Jewels are glowing with acceptance.

~~~~~

- I focus my inbreath into my Jewels, that is I feel my belly area rise with the inbreath, and I imagine that I can gently push my breath all the way into my Jewels.
- This inbreath is like a wave on the ocean being watched from a boat looking onto a sandy shore. I watch the wave building up to a crest, breaking, and rolling down the beach all the way into my Jewels, slowly counting to five.
- I watch my outbreath recede like a wave from the beach. It recedes from my Jewels into my belly and I watch my belly fall with the outbreath, slowly counting to five.
- I continue watching the flow of the waves, my inbreath, and my outbreath for about four to six long slow breaths.

OutBreath

- I start directing a focused breath into my Jewels using an outward "FFF" breath.
    - I breathe in through the nose.
    - I breathe out by pushing my breath through pursed lips between my upper teeth and my lower lips making a "FFF" sound.
    - I take a few outward "FFF" breaths noticing the resistance on the outbreath and the smooth flow of air on the inbreath.

~~~~~~

- I imagine a sphere around my Jewels with its center in either my Pearl or the base of my Lingam and reaching to about my navel and halfway to my knees. The sphere has a semi-permeable surface.
- I imagine directing this "FFF" breath into my Jewels and into my pelvis area and letting my breath fill the sphere with swirling bright and intense colors.
- Every "FFF" breath is bringing in another bright and intense color and releases it into the sphere.
- I am breathing fairly rapid and intense.
- I imagine the sphere being filled up with all these swirling bright colors.
- I imagine my Jewels and reproductive organs being charged up and fired up by these swirling bright colors.

Pleasure Fullness

- I imagine this first sphere filling up to the point where the colors explode through the semi permeable surface into a second sphere.

- This second sphere encompasses my whole body from head to toes and includes my outstretched arms.
- It also has a semi permeable surface.
- I am still making the "FFF" sound by breathing in through my nose and breathing out by pushing my breath through pursed lips between my upper teeth and my lower lips.
- I am breathing at about half the speed and intensity of the breath in the first sphere.
- I am aware of being stretched from the first sphere into the second sphere.
- When the various colors explode into the second sphere they become pastel colors, having about half the brightness and intensity as the colors in the first sphere.
- Every "FFF" breath is bringing in more pastel color and releases them into the second sphere.
- I am breathing slower and fuller.
- I imagine the skin all over my body being gently caressed by the swirling pastel colors.
- I imagine the pastel colors penetrating my skin into my arms, my legs, my head, my torso, every part of my body.
- I imagine the second sphere being filled up with all these swirling pastel colors.
- I imagine it filling up to the point where the pastel colors explode through the semi permeable surface into a third sphere.

~~~~~~

- This third sphere encompasses everything outside my physical body beyond the second sphere.

- I am still making the "FFFF" sound by breathing in through my nose and breathing out by pushing my breath through pursed lips between my upper teeth and my lower lips.
- I am now breathing very slowly, deliberately, and softly.
- When the various pastel colors explode into the third sphere they become luminescent, that is they are gently glowing with silvery and golden traces.
- I am aware of being stretched from the first sphere all the way into the third sphere.
- This third sphere is as large as I am willing to explore.
- It might reach just a few inches below my feet or above my head.
- It might reach all the way to the height of tallest mountain here on Earth.
- It might reach up to the Moon and the stars.
- And it might reach all the way into the next solar system, the next galaxy, the next universe, into infinity.
- I take a few deep and slow breaths, just breathing in and breathing out, resting in the awareness of being inside all three spheres.

InBreath

- I now focus on an inward "FFF" breath.
  - I breathe in by sucking my breath through pursed lips between my upper teeth and my lower lips making a "FFF" sound.
  - I breathe out through the nose.
  - I take a few inward "FFF" breaths noticing the resistance on the inbreath and the smooth flow of air on the outbreath.
- My awareness is stretched from the first sphere in my body all the way out in the third sphere.
- I notice the luminescent and silvery and golden glowing traces in the third sphere.
- Through the "FFF" inbreath I imagine drawing in the luminescent silvery and golden traces of the third sphere.
- Every "FFF" breath concentrates the luminescent traces more and more.
- I imagine concentrating them so much that they get drawn in through the semi permeable surface into the second sphere.

Pleasure Fullness

~~~~~~

- This second sphere encompasses my whole body from head to toes and includes my outstretched arms.
- I am aware of now being stretched from the first to the second sphere.
- I am still making the "FFF" sound by breathing in, sucking my breath through pursed lips between my upper teeth and my lower lips and breathing out through my nose.

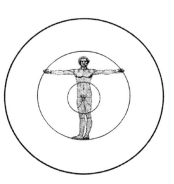

- I am breathing now at twice the speed and intensity of the breath in the third sphere.
- Through the "FFF" inbreath I imagine concentrating the pastel colors of the second sphere.
- Every "FFF" breath concentrates the pastel colors more and more.
- I imagine concentrating them so much that they get drawn in through the semi permeable surface into the first sphere.

~~~~~~

- This first sphere is around my Jewels with its center in either my Pearl or the base of my Lingam and reaching to about my navel and halfway to my knees.
- I am still making the "FFF" sound of breathing in by sucking my breath in through pursed lips between my upper teeth and my lower lips and breathing out through my nose.
- I am breathing now at twice the speed and intensity of the breath in the second sphere.
- Through the "FFF" inbreath I imagine concentrating the bright intense fiery colors of the first sphere.
- Every "FFF" breath concentrates the intense bright colors more and more.
- I start sucking my breath directly into my Jewels using the inward "FFF" breath.

~~~~~~

- I start breathing normally, letting go of the inward "FFF" breath.
- I rest in the awareness of being inside this first sphere.
- I notice any changes in my body, in my sense of well being, in my breathing.

~~~~~~

- I once again focus my inbreath into my Jewels, that is I feel my belly area rise with the inbreath, and I imagine that I can gently push my breath all the way into my Jewels.
- This inbreath is like a wave on the ocean being watched from a boat looking onto a sandy shore. I watch the wave building up to a crest, breaking, and rolling down the beach all the way into my Jewels, slowly counting to five.
- I watch my outbreath recede like a wave from the beach. It recedes from my Jewels into my belly and I watch my belly fall with the outbreath, slowly counting to five.
- I continue watching the flow of the waves, my inbreath, and my outbreath for about four to six long slow breaths.
- Anytime now I can access my three Spheres of Pleasure and experience their effect on my life in the hours, days, and months to come.

Completion

- When I am complete, I bring my awareness back to the world outside of me.
- I wiggle my toes and fingers.
- I stretch my body like a cat with a few lazy, long, full body stretches.
- I am back in my waking reality.

Suggestions

If you want to make sure that you experience more Pleasure Fullness in your life, independently from having any partner or a willing partner, try the Mandala exercise described in Breathing Exercise:
Color of Loving Fullness under Mandala Breathing.

Pleasure Exercises

Solo: The Three Pleasure Spheres

Here is an invitation for a ritual to awaken the three Spheres of Pleasure in your body.

Preparations

- ❖ If you want a conceptual context, read the part called "Definitions First" in the Mind Section of this chapter to familiarize yourself with the concept of pleasure spheres.
- ❖ Make sure you have some time and space to yourself, preferably not just before you go to sleep.
- ❖ Create a ritual space by lighting some candles, maybe some incense, putting on some music that helps you feel good.
- ❖ If you feel comfortable with it, set that ritual space up in front of a mirror.
- ❖ Have some massage oil handy, maybe even some aromatic oils that have a scent to your liking.

Exercise

- ❖ Place yourself in front of the mirror by either kneeling with a pillow between your legs for support or sitting in a comfortable position that allows you to touch both your body and your Jewels.
- ❖ Set an intention for this ritual. An example would be: "I am ready, willing, and able to invite more pleasure into my life by awakening my three Pleasure Spheres." Just say that sentence or any other more to your liking out loud three times.
- ❖ Take the massage oil and start applying it with loving touch to the first Pleasure Sphere: the Sexual Sphere.
- ❖ Apply the oil as lovingly as you can to your belly, your Jewels, your Rosebud, your bottom cheeks, your hips, and the small of your back.
- ❖ You might imagine sending your Loving Color (Chapter 1 Loving Fullness) through your hands and the oil into your first Pleasure Sphere.
- ❖ When you feel complete, close your eyes and feel inside of you. Be aware of your first Pleasure Sphere.

Fullness No Matter What

~~~~~~

- ❖ When you are ready for the next sphere, take some more oil and start applying it with loving touch to the second Pleasure Sphere: the Sensuous Sphere.
- ❖ Apply the oil as lovingly as you can to your stomach, your chest, your neck, your face (if you feel comfortable applying oil), your arms and hands, your upper back as far as you can reach, and your legs and feet.
- ❖ You might imagine sending your Loving Color through your hands and the oil into your second Pleasure Sphere.
- ❖ When you feel complete, close your eyes and feel inside of you. Be aware of your second Pleasure Sphere.

~~~~~~

- ❖ When you are ready for the third sphere, start pleasuring yourself sexually until you get close to orgasm. Once you are very close, pleasure yourself very slowly and deliberately, and relax into the pleasure, this time not to go over the edge, but to stay close to the edge.
- ❖ Close your physical eyes and "see" with your inner eyes. Sense into the space inside your eyes and head. Feel your awareness spreading beyond the confines of your physical body. Welcome to the third Pleasure Sphere: the Transcendent Sphere.
- ❖ Keep stimulating yourself gently and slowly.
- ❖ If you feel your energy getting too low, go back to more intense pleasuring, but slow down again before you go over the edge.
- ❖ See whether you can hang out on that edge of the third Pleasure Sphere as long as it feels good.
- ❖ When you feel complete, either give yourself a good orgasm, or just let your energy come down slowly and relax into it.

Suggestions

It might take several sessions to experience the pleasures of the third sphere, the transcendent sphere. You might just practice on the edge pleasuring for a while to be familiar with your own Point of No Return (see Pleasure Exercises in Heavenly Fullness) and the sensations just before that point, as that is the one where you can travel the farthest.

Partnered: Honoring the Divine in Each Other

For me pleasure experienced through the human body is one way of knowing and celebrating the Divine in my life. Here is an exercise I was taught by Andro, my first Tantra teacher who lives and teaches in Berlin, Germany. I adapted his idea to my own needs.

This is an exercise to open up your lovemaking to a new and possibly more intense level of pleasure. Even if at the beginning it feels like you are faking it, don't worry. Sometimes you just fake it till you make it…Play with it. Don't take it too seriously and let yourself be surprised.

Preparations

- Sit facing each other.
- Close your eyes and connect with yourself.
- Find your love for yourself and your partner inside of you.
- Hold hands and just look into each other's eyes till you feel connected with each other in love.

Exercise

- Women start.
- Both gently and passionately touch your partner's face with both your hands while saying out loud:
- "This is the face of the Divine. I love and honor the face of the Divine."
- Go through eyes, mouth, cheek, hair, using the above formula.
- Touch arms and hands, and legs and feet, again turning them into divine body parts.
- Move to the neck, back, buttocks, chest, belly, and last, but not least his Lingam.
- Explore touching his body parts with both love and turn-on. Turn this exercise into another form of foreplay…
- Come to completion by lightly stroking his body from head to Jewels, saying:
- "This is the body of the Divine. I love the body of the Divine, and my soul, heart, and body are ready and willing to make love with the Divine in you."

- ❖ Then men, do the same with your woman, moving from head through your woman's whole body, ending up with her Pearl and her Yoni, and completing the process by saying:
- ❖ "This is the body of the Divine. I love the body of the Divine, and my soul, heart, and body are ready and willing to make love with the Divine in you."
- ❖ Then let yourselves be carried into lovemaking.
- ❖ Feel free to change or add words or phrases. Experiment…
- ❖ Remember, have fun with it…

Mind

Definitions First

Let me start with some definitions. To me pleasure has three basic forms of expression:

- ❖ Sexual Pleasure
- ❖ Sensuous Pleasure
- ❖ Transcendent Pleasure

The best way to describe how these three forms of pleasure relate to one another and the human body is to imagine three concentric spheres with their center on the female Pearl or the base of the male Lingam (not its head—too much room for variations!):

The innermost sphere represents **Sexual Pleasure**, or sexuality, which is pleasure experienced through sexual organs. Even though hands, mouths, and breasts can be involved in sexual pleasuring, its focus lies in the Jewels. It is also the procreative aspect of pleasure, that is, engagement in sexual union can lead to the creation of children.

The next sphere represents **Sensuous Pleasure**, which can be experienced involving all five senses and our whole body like our skin, breasts, nipples, mouths, eyes, hands, feet, hair etc. This sensuous pleasure sphere includes sexual pleasure, but its focus has broadened to include experiencing pleasure throughout the whole body. (The dictionary definition of sensuous is: producing gratification of the senses or characterized by gratification of the senses).

The biggest sphere represents **Transcendent Pleasure** where we find pleasure beyond our bodily confines. It has the widest focus, reaches all the way down into the earth and all the way up into the heavens, but also includes both sexuality and sensuality. (The dictionary definition of transcendent is: extending or lying beyond the limits of ordinary experience, or being beyond comprehension)

Interestingly, each of the three forms of pleasure can serve as a gateway for the others. This means that the flow between all three spheres is not only from the Jewels (sexual) through the body (sensuous) to the non-physical realm (transcendent), but also from the non-physical to the body into the Jewels. Any experience can open up or narrow down in any direction. Here is an example: Eating a very juicy, fully ripened, delicious, golden yellow mango can get me totally sexually turned on, or it can open me up to being in transcendent bliss where I feel like I am the mango tree and my fruit laden heavy branches are being caressed by a tropical breeze. That's why I have included Pleasure Exercises in every fullness aspect, as every one can serve as a gateway into more and expanded experiences in our lives.

To me lovemaking is the most satisfying when elements of all three spheres are present. Here is an example: while being in sexual union I am sharing a juicy red strawberry with my partner in a wet French kiss, and after orgasming we look into each other's eyes and float out into space just looking in and through and beyond these beloved eyes.

It gets even better when we are with a partner who can meet us in all three spheres. That is a lover who revels in pure raw physical sex just as much as in the sensuous pleasure of stroking skin for an hour, as letting physical pleasure open up other dimensions and knowing we are both traveling out there only to return to another round of pleasure.

Pleasure also connects all the different fullness aspects like Loving Fullness or Guidance Fullness. Remember in the Introduction to this book, I described fullness as a horse that keeps the carriage in motion. Pleasure is that motion from one fullness to the next fullness. It is also like the amniotic fluid around and inside a fetus, as it soothes, contains, nourishes, and cleanses all the fullness aspects. And it is like pleasure glue holding all of it together—a glue as light as butterfly wings and as durable as steel.

~~~ A deep belly breath in ~~~

My Pleasure Story

I personally did not awaken to the joys of various kinds of pleasure until in my early thirties. By that time I had spent more time in my head than in my body, and basically was afraid of pleasure—not that I knew it then. I had discovered self-pleasuring and clitoral orgasms at the age of 18 when I read an article in a Cosmopolitan magazine. It got me started on a journey of daily self-exploration that was very satisfying and exciting but guilt ridden.

When I discovered partnered sex about a year later, I felt very disappointed, as it did not feel at all like what I could do with myself. And it stayed disappointing for another 15 years, even though I managed (with the help of my wasband Chris) to conceive and give birth to two children during those years. I attribute the disappointment to several factors: one, I was not able to experience Yoni orgasms (vaginal orgasms) and did not know how to add Pearl Orgasms (clitoral orgasms) into my lovemaking experiences. Two, I had not yet figured out how to bring my feelings and the sense of loving into sexual union. And three, I had no way of asking for what I really wanted—a typical woman's dilemma as I later found out. So I had a lot of headaches for a lot of years…

And then, as we say in German, "the monkey bit me" (da hat mich der Affe gebissen) and I caught the pleasure exploration bug. For the next ten plus years I dove into the world of sexual exploration, first with my wasband and after our divorce with a number of different partners. I found a community of fellow explorers in the greater San Francisco Bay Area and went for it through Tantric workshops, communication classes, and different sexual and sensuous healing modalities. This exploration became my path to self-discovery. It turned into my road to healing my childhood wounds. But most of all, it was my gateway into **knowing** without a doubt that I have a direct connection to the Divine, God, Spirit, or whatever you want to call that force that calls us to be all we came here to be…and way more. And that direct connection happens to go through my own body. The knowing is **in** my body, **in** my pleasure, **in** me.

Since then I have gone through many layers of experiencing all kinds of pleasure, and the discovery is not over yet, not for a long time. I feel I have just gotten started, and surely appreciate all the gifts that pleasure has brought to me and all the challenges it allowed me to go through more easily and more gracefully.

~~~ A deep sigh out ~~~

The Politics of Pleasure

Pleasure, that throbbing, that bodily sensation, that state of being, which for centuries has brought up and still brings up so much disagreement, has been one of the greatest tools to explore controversy for us human beings. There is nothing that can divide humanity so easily as different opinions about the proper or improper uses of pleasure.

For centuries most religions explored the effects of reducing pleasure to the purely procreative aspect as part of the Grand Experiment. At the same time they allowed a minority, usually relegated to the status of a "sect", to use pleasurable practices as a means to connect with their definition of the Divine. Here are some examples: Hinduism had Tantra. Its detailed sexual practices were even depicted on some of their sacred temples (for example the Madhya Pradesh Tantra Temple in Khajuraho, India). Christianity had Sex Magic until the inquisition burnt most traces of it at the stakes and called it witch burning. And Islam had its Sufi tradition that brought forth such sensuous mystics like Rumi and Rabia (a slave sold into prostitution who became a famous mystical poet).

In our Western society I see a number of strange and beautiful paradoxes at work. On one side I have observed that nearly every consumer product can be sold with intimations of sexuality. Full breasted blonde females as symbolic representations of sexuality are placed near or on consumer goods to fill the cash (or credit card) registers. Another way is the implied promise of sex appeal through the mere purchase of a consumer good that originally is not at all associated with sex, as when mere tooth paste is turned into something very sexy.

A number of consumer products experienced explosive sales **only** when they became associated with easy access to pornography. Both video recorders and CD-ROM players hit the **big** sales when video tapes and CD-ROMs featured pornographic content. And by the way, some of the first Internet companies to bring home real bacon instead of venture capital bacon were pornography sites. Because of that they were at the forefront of financing and implementing technological advances on the Internet that later became industry standards.

On the other side more people today seem to talk about sex, want sex, or dream of sex, than are actually having sex. I have a hunch that the quality of pleasurable experiences is also something that for a number of people has room for improvement. And I am not talking about some redecorating here and there, but about a general overhaul.

These paradoxes all are pointing towards the fact that pleasure and its various aspects are more explosive than the atom bomb, even though they are more easily accessible than a tooth brush—everyone of us has a body and has the ability to experience pleasure. All we need is an open mind, a willingness to explore, and not even a cent in our wallets. We do not even need a partner as the Solo Exercises in this book easily demonstrate. We **are** pleasure beings just by the nature of having a body that has the ability to experience pleasure.

~~~ *A deep belly breath in* ~~~

Some Pointers

The road into pleasure can be very simple because of its relatively easy access. All we need is our bodies and the openness to explore new sensations or new territory. But the impact of more pleasure is anything but simple in or beyond our bodies. This is not meant to deter anyone from exploring more pleasure. Knowing helps to integrate some of the side effects that accompany an increase of pleasure in our lives.

The Road to Feelings

In our Western culture pleasure energy is mainly directed downward and outward, that is, it is being expressed genitally and released for men through ejaculation, and for women through Pearl or Yoni orgasms. This coincides with the first sphere, the sexual sphere.

When we start reaching out for the next sphere, the sensuous sphere, we include the rest of the body in the experience of pleasure. The flow of energy then moves upwards, among other things, to the feeling center (see chapter 11 Feeling Fullness) and stirs the pot there. So far unexpressed or unacknowledged feelings suddenly receive a jolt of energy and start waking up.

Waking up these feelings is a blessing for those who are ready, willing and able to go for it. It turns into a major challenge if there is an attempt to keep the lid down on the pot. As I said earlier, pleasure is what keeps the wheel in motion and different body parts connected. One of the reasons that sensuous whole body pleasure and feelings are connected is that energetically, there is no difference between the opening up to physical sensations and the opening up to emotional feelings. Both are the result of more flow of energy through the body beyond the Jewels, and thus cannot be selectively shut off or turned on. You either open up to more sensations, **both** physical and emotional, or you close down sensations, **both** physical and emotional. When floodgates are open, all the water flows out, not just parts of it, and when they are shut, all the water becomes stagnant, not just part of it.

Another aspect of the open floodgates is that we also cannot selectively open up to only the "good" feelings like pleasure, joy, and love. When we open ourselves up to more pleasure throughout the whole body, all the difficult feelings like anger, sadness, jealousy, fear etc. have a way out, too. When the dam opens, not only do just the fish we like flow out, but all the creatures of the bottom and the dark come out, too.

Said in another way, if we want to be in control in terms of **what** feelings we experience, we cannot be asking for more pleasure. If we are willing to let go of control, we get both the pleasurable and the challenging feelings. But let me tell you, experiencing more and richer pleasure is worth every difficult feeling along the way. There are just more feelings to enrich our lives and there is just more fullness.

~~~ A deep sigh out ~~~

For Women in Particular

Women overall have more leeway in our Western culture to experience and show feelings. That is why one typical complaint from women is that lovemaking with their partners is not sensuous enough for them. Women often would like more of their bodies involved in lovemaking, in other words, they are asking for feelings to be involved in lovemaking. This is easier for women as they usually are more open to experiencing and expressing feelings.

When we women reach for more pleasure, for most of us the increase in feelings is not quite as overwhelming as it typically is for men. But we women have another aspect to deal with: in my experience and understanding a woman's potential for pleasure can be almost limitless. A woman's Pearl is the only human sexual organ whose **only** function is pleasure. Female breasts are both for breast feeding and pleasure, a Lingam is designed for urination, impregnation and pleasure, a Yoni for conception, birthing and pleasure. Only the Pearl and its internal expression, the Sacred Spot (or G-Spot in medical terms), have no other "useful" function besides pleasure. (A case can be made that men's nipples represent the female pleasure aspect in a man, as they do not serve any other purpose than pleasure, but it usually takes some practice to sensitize them.)

Another reason women's potential for pleasure can be considered almost unlimited is that most women do not loose their energy after orgasm as men often do. Many men are ready to almost instantly fall asleep after ejaculatory orgasm (I consciously make a distinction here between ejaculatory and energetic orgasms for me—see "Sexual Energy Ecstasy" book). Many women can keep coming and coming and coming…especially once they have opened themselves up to experiencing greater levels of pleasure in their lives.

So what makes it difficult for women to go for more pleasure? Historically there have been a myriad of ways to either suppress a woman's pleasure potential as much as possible, or to make use of it, but not on a woman's terms. Over the last 2000 years, women have been burned at the stakes, sold into slavery, worn out and old as breeding machines, exploited via prostitution, kept under lock and stock as wives, or induced to follow ever changing fads of commercial trends that have little to do with the experience of actual pleasure. (see the video "Burning Times" which makes that point quite poignantly).

~~~ *A deep belly breath in* ~~~

What DO Women Want?

It has only been for the last 50 years that women have started to claim back some of that right to pleasure on their own terms and without fear of repercussions. That reclaiming of pleasure for women has wider implications than just another happy woman. As a woman's potential for pleasure is almost unlimited, if she is not able to live in pleasure, and I am not only talking sexual pleasure here, an essential part of her nature is not invited to the table. The saying "If Mama ain't happy, no one's happy" points in the right direction. Let me express the same idea in a positive way. A woman who lives in pleasure by her own choice and by her own definition and feels supported in that pursuit by her partner and even the community around her, radiates joy and contentment that effects **all** who are around her in a positive way. The rightful pursuit of pleasure brings out the best in us women.

The challenge here is that both today and historically in our Western culture "what women want" does not matter too much. And I am not talking about the diamond ring, the pearls and the Benz Convertible—those are just substitutions for the real thing. Interestingly the right answer to the nearly stereotypical and often exasperated question "What **does** a woman **really** want?" cannot be reduced to one thing.

What a woman wants is the process of continuously being given room and support to explore that question into deeper and deeper realms. Any man grasping that concept will be most likely a very, very happy man for quite some time. To be a woman's supportive and equal partner on her journey into what she wants is deeply rewarding for a man who loves her. The spillover from a woman's continuous quest into pleasure covering all pleasure spheres is very beautiful and enriching for anyone supporting it, both as an individual and as a community.

~~~ A deep sigh out ~~~

For Men in Particular

Let me preface this section with the remark that I love men. I love your sexuality and the fire it ignites in me. I love your bodies, particularly your smells. I love your minds and what you can create with them. I love your hands and what they can do when you touch me, or hold the children, or fix my computer. And I honor your journey into fullness, being quite aware that though we are on the same path, we travel using different means and at different speeds.

Men in Western culture (and more or less the rest of the world) have had more leeway to express their pleasure sexually than women, though the majority of it has been and is still experienced mostly genitally. At the same time, it has been more difficult socially for men to acknowledge and express their feelings. I see a big opportunity here for men: in opening up to more sensuous whole body (and transcendent) pleasure you open the floodgates to feelings, while at the same time opening up to greater depth of pleasure.

The challenge here is to learn and practice safe ways to express these feelings, and by safe I do not mean the traditional outlet of recreational substances like alcohol, cocaine, and marihuana, which allow for feelings to surface and be released, but in unconscious and often destructive ways. The substance use ultimately only serves as a pressure valve to temporarily release pent up feelings, but will not help integrate the safe expression of those feelings into every day life. There is always a return to the original status quo, until the next round of recreational drugs.

A man, who is not only in touch with his feelings but also comfortable expressing them safely, achieves a whole new sense of freedom and independence—from women. So often men need women in their lives to provide them with the richness of the feeling world, the warmth of knowing themselves connected, and the chance to be soft and open. At the same time that emotional dependence scares men and leads to the "commitment shuffle" so many men do—one step forward, two steps back. It is no fun feeling dependent on someone as an adult. It's enough that we are dependent as children.

Men also tend to need women as sexual objects to pour their pent up feelings into, because ejaculatory orgasm will create a temporary release of those feelings into the woman. And then men wonder why women loose their sweetness and turn bitter and angry over time. (Women have their own part in that game, but that is another story.)

Men do not only temporarily release the pent up feelings, but they also loose their energy and therefore often need to go to sleep right after ejaculation. Men who know how to separate ejaculation from orgasm, that is experience orgasms sensuously throughout their whole bodies without ejaculation and have learned to be in touch with their feelings, generally have much more staying power and do not experience the instant loss of energy. They also see themselves emotionally more easily as an equal to their women, and when they make a commitment to the relationship, it comes from a sense of self-reliance and strength.

~~~ A deep belly breath in ~~~

Communication—Communication—Communication

When we are engaging in that kind of intense exploration, it is imperative to learn and practice safe communication techniques. I would not recommend a deeper exploration into full body pleasure without the support of "good" communication skills like:

- ❖ I am able to identify my feelings even if all I can do is locate a sensation in my body, for example: "My belly is very tight."

- ❖ I am able to express my feelings without needing to blame, for example: "I am feeling very angry right now" instead of "You are making me angry."
- ❖ I am able to express my needs without making them into a conditional demand, for example:" Right now I would like to be held in your arms. Would you be willing to do that for me?" instead of "If you don't hold me right now, I am never going to talk to you again."
- ❖ I have an agreement with my partner to follow some form of communication structure in these intense emotional situations. See More Section in Chapter 11 Feeling Fullness for a list of different communication techniques.

Safe communication techniques are a must in these pleasure explorations because we are literally playing with emotional fire when we call our blocked feelings into play. But it is a cleansing and healing fire, this fire of our pleasure.

~~~ *A deep sigh out* ~~~

Social Ramifications

Inviting more pleasure into our lives also has social ramifications, and they apply to both genders. We live in the Grand Experiment of a consumer goods oriented society. It works so well precisely because it can keep selling what I call "substitutions for the real thing". We all do strive for a life full of happiness, joy, and pleasure, and in the USA even have a legal right to the pursuit of happiness guaranteed by the Bill of Rights.

Here are some of the terms of the Grand Experiment as I see them: can the consumer industry invent, produce and sell enough substitutions like technical toys (computers, game stations, television, VCRs etc), gadgets (cell phones, pagers etc), larger toys (houses, boats and cars) that promise happiness by purchasing them? Interestingly they are never the "real thing". All that happens is that usually after an initial short phase of joy and satisfaction, the next substitutions need to be pursued and purchased, only to wear out soon again. In my opinion no real lasting satisfaction can be found in the continuous pursuit of external substitutions for the real thing. How can anything outside ourselves bring us the so much desired happiness which can ultimately only be found inside of us?

So if in the above scenario we turn our attention to the "simple pleasures" of life like our bodies, our five senses, in short the basics, in my experience life becomes immensely pleasurable without the constant need for new products and gadgets. If we allow the consumer goods machinery to only run in the background instead of running our lives, we might just have a chance at happiness. The saying of the sixties "drop out, drop in" already described that process very nicely.

My invitation here is to try an experiment for a year: does my life become fuller and more satisfying if I "drop" into myself, and can I find real happiness there? Follow the suggestions of this book for a year and my sense is that you will be pleasantly surprised. If you are serious about that idea, visit my web site at www.FullnessNoMatterWhat.com. There you will find all the support you need for that experiment.

~~~ A deep belly breath in ~~~

Transcendence

There was a reason so many of the world's religions have not and still are not keen on practices that lead to a life where pleasure is an integral part of our daily existence. And I am not talking about a so-called hedonistic approach to life, where pleasure becomes the one and only goal in life. I am talking about a life where the experience of pleasure is wholly integrated into all the other aspects of a full life.

Opening ourselves up to finding pleasure in the third concentric sphere means we are ready, consciously or not, not only to feel pleasure in our Jewels and the rest of our body (sphere one and two) but are willing to reach beyond out bodies. When we reach beyond our bodies, there is a possibility of encountering something much larger than our self and/or our body. We might find a direct and very personal connection into a whole new world. I call this the transcendent aspect of pleasure. Here are the three definition of transcendent and they all fit my interpretation of it:

- ❖   1: exceeding usual limits
- ❖   2: being beyond comprehension
- ❖   3: transcending the universe or material existence

There is a challenging aspect here when we reach for the transcendent aspect of pleasure. In my opinion it is a challenge to one of the most fundamental reasons for the existence of most religions. This transcendent encounter can occur without any need to be sanctioned by a priest, or interpreted by a church leader, or even mediated by the whole religious structure as to its rightfulness, properness, and appropriateness.

There is a directness and an immediacy available to us that has no need for outside validation. This encounter is deeply personal and unique to each one of us. Each one of us has the ability to become the sole authority into a world that is both outside and inside of us. This world to me is too vast to be easily named, and most often defies any use of words. And it is ours to experience any time we dare to open ourselves up to ever larger realms of pleasure.

In other words, in another Grand Experiment of the last 2000 years the religions of this world have needed us to give them authority over our spiritual life. The easiest way to be that authority and stay in control was to condemn pleasure. Pleasure is one of the main gateways into the proverbial heaven of the religions, except that this heaven is here on earth, and does not need any external authority to open its pearly gates for us.

What we do have need for are guides into that realm, as it reaches beyond the confines of the logical mind. In our Western culture that kind of exploration easily scares us and we give up, as we do not know how to be friends with matters not explainable or understandable through logic. The guides I am talking about are those who have reached into those realms and have returned, not only to tell the tale, but to live a different life.

Once we know without any doubt, that there is transcendence, that is, once we know there is more available to us than just this bodily existence, and that we are an integral part of it, we are forever changed. That is the promise here, literally the Promised Land, when we continuously explore ever deeper levels of pleasure.

~~~ A deep sigh out ~~~

Soul

They try to say what you are, spiritual or sexual?
They wonder about Solomon and all his wives?

In the body of the world, they say, there is a soul
And you are that.

But we have ways within each other
That will never be said by anyone.

~~ Rumi (Coleman Barks Translation) ~~

~~~~~~~~~~

I often think that the senses are the gateway to the soul;
we should celebrate them more.

~~ Ellis Peters, The Leper of St. Giles ~~

~~~~~~~~~~

Getting an education was a bit like a communicable sexual disease.
It made you unsuitable for a lot of jobs and
then you had the urge to pass it on.

~~ Terry Pratchett, Hogfather ~~

~~~~~~~~~~

A Woman's Song

I'm strong she said
And looked at her creation
I'm strong she said
And looked at the destruction
Of that which was no longer true

I'm strong she said
And looked at her fierce love
I'm strong she said

Pleasure Fullness

And looked at all her ruthlessness
To cut away the worn out and the old

She looked at her old self
And saw that is was good
The way that she had been
And then she left to make a home
For her new life

She said I'm good no matter what I do
She said I love myself no matter who I am
She said I'm loved no matter where I go

And then she laid her wings to rest
Just for a while and sang a song
Of love and joy and happiness
While looking at the wasteland she had laid
There were the first seeds of a new life
For her and all the others she had freed
By her own strength
By her own truth
By her own joy

~~ Ulla! ~~

~~~~~~~~~~

More

Suzie Heumann and Susan Campbell, Ph.D. *Everything Great Sex Book.*
http://www.tantra.com/catalog/20-076/R_home

Patricia Taylor. *The Enchantment of Opposites: How to Create Great Relationships.* To order this book:
http://doctorg.com/enchantmentofopposites.htm

Patricia Taylor. *Expanded Orgasm: Soar to Ecstasy at Your Lover's Every Touch.*

Jenny Wade. *Transcendent Sex: When Lovemaking Opens the Veil.* In this book the author interviewed a number of people who had "transcendent" sexual experience that were not induced by either drugs or meditative techniques.

Louis Meldman. *Mystical Sex.* One of the best books on transcendental pleasure I have found.

Charles and Caroline Muir. *Tantra: The Art of Conscious Loving.* A very practical and technique based approach to Tantra.
www.sourcetantra.com

Documentaries
Ancient Secrets of Sexual Ecstasy for Modern Lovers (video) is a both exquisitely beautiful and very informative video on Tantric concepts and practices.
Secrets of Female Sexual Ecstasy (video) was groundbreaking in its visual presentation of female ejaculation.
Tantra: The Art of Conscious Loving (video) is a companion piece to the Muir's book by the same title. Shot on Maui in Hawaii it is an esthetically pleasing visual introduction to the art of loving consciously.
Partner Play: More Passion with Sensual Yoga and Touch (video) gives couples and partnered singles a variety of simple, fun tools to build intimacy and connection. It features a flowing series of non-sexual, sensual techniques, including easy partner yoga, massage, and Tantric partner focusing.
Women and Spirituality: Burning Times (video) is a three part deeply moving documentary on the history, background and practices of witch burnings in the Middle Ages.

Movies
Dangerous Beauty (video) A woman positive, sex positive, erotic, mainstream film with a happy ending that is revolutionary in my opinion. One of my all time favorite movies!
Bliss (video) Far from blissful, this is an impressive and serious movie about the rebuilding of a troubled marriage.
Wild Orchid (video) This erotic and exotic movie has some very sensuous images and one of the most unusual lovemaking movie scenes at the end.
Kama Sutra (video) is a lush and voluptuous tale about two young women who grow up to pleasure a King in 16th century India—one as his wife, and the other as his courtesan. Beautiful images—baaad ending though.

www.tantra.com A great portal site to find articles, book reviews, and tasteful products for a better sex life.

11

Feeling Fullness

Missing You All

I miss you Chris
Once the man for the rest of my life
The first man I deeply loved
Gave myself to and waited for
The father of my growing children
The man who shared his dreams and riches
With me for a while and then got lost
The center of my life for so long
In the absence of my own

I miss you
And right now I feel
That I have lost you

I miss you Felix
My first born
Silver-haired and brightly blue-eyed boy
It took so long for me to let you in
And I am still learning more to open up
You magical child of ten years with wonderful hugs
Who is starting to see me as more
Than just a Mother since I left

I miss you
And right now I feel
That I have lost you

I miss you Emily
My sweet daughter child
So full of joy and centeredness
I miss your kissy-wissies and soft hugs and cuddles
And your clear presence in my life
You gave me the first taste of miracles
When you showed up in my life
As desired and as planned
I wanted you and you came to me

Feeling Fullness

I miss you
And right now I feel
That I have lost you

I miss you my Unborn One
With all the possibilities of a new life
Coming to me in these strange times
A time of losing everything I once held dear
You little precious spark in me
Who fond me in the darkness in Los Angeles
And left quite voluntarily just for the asking
Through quite ecstatic blending
Of pleasure and of pain
While my voice sang your leaving song

I miss you
And right now I feel
That I have lost you

I miss you Ulla
Painting day and night
And basking in your new found colors
Wild and unexpected
In this slender and slim body
Beautiful and radiant and available
Now there are these layers of protection
Inside my mind and outside on my hips

I miss you
And right now I feel
That I have lost you

~~ Ulla! ~~

Body

Someone once said that we humans have feelings so that we know that we change and grow. When we change and grow, we feel good. When we stay stuck, we feel bad. What a wonderful idea, feelings as a useful feedback loop for our personal changes.

Breathing Exercise: Anemones of Feeling Fullness

This breathing exercise is an invitation to explore our own fullness from our belly, this soft, often rounded place, which to me is a gateway into the wonderland of feelings. I call it the Anemones of Feeling. One feature among several that allows for a rich human experience is the fact that we can experience a wide range of feelings, can feel them within ourselves and express them in various ways. Here is your chance to open yourself up to exploring your own feeling seascape.

Preparations

Specific instructions for this particular exercise:
Have pen and paper ready to write something down.

This Breathing Exercise is designed to be experienced while you are reading it, preferably out loud to yourself, if you are in a position to do so. If not, at least mouth the words; it will help you slow down and stay focused. If you are with a partner who is open to sharing this exercise, take turns reading it out loud to each other. Make sure you are in a position to relax while you are reading, without falling asleep too quickly.

If you want to intensify this exercise, invite your spirit guides and angels, known or unknown, seen or unseen, to join you in this experience.

Exercise

❖ I bring my awareness to my belly area by placing my hands on my belly in a comfortable position.

- ❖ I appreciate my intestines doing such a wonderful job of digesting food, extracting nutrients and disposing of the waste. I am becoming aware of the soft gurgling sounds of my intestines.

~~~~~~

- ❖ If I feel any discomfort or tightness in my belly, I notice it, and then totally accept it by directing my very own Loving Color into the tender or tight area. I bring that Loving Color of acceptance into every area of discomfort, one after another, until my belly is glowing with acceptance.
- ❖ I focus my breath once again into my belly area. I feel my belly area rise with the inbreath, slowly counting to five, and fall with the outbreath, again slowly counting to five.
- ❖ I continue watching the rise and fall of my upper lungs for about four to six long slow breaths.

~~~~~~

- ❖ I imagine a number of circles looking like soft sea anemones that open and close inside my physical belly.
- ❖ These anemones have the outer dimensions of my belly. Its inner dimensions are much larger.
- ❖ These are my feeling anemones.
- ❖ I notice the size of my feeling anemones:
    - ➢ Are they big and fat?
    - ➢ Are they average size?
    - ➢ Are the small and tight?
- ❖ Their size is dependent on how I relate to my feelings:
    - ➢ If my feelings have been sitting inside of me for a very long time, unexpressed and unacknowledged, they are quite big, tight lipped, and ready to burst.
    - ➢ If I am at ease with both acknowledging and safely expressing my feelings, they vary in sizes and open up to share their luscious colorful insides.
    - ➢ If I have been ignoring my feelings overall, they might look tiny and compacted and show a prickly outside.
- ❖ I notice their size and the state they are in.

- ❖ I totally accept them in their particular state by directing a soft accepting breath into my feeling anemones until they are glowing with acceptance, no matter what size or state they are in.
- ❖ Acceptance is the fluid that nourishes my anemones, that invites them to open up and share their luscious insides.
- ❖ The more acceptance I can breathe into my belly, the more fluid will be available to the anemones to flourish in.

Invitation

- ❖ I now invite as many feeling anemones in my belly to open up and share their wisdom with me.
- ❖ I am ready to be friends with my feeling anemones that is I am ready to acknowledge their existence, to hear what they have to say, and to find a way to safely express them.
- ❖ I am going to say hello to the following feeling anemones and connect with them, one by one. Just a simple hello.
- ❖ I notice a change, whatever it might be.
- ❖ I notice a color and/or maybe a texture for each feeling anemone.
- ❖ Hello Joy! You are my Joy feeling anemone.
  - ➢ I sense your color as _____.
  - ➢ I feel your texture as _____.
- ❖ Hello Grief! You are my Grief feeling anemone.
  - ➢ I sense your color as _____.
  - ➢ I feel your texture as _____.
- ❖ Hello Anger! You are my Anger feeling anemone.
  - ➢ I sense your color as _____.
  - ➢ I feel your texture as _____.
- ❖ Hello Fear! You are my Fear feeling anemone.
  - ➢ I sense your color as _____.
  - ➢ I feel your texture as _____.
- ❖ Hello Envy! You are my Envy feeling anemone.
  - ➢ I sense your color as _____.
  - ➢ I feel your texture as _____.

Feeling Fullness

- ❖ Hello Jealousy! You are my Jealousy feeling anemone.
    - ➢ I sense your color as _____.
    - ➢ I feel your texture as _____.
- ❖ Hello Guilt! You are my Guilt feeling anemone.
    - ➢ I sense your color as _____.
    - ➢ I feel your texture as _____.
- ❖ Hello Loneliness! You are my Loneliness feeling anemone.
    - ➢ I sense your color as _____.
    - ➢ I feel your texture as _____.
- ❖ Hello _____! You are my _____ feeling anemone.
    - ➢ I sense your color as _____.
    - ➢ I feel your texture as _____.
- ❖ Hello _____! You are my _____ feeling anemone.
    - ➢ I sense your color as _____.
    - ➢ I feel your texture as _____.
- ❖ Hello _____! You are my _____ feeling anemone.
    - ➢ I feel your color as _____.
    - ➢ I sense your texture as _____.
- ❖ I thank all the feeling anemones that honored me with their presence.
- ❖ I notice any changes in my body, in my sense of well being, in my breathing.

~~~~~~

- ❖ I once more focus my breath into my belly area. I feel my belly area rise with the inbreath, slowly counting to five, and fall with the outbreath, again slowly counting to five.
- ❖ I continue watching the rise and fall of my upper lungs for about four to six long slow breaths.
- ❖ Anytime now I can access my Anemones of Feeling and experience their effect on my life in the hours, days, and months to come.

Completion

- When I am complete, I bring my awareness back to the world outside of me.
- I wiggle my toes and fingers.
- I stretch my body like a cat with a few lazy, long, full body stretches.
- I am back in my waking reality.

Suggestions

This particular Breathing Exercise can be intense. Give yourself lots of space and rest to integrate afterwards. Spend time in nature. Drink lots of clear fluids like water or clear fruit juices for the next couple days.

If you want to make sure that you experience more Feeling Fullness in your life, try the Mandala exercise described in Breathing Exercise:
Color of Loving Fullness under Mandala Breathing.

Pleasure Exercises

Solo: Add Sexual Pleasure into Your Feelings

When we connect our feelings with physical pleasure, it definitely intensifies them. It also helps move us through the feelings quicker. For example, I am aware that there is some conflict brewing at work. I have noticed that a certain situation is keeping me feeling on edge, but I don't quite know what it is. Something is bubbling beneath the surface, and won't leave me alone. This is a perfect situation to add a little bit of sexual dynamite into the stuck situation to help me clear it up.

I believe that if we are feeling bothered, that is, we are feeling an emotional charge about a person or a situation in our life, there is always something we can do to move that charge. Most of the time we cannot change the person or the situation, but we can change our response to the person or situation. Getting to the bottom of unclear emotions, or intensifying them in order to clear the emotional charge out of our system is something we can always do.

Feeling Fullness

Preparation

- Make sure you have some time and space to yourself, preferably not just before you go to sleep.
- Have an emotionally unclear or charged situation handy in your awareness.

Exercise

- Start pleasuring yourself, and build up some sexual charge, the higher the better.
- **But** stop when you get to close to your point of no return, because the idea here is to mix the sexual and the emotional charge together.
- Start thinking about the emotional charge that you are experiencing or the person that you are feeling strongly about.
- Start touching yourself sexually again and see whether you can intensify the emotional charge.
- Don't be surprised if all of a sudden you feel deep emotions, that is, tears start flowing, or you feel angry and want to hit something. Go with the feelings. Hit that pillow in anger! Let the tears flow! Just totally get into the feelings.
- If you feel you are loosing the connection with your feelings, add more sexual energy again.
- At some point you will feel complete, spent, emotionally drained.
- Now you have two options:
  - You can either just rest in the sense of feeling clear, exhausted, spent.
  - Or you can pick up your self-pleasuring again and give yourself an orgasm.
  - Or just touch yourself sensually.
- Notice what feels different. You will most likely experience more pleasure. Any time we clear emotional charges there is more room for pleasure!

Suggestions

That is why I love mixing sexual pleasure and emotional releases! Nowhere else is there such instant feedback as when releasing feelings creates some form of change! There is **always** more pleasure, even if in small increments, after emotional clearings.

Offering our bodies sexual and/or sensual pleasure after emotional clearings is also a way to create balance after all the pain, the anger, the difficulty. It soothes the body and lets it know that all is well again.

Partnered: Gibberish Releases

Here is a sure different kind of foreplay!

Being in a healthy relationship in this complex world is quite a feat. Keeping the relationship free of built up emotional charge and sexually and sensually juicy is an even greater feat. If we do not discharge or clear pent up feelings, it creates emotional distance, called a "withhold": something is being withheld. And interestingly enough withholds, that is, unreleased feelings, have a direct effect on our pleasure life: withholds diminish our desire to be intimate sexually. In other words, if we do not feel intimate emotionally towards our partner, it is much harder to feel intimate sexually.

In order to discharge pent up feelings we typically try to process them verbally, that is find a safe way to express our feelings while making sure that we are getting heard. Here is an easy and fun way to discharge these built up feelings without words. The idea here is to get to the emotions directly via "gibberish", that is the expression of feelings through sounds or nonsense words. Instead of either expressing our feelings directly and thus running the risk of hurting our partner, or toning our feelings down via safe communication techniques (which definitely have their place), gibberish allows us to go directly to the feelings but in a nonverbal way.

Preparation

- ❖ Agree to have a Gibberish Release before making love.
- ❖ Agree not to use any real words of any language that either one or both of you know.
- ❖ Sit facing each other either on your bed or on the floor.
- ❖ Wear loose and comfortable clothing or no clothes.

Exercise

- ❖ Both start breathing deeply into your belly.

Feeling Fullness

- Inhale through your nose.
- Exhale through your mouth pursing your lips, pushing your breath out.
- Inhale and exhale like this for about ten to fifteen breaths.
- Start making sounds as if you are having a conversation but without words, that is, go back and forth babbling.
- As you have no verbal content, all that keeps you going is emotional charge.
- Keep responding to each other's emotional offers. Play with them.
- For example:
  - Toss anger back and forth like a tennis ball.
  - Softly juggle sadness between you.
  - Hurl rage back and forth like a big heavy rock.
  - Dance around yuckiness. Or frustration. Or hurt.
- Converse in gibberish until you feel done. You now when that happens. You feel clean and clear and complete.
- Now make love and watch your passion!

Suggestions

This process takes discipline, because we are so used to jumping into words when our feelings come up. But if you stay away from words and really just use gibberish, watch how quickly you can clear up emotional storms, even hurricanes. It is worth the initial effort. And worth the intensified pleasure, let me tell you.

Mind

Part of the Grand Experiment of our Western culture has been a tendency to suppress the free expression of feelings except when sanctioned by the use of recreational drugs like alcohol, marihuana etc. Certain feelings have always been acceptable in ritualized contexts like tears at weddings and funerals, joy at birthdays and parties etc, though often again with the help of recreational drugs. This means as a society we are not very used to experiencing the wide range of feelings available to us. We also do not have learned to safely express feelings when they do come up, nor do we teach safe expression of emotions to our children, neither at home nor in our educational institutions.

Remembering how to experience our feelings and to safely express them is important because our feelings are another gateway to fullness. The process of making friends with a wide range of emotional expressions brings with it both a richness of experience and a fluidity that qualitatively changes our lives: it makes them simply sumptuous without the need of expensive entertainment toys and extravagant thrills. Say goodbye to boredom and tediousness and say hello to rich intensity and presence of living, once feelings flow freely through us.

Especially human interactions become so much more satisfying when feelings are allowed to be part of it. In my opinion, both soap operas (predominantly indulged in by women) or sports programs (predominantly indulged in by men) on TV are such a hit, exactly because they present us with a wide range of emotions, except that they are only second hand fare through the use of cameras and TVs.

Wouldn't life be so much richer if we could personally experience the range of feelings produced and seen daily on TV and videos? For me a life lived from fullness definitively includes a wide range of emotions that can come and go as easily as they do in little children, except that I have learned to express them much more safely than little children are known to do.

In my own life I have been on quite a journey towards the richness of a life full of various feelings. Until in my thirties I was only able to express feelings via either tears (and I cried easily and a lot) or laughter (but not the full belly laughter—more a nervous avoidance laughter). When my journey into pleasure began, it was paralleled by my journey into feelings. I found out that every feeling, no matter how undesirable its expression seemed at first, has a gift to offer when it is allowed to freely flow through me. One of the key elements to that free flow is acceptance.

~~~ A deep belly breath in ~~~

The Five Attitudes of God

When we are feeling confronted with difficult feelings or overwhelmed with too much emotion, the most important thing to remember is that accepting them wholeheartedly for just that very moment is the very first step to coping with them. All we need to do is to accept whatever we are feeling for that moment. And for the moment does not mean for the rest of our lives.

Feeling Fullness

Here is a practical formula that has worked really well for me. I found it in Neale Donald Walsh's book "Conversations with God: Part 3". He calls it "The Five Attitudes of God" and it looks like this:

"I totally Joyfully, Accept, Love, Bless and Thank…"

My suggestion is to remember this formula and practice saying it by heart. Another way is to hand write or print it up and tape it to your mirror, your steering wheel in your car, your refrigerator, etc. Use it every time you are feeling confronted with difficult feelings. If for example you are in the grips of envy, just say to yourself three times:

"I totally Joyfully, Accept, Love, Bless, and Thank myself for feeling envious."

Once that is said and done, most likely something has changed. Notice the changes:

- ❖ The intensity of the emotion might go away.
- ❖ Your breathing might slow down.
- ❖ The sharp pain in your insides might lessen.
- ❖ Your feel like you are yourself again instead of a monster.
- ❖ There is some space inside your self.

The more often we can allow ourselves to be with our emotions, letting them flow through us, the easier it becomes and the richer our lives are just for this range of feelings flowing through us.

~~~ *A deep sigh out* ~~~

A Guide to Feelings

With the help of this formula it is possible to learn to be with our feelings. And sometimes just being with them is more than we can handle. It takes finding a way to safely express them, to encourage the flow, to practice becoming friends with the various feelings. Here is my (partial) list of emotions, some suggestions on how to safely let them out of the cage, and the gift they bring, once they have been allowed out.

JOY

What can I say? When we are feeling joyful, the best thing is to revel in it, knowing full well that is can and most likely will change any minute. If we welcome that change, the other, darker feelings (see below) that sometimes use joy as a gateway, can more easily reveal their gifts to us. Then we can get to the point where it really does not matter anymore **what** we are feeling as long **as** we are feeling. As Dr. Peebles taught me: "You don't have to like your experiences (or feelings), but you have to like the fact that you are having these experiences (or feelings)."

Joy's Gift: Lightens up a Moment, an Hour, a Day

GRIEF

There is a richness in those periods of grief, when all we want to do is sit down in a safe place and cry, or if tears don't flow easily, be with that bottomless sadness. That sense of deep heartbreak, often after the loss of a relationship or the death of loved one, can come on so strongly that we don't know whether it will ever end again. But it always does, especially when we allow grief to do its work of helping us adjust to the new situation, to a life without someone or something special. Here are a couple ways how to invite Grief into your life:

Find "Sad" Music and Let the Flood Gates Open

Find some music that brings up tears for you. For some of us it is the corniest Country and Western songs. For some it is a love song that reminds us of days gone by. Just find one and go for it. Just let your self cry, or just feel sadness from the bottom of your heart.

Find "Sad" Videos and Let the Story Bring You to Tears

Go to your video store (or library if they rent out videos) and rent a bunch of romantic, or no-happy-end or idealistic movies that you know will have chance to move you to tears. Turn off your phone, get the box of tissues ready, and go for it.

Grief's Gift: Integration and Adjustment after a Loss

ANGER

That fiery, explosive force called anger or rage can come upon us all of a sudden, wanting to blast its way out, just for the sake of blasting. Or it can sit and smolder for quite while until it finds it s way out. It is an art form to learn to experience its cleansing capacity without the use of numbing alcohol. Here are a few ways I found that allowed me to safely move that blasting force without doing harm to myself, others, or furniture.

Cleaning House

I LOVE to clean my house when I am feeling angry. I usually have so much energy when I am feeling anger move through me, that I love to use it to do something constructive. And boy, do I get my house looking spick and span when I am in that angry mood!

Breaking off Dead Branches from Trees

Here is a very effective way to express anger safely: I like to go for a hike in the woods, as far away from people as I can. I find a sturdy dead and use it to break other dead branches from trees. I really hit the dead branches hard with all my anger! It feels so satisfying to hear those dead, old, useless branches snap off and crash to the ground. Yeah!

Anger's Gift: Deeply Cleansing like Spring Cleaning a House

FEAR

FEAR is an acronym for "False Evidence Appearing Real", that is if we buy into fear, we can scare ourselves mightily. If we dare to look behind the curtain, we see an old man (or woman) rattling and whistling pretending to be "The Wizard of Oz". Any time we get scared, that is, when we feel that tightness in our stomach, it offers the opportunity to look behind the curtain, asking the question: what is really going on?

Seeing Fear as Excitement

Fear in its evolutionary origin had the function of warning us. It provided additional adrenaline to sharpen our senses and our wits in situations that were outside our normal habitual experiences. Excitement has the same effect. The only difference is that we associate fear with negative, detrimental experiences, and excitement with positive, invigorating adventures. One way to deal with fear is to just rename its symptoms as excitement, because the real issue is not fear in itself, but the fear of fear.

Fear's Gift: False Evidence Appearing Real

ENVY

Being green with envy—what a rush! What a yucky rush. But it is in there, part of the whole spectrum of human feelings. Not one of the pretty ones for sure. But when I let that particular one out, accepting it as much as I can brings me the gift of loving myself more. The only way not to let envy run my life is to treat myself well. It is not necessary to buy a Jaguar Convertible if I find the Joneses next door have gotten one that spikes my envy. But it helps to give some attention to myself.

Giving Myself a Treat

When envy hits me, I really get into it. I wallow in its sharp edges, it painful stabs, just ride it. When I come out on the other side, (which is what usually happens when we really get into a particular feeling) I give myself a delicious treat. Either something really good to eat or a massage, or a trip to the second hand store, or whatever makes me feel really good.

Envy's Gift: Self-Love

JEALOUSY

Jealousy has been the hardest feeling to deal with for me. I feel so ugly, unworthy and awful when this ugly beast has me in its claws, that I needed a lot of exposure to it to become friends with it (and let me tell you, open relationships do wonders for the continuous appearance of that beast). But I learned to be with its gift, which for me was humility, and gleaned a few pointers from those experiences:

Step one: Admit to Myself that I am Feeling Jealous

As this beast is so ugly and ferocious in its appearance, the last thing anyone wants to do, is own it. But it is the first step to taming it. Admit to yourself: "I am feeling jealous." Not "You are making me feeling jealous." Just I am feeling jealous. Period. And that alone is no a small feat.

Step two: Admit my Jealousy to my Partner

The next step that is both humbling me and taming the beast further, is to go to my significant other (who most likely has been instrumental in waking up the beast) and very gently and softly say: "I am feeling jealous." No expectations that s/he change her/his behavior. No conditions such as: "If I admit to being jealous, you need to do this and that for me." Just the pure sharing of a very vulnerable state of this ugly feeling will stop feeding the beast, and it will actually shrink to a much smaller size, if not vanish all together.

Step Three: Make some Connection with your "Rival"

This is the hardest one, but it definitely tames the beast for good. Jealousy works best on an empty canvas. The less we know the person who has shown up as a rival, the more we can project **everything** that we believe we are not, onto that empty canvas. Our rival becomes the most beautiful, handsome, sexy, juicy, intelligent, you-name-it person compared to me. The minute we know more about that person, and connect through a face-to-face talk, a phone call, or a walk, the less empty the canvas becomes. The more details can be painted on that canvas, the less my supposed inadequacies stick to it or have room on it.

Jealousy's Gift: Humility

GUILT

If guilt shows up to knock on our door, it points to something not completed in our lives. One way of dealing with guilt is to say to yourself three times (if possible, out load): "If I could have done anything different, I would have." That particular attitude helps put the lid on the past in a useful way. It is over. It is done.

Guilt's Gift: A Reminder that the Past is DEFINITELY Over

LONELINESS

You know these beautiful love songs on the radio, the ones that talk about love ever lasting till the end of time for ever and ever true and sweet and deep? The ones I so fervently want to believe in, but that my years of experience have shown me not to be true? The ones I often only dare to listen to alone and in private? I found if I listen to these love songs when I feel lonely, and treat them as if they are addressed to Spirit, God, The One, Yahweh, or whatever name I give to that larger entity, instead of a human lover, they work!

My sense is, in a world where very little true connection to the mystery has been left, all that longing for the perfect union has been focused on a human partner, where it hardly ever lasts forever and is a continuously changing experience full of valleys and peaks. **But** the connection to the **One** has all these qualities of perfection, eternity etc…This listening to love songs as devotional songs to the One while feeling lonely can be very satisfying and fulfilling.

Loneliness' Gift: Longing for Union with God, Spirit, Yahweh, The One

~~~ *A deep belly breath in* ~~~

Through the Body into Feelings

For some of us it is not a question of: "How do I deal with being overwhelmed by my feelings?", but more, "How do I know what I am feeling?" From the Hendricks I learned a beautiful and simple approach into our world of feelings. They called it "Body Centered Transformation". Here is how it works: quite often we have a sense of sitting on some emotional charge, but we cannot quite feel our way into it. There is just an unease, a tightness, a Grrrrrrr! One of the easiest way to connect to that Grrrrrrr! is to do the following:

- ❖ First, I acknowledge a Grrrrrrr! or whatever is present.
- ❖ I close my eyes and check my body.
- ❖ Where in my body is that Grrrrrrr! located?
- ❖ I notice my posture, the location of my arms and hands, the location of my legs and feet.

- I notice maybe a tightness, butterflies, a knot, stress, anything unusual happening in my body that stands out.
- I sense into that unusual happening in my body.
- I extend my breath directly into that space.
- I send my awareness directly into it and just accept it.
- I let a story, a memory, a word come up, something that is associated with that unusual happening in my body.
- That story, or memory, or word will lead me to the feeling that I have not been able to quite access.

This is just a taste of how to use your body as the entry point into your world of feelings. If you want to know more about that approach, please check out the More Section at the end of this chapter.

~~~ *A deep sigh out* ~~~

The Tunnel of Not Knowing

Once we invite a life lived from fullness and open ourselves up to a wider landscape of feelings, we find out, among other aspects, that we are not anymore the ones running the show. Yes, life gets richer, more intense with increasing glimpses of clarity. But there is also a shadow side, a darker side, and it is an equally important part of the journey. Ever so often we can enter into a phase in life that I call "The Tunnel of Not Knowing" (sometimes I also refer to these phases as Madness). These have been and still are phases in my life where I feel totally disconnected from myself, the world around me, and any reason for being here.

A psychologist might diagnose these phases as "depression", and prescribe anti-depressants. My suggestion here is not to fall back on "Mother's Little Helpers" as the Rolling Stones put it so wonderfully in one of their early songs. If you can, ride that phase out, hang in there through all its terror, anxiety, craziness, or whatever it will bring up for you. Remember, it is just a tunnel. It might feel like a dark hole with no way out, but it is just a tunnel, which granted, might have been dug quite deep. But it will lead back to the surface, in most cases.

Anti-depressants take away that razor's edge that hones our experience to its fullest. In my opinion, by taking anti-depressants we miss the chance off blossoming into our next level of fullness. A blossom (at least in continental climates with distinct summers and winters) has to go through the dark of winter before it can open up into its new glory in spring. By taking off the edge of pain, terror, and anxiety, it takes away the chance to literally work our way through all those difficult parts of us. If we don't wrestle our way through, we can get stuck in the mediocrity of not feeling deeply and of a false safety. We have not really worked our way through all those dark places within us.

Here is an interesting story: Someone was watching several cocoons ready for butterflies to emerge. They were already partially broken open, and you could see the butterflies in the process of breaking free of the cocoon's shell. The person watching these butterflies struggling wanted to help and decided to take a stick and break open one of the cocoon's shell. He succeeded in making it easier for this particular butterfly to emerge from the cocoon and it came out sooner than the others around it. Interestingly it had a lot less strength and vitality than all the others did that had struggled to break out of their shells on their own.

Why do these tunnels show up in the first place? I do not understand all of it, and I grudgingly learned to be OK with not knowing. One thing I do know: when we invite fullness into our lives, we are inviting more love (and joy and light) into our lives. Love brings out anything unlike itself. If you bring more light into a room, the shadows become deeper.

Luckily, on the other side of that tunnel lies another level of fullness, bringing so much more to us than we ever could imagine, that it is worth every moment of having spent in that dark, long tunnel.

~~~ A deep belly breath in ~~~

Symptoms

Here are some of the symptoms we might experience while in the tunnel experience:

- ❖ My monkey mind is going on a scathing criticizing rampage day in, day out.
- ❖ Nothing makes any sense anymore.
- ❖ Sadness and grief are coming up like someone opened the flood gates, and I have nowhere to go with all those overwhelming feelings.
- ❖ I am going crazy on the inside while still functioning on the outside, that is on the outside I am going to work, I take care of my kids, house, cat,

dog etc. wile on the inside I feel ready for the straight jacket and the loony bin any minute.
- ❖ Life feels totally empty, meaningless, devoid of joy, laughter, and happiness, and none of it will ever come back.
- ❖ If I just make it through the day somehow without falling apart, and then can fall asleep, I will be OK.
- ❖ It feels like I have gone mad and will never find my way out again of this madness.
- ❖ I do not know how to talk about what is going on as I have no words for it.
- ❖ I do not understand what is going on and that is driving me crazy.
- ❖ I have no energy, no motivation to do anything at all.
- ❖ Life will never be OK again, I will be stuck in this mudhole forever.
- ❖ There is no one to help me, to understand me, to tell me or show me that I am OK, even my partner/husband/family feels miles away.
- ❖ And more…

The bad news is that we never know what will push us into the tunnel (btw, some of us dig ourselves nicely into our own tunnel, thank you very much—we don't need anyone's help) and how long we will stay in the tunnel.

The good news is that having come through that tunnel I found it worth every moment of pain, terror, fear, and craziness. Having come through a number of tunnels, and they were frigging deep, long and dark, I know. This book is the direct result of the worst tunnel I crawled through for about six months (ask my friends…the ones I have left). But, since I came through the tunnel, I have been blessed with clarity, insight, and a flood of creativity that is literally mind blowing.

~~~ *A deep sigh out* ~~~

What to Do

Here are some suggestions on what to do when in the midst of a dark tunnel experience:

- ❖ First and foremost and most important (and also helpful) is to accept that we are in a tunnel phase, (whether we are digging ourselves into it or have fallen into it). Acceptance eases the stress. If we resist it or even fight it, it only gets worse. Let me tell you from experience…

- It also helps to name it, as in "I am in a tunnel phase"—the monkey mind does better with a descriptive name like that.
- Read the Soul Sections in all chapters. These sayings helped me through some of my darkest moments. Try reading them first thing in the morning and last thing before you go to sleep at night.
- Find books or websites that refer to "the dark night of the soul". I found some help there.
- Get professional help if it gets too bad and you think you are becoming suicidal, but my suggestion is to try staying away from anti-depressants.
- Distraction works very well for me. I have survived tunnel phases by either watching lots of videos, or by listening to books on tape (both Ellis Peters and Terry Pratchett helped me through two of my tunnel phases—see reviews of their books). I found it helpful to pick videos or books that depict overall positive situations. Happy endings work well for me.
- Reach out to others. The tendency here is to hole up and disconnect, but connecting with other tunnel crawlers definitely helps.
- Connect with other tunnel crawlers through the chat room on my website (check www.FullnessNoMatterWhat.com) for its implementation.
- Remember—it is just a tunnel and there is an end to it—always.

~~~~~~~~~~~

Sometimes The Light Stops Shining

Sometimes the light stops shining
And everything feels dark and empty
Like nothing matters or makes sense

I do all that needs doing
I feed all that needs feeding
I sit and sit and sit alone

I get no calls nor invitations
No lovers beckoning to play
Just emptiness and loss and tears

Feeling Fullness

Now all that's left is hiding in the dark
And dream of days of light and joy
And wait and trust and know
That love is back
That joy is here
That light is all

~~ Ulla! ~~

~~~~~~~~~~

Soul

There is a brokenness
out of which comes the unbroken.
There is a shatteredness
out of which comes the unshatterable.
There is a sorrow beyond all grief
which leads to joy.
And a fragility
out of whose depth emerges strength.
There is a hollow space too vast for words
through which we pass with loss.
Out of whose darkness
we are sanctioned into being.

~~ Unknown Source ~~

~~~~~~~~~~

Anfangs wollt' ich fast verzagen,
Und ich glaubt', ich trueg es nie;
Und ich hab es doch ertragen—
Aber fragt mich nur nicht wie.

At first I was ready to give up
And I believed I could not do this
And I ended up getting through it
Just don't ask me how.

Fullness No Matter What

~~ Heinrich Heine (Ulla's Translation) ~~

~~~~~~~~~~

If you look into the dark,
the paranoid theater of the mind
will perform for you.
But if you look into the light,
who knows what wonders you might see.

~~ Professor Teru in RUBY 4 ~~

~~~~~~~~~~

THE GUEST HOUSE

This being human is a guest house.
Every morning a new arrival.

A joy, a depression, a meanness,
some momentary awareness comes
as an unexpected visitor.

Welcome and entertain them all!
Even if they are a crowd of sorrows,
who violently sweep your house
empty of its furniture,
still, treat each guest honorably.
He may be clearing you out
for some new delight.

The dark thought, the shame, the malice,
meet them at the door laughing,
and invite them in.

Be grateful for whoever comes,
because each has been sent
as a guide from beyond.

~~ Rumi (Coleman Barks Translation) ~~

~~~~~~~~~~

The most beautiful thing we can experience is the mysterious. It is the source of all true art and all science. You, to whom this emotion is a stranger, who can no longer pause to wonder and stand rapt in awe, are as good as dead: Your eyes are closed.

~~ Albert Einstein ~~

~~~~~~~~~~

The duke had a mind that ticked like a clock
and, like a clock, it regularly went cuckoo.

~~ Terry Pratchett, Wyrd Sisters ~~

More

Frederic F. Flach, M.D. *The Secret Strength of Depression*. The author makes a good case for looking at the positive aspects of depression.

Marshall B. Rosenberg. *Nonviolent Communication: A Language of Life*. A very practical, step by step approach to changing our ways to communicate. I use it a lot, when I remember.
http://www.cnvc.org

Active Listening: http://www.studygs.net/listening.htm I learned this technique when my children were small and I needed a different way to hear what it was they were actually telling me.

Sharon Ellison. *Taking the War out of Words: Powerful Non-defensive Communication*. Sharon has developed a very gentle but most effective way to deal with verbal or physical aggression directed towards you. www.pndc.com

Ruby 1 to 6. ZBS Productions in New York, NY. Contemporary audio drama with the swish of satin and the bite of a piranha! www.zbs.org

12
Knowing Fullness

Is it possible?

Is it possible
That I am running
Have been running for years
From the feeling of sheer ecstasy
From feeling a bliss so unspeakable
That the little one went into hiding
As not to be swept away or torn apart
By the immense joy welling up in her
Over and over again

Is it possible
That I am not running
Have not been running for years
From the feeling of pain
My old familiar safe companion
One acceptable to everyone around me
And one so easily copied by a little one
Who wanted to be one of Them
So much and oh so urgently

Yes it is possible
That feeling pain has not been my task
That going deep into the darkness of my hell
Has been the easy part of my long journey
And it is time now to explore the joy
To let it well up large in me
Always and all ways
In all its glory and pure beingness
That had been promised
A long time ago

~~ Ulla! ~~

Body

What do I know? What do I not know? Who do I know myself to be? How do I know what I know? Knowing has been and still is a rich gold mine that keeps us digging ever deeper to find answers to some of the important questions we humans keep asking.

Breathing Exercise: Caves of Knowing Fullness

This breathing exercise is an invitation to explore our own fullness from the solar plexus, a place where we can find answers to all our questions. I call it the Caves of Knowing. Our universe is built on answers and solutions, not questions and problems. Whenever we have a question, by definition, it means that there is an already existing answer. The fact that a question comes into our awareness means that there is already an answer. The answer comes first.

Preparations

This Breathing Exercise is designed to be experienced while you are reading it, preferably out loud to yourself, if you are in a position to do so. If not, at least mouth the words; it will help you slow down and stay focused. If you are with a partner who is open to sharing this exercise, take turns reading it out loud to each other. Make sure you are in a position to relax while you are reading, without falling asleep too quickly.

If you want to intensify this exercise, invite your spirit guides and angels, known or unknown, seen or unseen, to join you in this experience.

Exercise

- ❖ I bring my awareness to my solar plexus area and place my hands on my physical stomach in a comfortable position.
- ❖ I appreciate my physical stomach for doing such a wonderful job of receiving food and adding acid to break it down into all its various components.

~~~~~~

Fullness No Matter What

- If I feel any discomfort or tightness in my stomach area, I notice it.
- I totally accept any discomfort by directing my very own Loving Color into the tender or tight area.
- I bring that Loving Color of acceptance into every area of discomfort, one after another, until my stomach area is glowing with acceptance.

~~~~~~

- I focus my breath into my stomach area. I feel my stomach area rise with the inbreath, slowly counting to five, and fall with the outbreath, again slowly counting to five.
- I continue watching the rise and fall of my stomach for about four to six long slow breaths.

~~~~~~

- I imagine a cave in and around my physical stomach.
- This cave has outer dimensions of my stomach. Its inner dimensions are like a great hall. It is called the Cave of Understanding.
- I imagine myself entering that cave by projecting my awareness into this imagined cave. I see myself, feel myself, sense myself inside this cave. I let it surround me on all sides. I know that I am inside of it.
- I now imagine myself moving, walking, gliding, flying, through it to the opening at the other end of this cave.
- I imagine myself moving through that opening and find myself in a larger cave. It completely surrounds the Cave of Understanding.

~~~~~~

- This second cave is called the Cave of Intuition.
- I imagine myself entering that cave by projecting my awareness into this second imagined cave. I see myself, feel myself, sense myself inside this cave. I let it surround me on all sides. I know that I am inside of it.
- I now imagine myself walking, moving, gliding, flying, through it to the opening at the other end of the cave.
- I imagine myself moving through that opening and find myself in an even larger cave. It completely contains both the Cave of Understanding and the Cave of Intuition.

Knowing Fullness

~~~~~~

- This third cave is called the Cave of Communion.
- I imagine myself entering that cave by projecting my awareness into this third imagined cave. I see myself, feel myself, sense myself inside this cave. I let it surround me on all sides. I know that I am inside of it.
- In those three caves, which are both inside my body and in other dimensions, anything anybody has ever experienced, thought, done, and imagined, has been stored and is accessible just for the asking. It is called Universal Knowing.
- These three caves are three different entry points into Universal Knowing.

~~~~~~

- I imagine sending a question into the vastness of all three caves.
- And wait.
- There is always an answer.
- I either receive my answer directly, or I know it will come to me in its own time.
- I just revel in the vastness of the knowing that is available to me any time, just for the asking.
- I notice any changes in my body, in my sense of well being, in my breathing.

~~~~~~

- I once more focus my awareness into my solar plexus area.
- I breathe into my solar plexus area, slowly counting to five on the inbreath, and again slowly counting to five on the outbreath.
- I sense the inbreath slowly raising up my stomach.
- I sense the outbreath slowly letting my stomach come down.
- I continue watching the raising of my stomach on the inbreath, and the falling of my stomach on the outbreath for about four to six long slow breaths.
- Anytime now I can access my Caves of Knowing and experience their effect on my life in the hours, days, and months to come.

Completion

- When I am complete, I bring my awareness back to the world outside of me.
- I wiggle my toes and fingers.
- I stretch my body like a cat with a few lazy, long, full body stretches.
- I am back in my waking reality.

Suggestions

These three caves inside the physical stomach are available for exploration any time. This kind of suggestive way of working with the imagination receives its actual power from repetition. The more often we use it, remember to apply it, the more powerful its capacity becomes to provide us with all the answers we will ever need. Play with it; use it to look for answers to all the questions you have. By the way, the answer can come in many shapes and forms:

- Some of us will hear an answer as if a voice is talking inside our head, but it is not quite the critical, monkey talk, chatterbox voice that we usually hear.
- Some will sense an answer as if we know it without words like: "Yep, that's it."
- Sometimes during the rest of the day or the next day the answer will find its way to us in the shape of a sentence in a book, something someone mentions to us in a conversation, a picture we see, or anything that catches our attention.
- The answer usually comes with its own sense of clarity. Bang. Here it is. That is at least how I recognize it.

If you want to make sure that you experience more Knowing Fullness in your life, try the Mandala exercise described in Breathing Exercise:
Color of Loving Fullness under Mandala Breathing.

Pleasure Exercises

High energy states that accompany physical excitement, intense and prolonged sports activities, feeling joyful, being out in nature, dancing, taking psychoactive substances, and of course, any form of lovemaking offer the gift of clarity.

In other words, when we find ourselves in high states of energy, either alone or with a partner, we usually have an easier access to "the bigger picture" of our lives and to more clarity. How come high states of energy and clarity go together? Here is an analogy: slow moving water usually is full of mud. You cannot see through it. Fast moving water on the other hand stays clear and you can see the bottom more easily.

In this context it is important to remember that we live in a universe built on answers, not on problems. This means that the answers exist before the questions arise. In other words, just because we have a question, it signifies that the answer is already present. There could be no question, if there was not an already existing answer available.

My suggestion here is get high on lovemaking and ask your questions knowing that the answer is already waiting for you…

Solo: High Energy Oracle for One

Preparations

- Take some time to write down a few questions that you would like answers to.
- **Not so good questions** to ask in this context (too hard to get clear answers): dates and times, specific details, an outcome that you are very attached to.
- **Good questions** to ask: What is the bigger picture of this situation? Yes or no questions. New insights, overlooked aspects, a deeper meaning. What do I know to be true?

Exercise

- Get yourself nicely turned on through fantasies, videos, sexy stories, sex toys, or whatever gets you sexually aroused.
- Build as much sexual energy as you can stand and get very close to "your point of no return".
- Stop.
- Just keep contracting your PC muscles gently, to hold the energy, but don't go over the edge.
- Read out loud the first question you have.

- ❖ Close your eyes and build some more sexual energy again, get turned on again, and listen inside.
- ❖ The answer can show up in many forms. See Suggestions in the Breathing Exercise a couple pages back.
- ❖ Keep asking your questions and keep getting turned on until you have no more questions to ask!

Suggestions

If you feel like experimenting, try asking your question/s right after you have had an orgasm (if you can remember to think! Duh!). The time right after an orgasm is another high energy state conducive to clarity.

Try it out. What do you have to loose? The worst that can happen is that you will just have had some good sexual pleasure, but no answers. But you could also end up with clear answers to some of your questions.

You can also try this High Energy Oracle with your partner. It works best when taking turns stimulating each other manually or orally, that is one of you receives and finds the answers, the other pleasures and asks the questions. You can also explore answering each others' questions as there is less attachment to other people's answers. Just explore and remember to have fun with it.

Partnered: Washing Your Partner's Jewels

Preparations

- ❖ A good size bowl filled with warm water that is more on the hot than the cool side
- ❖ A clean terry wash cloth
- ❖ A soft towel

You can either just spontaneously decide to wash your partner, especially after lovemaking as an added treat. Or you can turn it into a special ritual and decide up front who will be the receiver and who the giver.

As the **receiver** make yourself comfortable on your back, relax, close your eyes, and find out how much pleasure are you willing to receive, to let in.

As the **giver** you get to be in charge here. Make sure you feel connected to yourself and your love for your partner.

Either way, enjoy the experience.

Exercise

It's easy. Dip the wash cloth in the hot water, wring it out and start washing your partner's body. Whenever the wash cloth starts feeling cool, dip it back into the hot water and wring it out again.

My suggestion is to start with the belly. Use very slow deliberate movements. Spread her/his legs, wash the inside of his/her legs, and slowly move to the Jewels. Make sure the wash cloth is nicely hot when you wash the Jewels. It feels so delicious, that hot loving, intimate touch between your legs. Yumm!

Dip the wash cloth one more time into the hot water and wring it out.

Women as Givers: wrap the hot washcloth all around his Lingam and Twin Globes. Use both of your hands to hold the wash cloth in place. Just hold "the whole package" for a few minutes while applying gentle pressure.

Men as Givers: fold the washcloth once and place it on her Jewels. Start at the top of her pubic bone, across her Pearl, and down to her Yoni. Then place the heel of one hand on her Pearl and the other hand on her Yoni and press hard. She'll let you know when it is too hard. Just hold that pressure for a few minutes and watch her relax deeply.

When you feel complete, take the towel and, again, slowly and deliberately dry off the areas that you washed with a dry towel.

If you want to, then cuddle up with your partner and hold him or her. You might see tears or feel intense emotions well up in your partner as most likely the last time anyone was washed with a warm wash cloth was as a small child.

You can also use this exercise as a form of foreplay, to relax your partner, make him or her feel loved, appreciated, and comforted. It might take your lovemaking to a whole new level of intimacy and closeness. You might feel more open and vulnerable while making love, which often intensifies the experience as we feel more connected to our partner.

Mind

Knowing—An Inquiry

We live in a culture that places a lot of value on understanding, the five senses, and learning from outside sources. We go to school to study all kinds of information (useful or not) and interestingly are finding out that in these "fast times" this information is quickly outdated. I call our times "fast times" as the technological imprint on our society has been speeding up ever faster. New technological tools and gadgets are becoming obsolete through the introduction of the next generation within shorter and shorter time spans.

But there is more than just informational data available to us. To me there are three kinds of Knowing:

- Understanding
- Intuition
- Communion

Understanding is a form of Knowing accessed through the five human senses: sight, smell, sound, taste, and touch. It is processed in the form of thoughts and it follows the rules and laws of this material world, the 3rd dimension. Cause and effect and logic are part of its rules. It is the world of science like engineering, chemistry, or physics. It is the world of words and numbers and mathematical symbols. It serves us well in practical 3rd dimensional projects like building bridges, flying airplanes, and using computers. And it has its limitations in dealing with the worlds of feelings, art, and relating with each other.

Intuition is a form of Knowing accessed through feelings and processed through the inside of our bodies. Although it is often perceived inside our bodies, it reaches into the realms beyond the five senses into the 4th dimension like psychic knowing, a term used for all kinds of knowing like precognition, deja vue, remote viewing, psychokinesis, channeling, or inner sight etc. It also includes vague knowing like "having a hunch" or "following my intuition".

Communion is a form of Knowing that happens outside of words and thoughts. It is characteristic of the 5th dimension. When we know something from the place of communion, it is experienced from a place of Oneness. There is no separation. It is an instant connection without any sense of boundaries.

An example would be sitting in front of an old sequoia tree and being one with that tree. Communion can be experienced when taking psychoactive or hallucinogenic substances like LSD, Peyote, or Psilocybin.

All I am doing here is offering more options in the way we "know" things. For example I "know" without a doubt that God exists. To me it is not a man with a beard who sits in heaven and keeps score of my good and my bad deeds. It is something I cannot describe, or easily put into words, but I have no doubts about its existence. I also know that I am part of it, and that it is the basis of my daily life and most of my actions.

This is an invitation to open up to some of these other options, even just for the sake of curiosity. I leave you with the following question: What do I know without knowing exactly how I know?

~~~ *A deep belly breath in* ~~~

Soul

In the creation of individual reality, thought control,
or what some might call prayer—is everything.
Thought control is the highest form of prayer.
Therefore, think only on good things, and righteous.
Dwell not in negativity and darkness.
And even in moments when things look bleak
—especially in those moments—
see only perfection,
express only gratefulness, and then
imagine only what manifestation of perfection you choose next.
In this formula there is found tranquility.
In this perception there is found peace.
In this awareness there is found joy.

~~ Neale Donald Walsh, Conversations With God ~~

~~~~~~~~~~

There are two kinds of intelligence: one acquired,
as a child in school memorizes facts and concepts
from books and from what the teacher says,

Fullness No Matter What

collecting information from the traditional sciences
as well as the new sciences.

With such intelligence you rise in the world.
You get ranked ahead or behind others
in regard to your competence in retaining
information. You stroll with this intelligence
in and out of fields of knowledge, getting always more
marks on your preserving tablets.

There is another kind of tablet, one
already completed and preserved inside you.
A spring overflowing its springbox. A freshness
in the center of the chest, this other intelligence
does not turn yellow or stagnate. It's fluid,
and it does not move from outside to inside
through the conduits of plumbing-learning.

This second knowing is a fountainhead
from within you, moving out.

~~ Rumi (Coleman Barks Translation) ~~

~~~~~~~~~~

Each problem has hidden in it
an opportunity so powerful
that it literally dwarfs the problem—
IF you just look for the hidden opportunities
instead of dwelling on the problem.

~~ Unknown Source ~~

~~~~~~~~~~

Alle Buecher dieser Welt
Bringen dir kein Glueck,
Doch sie weisen dich geheim
In dich selbst zurueck.
Dort its alles was du brauchst
Sonne, Stern und Mond,

Knowing Fullness

Denn das Licht, danach du fragst
In dir selber wohnt.
Weisheit, die du lang gesucht
In den Buechereien,
Leuchtet jetzt aus jedem Blatt
Denn nun ist sie dein.

All the books of this world
Cannot bring you joy
But they point in secret
Back into yourself.
All you ever need is found there
Sun and stars and moon above
As the light that you are wanting
Lives inside of you.
All the wisdom you have searched for
In the libraries around
Radiates from every leaf
For one reason—now it's yours.

~~ Herman Hesse (Ulla's Translation) ~~

More

Book Review: Terry Pratchett's Disc World Novels

Imagine a world that is shaped like a planet size disk. This disk rests on four huge elephants, which again rest on an even huger turtle. This contraption is called Diskworld and hurtles through space. It is a great playing field to let Terry Prachett's wildly creative imagination combined with a Renaissance man's breadth of knowledge loose to comment on anything and everything. He makes fun of about everything in witty oneliners, some of which I could not resist quoting in every Soul Section. He slaughters any holy cow possible and turns the carcass into creative and delicious entrees. And he quotes anything and everything from Shakespeare to Churchill to popular songs to James Bond—you name it—he quotes it (and you can read about every quote and its origin on a website created by dedicated fans—see L-Space references at the end).

Nothing is safe, nothing is sacred and everything is game in a sea of creativity, wit, and a deep understanding of the human psyche and way beyond. In his close to 30 novels the native British author just won't quit coming up with unique perspectives on our modern day society, even though his Diskworld technologically has only reached the use of horse drawn coaches. That does not hold Pratchett back from transposing modern day technologies into pre-electricity gadgets. The Hex (the one and only computer based on an ant farm kit), the klacks (a fax-like transmitting system using line of sight towers and paddles), and a movie camera (a box with 3 miniature demons in it painting pictures and turning the handle whips all three of them into continuous action) are just a few examples of his ingenuity.

On the Diskworld it's the Century of the Fruitbat and the complex multi-ethnic society in the city of Ankh-Morpork includes the following species: silica based trolls (whose brains work faster in colder climates), dwarves (who escaped from the gold mines in Uberwald), werewolves (as a uniquely gifted police officer), zombies (very important man in the undead community), vampires (who hold AA meetings for vampires sobering up on tomato juice and serve the city as lawyers), and many more characters. Any idea or mythological concept is taken all the way to its logical conclusion and way beyond like Jewish Golems in "Feet of Clay" or aging heroes called the silver horde in "Interesting Times".

This "modern" city of Ankh-Morpork is based on a self regulating system of guilds. Among them the Guild of Thieves (you pay a yearly fee for a plaque on your house which exempts you from robberies), the Guild of Seamstresses (in the process of renaming themselves the Guild of Negotiable Affection), the Guild of Fools (always so serious in their pratfalls, red noses, and water spraying flowers), and the Guild of Assassins (everyone's head has a price).

Every book has a major theme like opera (Masquerade), the music industry (Soul Music), Hollywood movies (Moving Pictures), Australia (The Last Continent), China (Interesting Times), fairies (Lord and Ladies), diplomacy (The Fifth Elephant), religions (Small Gods), time (Thief of Time), death (Mort and Reaper Man), and Christmas (Hogswatch), to name just a few. Remember, there are close to thirty novels, and therefore close to thirty themes, and he is not done writing yet (luckily).

Pratchett's books have sold over 25 million copies worldwide, but strangely enough, I found only one person in my circle of friends who knows of his novels. I myself had stumbled across them by chance when looking for a new book on tapes, and could not believe my ears when I started listening. I kept laughing so hard that I was hooked. That was a year ago and since then I managed to listen to all his books on tape available through the public library. His humor, his insights and his both simple and complex concepts have kept me sane in this last winter when his Diskworld held a place for me to reassemble my personal world. Thank you, Terry Pratchett, for the gift of your writing in my life.

The L-Space (Library Space where all libraries on the Diskworld are interconnected) http://www.ie.lspace.org A very informative website concerning anything you would like to know about Terry Pratchett and the Diskworld.

Audio Tapes of most of Terry Pratchett's books through Isis Audio is the world's leading publisher of unabridged audio books. Their website provides details for thousands of titles. http://www.isis-publishing.co.uk

The Donut

All of it

All of it is life
All of it is me
All of it is you
And all of it is us

~~ Ulla! ~~

Body

Guess what: in the Donut it all comes together. This is it. This is Fullness in the body and around it. Tangible, effortless, and easy.

Breathing Exercise: Whole Body Breath

Here is an invitation to explore the fullness of all aspects in the shape of our own donut shaped energy flow inside and all around our bodies.

Preparations

This Breathing Exercise is designed to be experienced while you are reading it, preferably out loud to yourself, if you are in a position to do so. If not, at least mouth the words; it will help you slow down and stay focused. If you are with a partner who is open to sharing this exercise, take turns reading it out loud to each other. Make sure you are in a position to relax while you are reading, without falling asleep too quickly.

If you want to intensify this exercise, invite your spirit guides and angels, known or unknown, seen or unseen, to join you in this experience.

Exercise

- ❖ I bring my awareness to my upper chest area to where my collar bones, my shoulders, my arms, and my hands create the structural connection between my head and my torso in the vertical line, and my torso and my arms on the horizontal line.
- ❖ I am appreciating my collarbones, my shoulders, and my neck for doing such a wonderful job of connecting different parts of my upper body.
- ❖ I place my hands on my chest in a comfortable position.
- ❖ I bring my breath into the upper parts of my lungs, and open up my collarbones, my shoulder and my neck area.

~~~~~~

- ❖ If I feel any discomfort or tightness in my upper chest area, my neck, or my shoulders, I notice it

Fullness No Matter What

- ❖ I totally accept any discomfort by directing my very own Loving Color into the tender or tight area.
- ❖ I bring that Loving Color of acceptance into every area of discomfort, one after another, until my upper chest area, my neck, and my shoulders are glowing with acceptance.

~~~~~~

- ❖ I feel my upper lungs rise and my shoulders stretch with the inbreath, slowly counting to five, and fall with the outbreath, again slowly counting to five.
- ❖ I continue watching the rise and fall of my upper lungs for about four to six long slow breaths.

~~~~~~

- ❖ This is an invitation to breathe my Color of Loving through all the twelve aspects of fullness inside my body, outside my body, and around my body.
- ❖ I start breathing into my heart. I am activating my particular Color of Loving. I breathe three deep breaths into my heart. I let my Color of Loving expand in my chest until in reaches all the way into the Peace Room underneath my collarbones.
- ❖ I imagine breathing my Color of Loving on my inbreath into the Peace Room until it is all lit up. I breathe three deep inbreaths into my Peace Room.
- ❖ I imagine breathing my Color of Loving on my inbreath into my throat and igniting my Ray of Creative Expression. I breathe three deep inbreaths into my throat.
- ❖ I imagine breathing my Color of Loving on my inbreath into my forehead. My Ray of creative Expression lights up my Vessel of Inspiration. I breathe three deep inbreaths into my forehead.
- ❖ I imagine breathing my Color of Loving on my inbreath into the top of my head. My Vessel of Inspiration turns on my Fountain of Gratitude. I breathe three deep inbreaths into the top of my head.
- ❖ I imagine breathing my Color of Loving on my inbreath into the space about two feet above my head. My Fountain of Gratitude sparkles all the way up into the Light Blue Tetrahedron of Heaven. I breathe three deep

The Donut

inbreaths into the space above my head. The Fountain of Gratitude crests and falls back down all around my head.

~~~~~~

- ❖ I now shift from putting my focus on my inbreath to putting it on my outbreath.

~~~~~~

- ❖ I imagine letting the Color of Loving drop down and around my head on my outbreath. It drops into the space around the back of neck to light up my Sofa of Guidance. I imagine saying hello to all my friends sitting on the Sofa, seen or unseen, known or unknown. I let three deep outbreaths fall into the space around the back of my neck.
- ❖ I imagine letting the Color of Loving drop down and around my upper body into both of my hands on my outbreath. All my friends on the Sofa help me weave my Web of Connection between both of my hands. I let three deep outbreaths flow into my hands.
- ❖ I imagine letting the Color of Loving light up both of my Jewels of Integrity in both of my hands on my outbreath. I let three deep outbreaths flow into my hands.
- ❖ I imagine letting the Color of Loving drop down and around my lower body and my legs into the space about two feet below my feet on my outbreath. My Honey Colored Tetrahedron of Earth lights up and sparkles. I let three deep outbreaths flow into the space below my feet.

~~~~~~

- ❖ I now shift from putting my focus on my outbreath to putting it on my inbreath.

~~~~~~

- ❖ I imagine breathing my Color of Loving into both soles of my feet on my inbreath. My Honey Colored Tetrahedron of Earth sparkles all the way into my Bubbles of Laughter. I breathe three deep inbreaths into the soles of my feet.
- ❖ I imagine breathing my Color of Loving into the back of my thighs, into my pelvis, and into my lower back on my inbreath. My Bubbles of

- Laughter have bubbled all the way up into my Seat of Security. I breathe three deep inbreaths into the back of my thighs, into my pelvis, and into lower back.
- I imagine breathing my Color of Loving into my belly on my inbreath.
- My Seat of Security is holding space for my Anemones of Feelings. I breathe three deep inbreaths into my belly.
- I imagine breathing my Color of Loving into my stomach on the inbreath. My Anemones of Feelings gently sway all the way into my Caves of Knowing. I breathe three deep inbreaths into my stomach.
- I imagine breathing my Color of Loving once again into my heart.
- I have come full circle connecting all my aspects of fullness via my Color of Loving and using my breath.
- I know myself fully connected and protected in that Donut shaped breath.
- I notice any changes in my body, in my sense of well being, in my breathing.

~~~~~~

- I once again feel my upper lungs rise and my shoulders stretch with the inbreath, slowly counting to five, and fall with the outbreath, again slowly counting to five.
- I continue watching the rise and fall of my upper lungs for about four to six long slow breaths.
- Anytime now I can access my connection to all the fullness aspects through the whole body breath and experience its effect on my life in the hours, days, and months to come.

Completion

- When I am complete, I bring my awareness back to the world outside of me.
- I wiggle my toes and fingers.
- I stretch my body like a cat with a few lazy, long, full body stretches.
- I am back in my waking reality.

The Donut

Suggestions

Now you have your very own Donut of Fullness available and at your disposal at any time you feel the need to reconnect into your own fullness. This Donut shaped energy both energizes and protects you. It both anchors you in your earthly existence and lets you draw down your heavenly aspects. It is a reminder towards completeness and connection.

Here is the short version of the sequential order for all Fullness Aspects:

>Start with the **Color of Loving**
>Into the **Peace Room** and
>Through the **Ray of Community**
>Into the **Vessel of Inspiration**
>Into the **Fountain of Gratitude**
>Into the Inverted **Tetrahedron of Heaven**
>Out and down and around the head
>Pass by the **Sofa of Guidance**
>Through the **Hands of Connecting**
>And the **Jewel of Integrity**
>All the way down below the body
>Into the **Tetrahedron of Earth**
>Up into the **Bubbles of Laughter**
>Up into the **Seat of Security**
>Up into the **Anemones of Feelings**
>Through the **Caves of Knowing**
>Back into the **Color of Loving**

Pleasure Exercises

Solo: Mandala Pleasure Breathing

Preparations

❖ Have some time and space to yourself, preferably not just before you go to sleep.

❖ Make sure that you have read at least once through the Whole Body Breath in this chapter.

Fullness No Matter What

- ❖ Make a photocopy of the Donut Mandala at the beginning of this chapter.
- ❖ If you want to get into the spirit of it, get out your watercolors, crayons, felt markers, or colored pens, and color in your Mandala.
- ❖ Find a position where you can both comfortably pleasure yourself and are able to look at the Donut Mandala at the same time. You might want to either pin the Donut Mandala to the wall, or lay it on a pillow next to your face, or dangle it on a string in front of your face, or any other creative way that makes sure you can touch yourself while seeing the Mandala.

Exercise

- ❖ Start by focusing your breath into your chest area by breathing in through the nose and breathing out through the open mouth. Just slowly breathe in and out for about ten breaths. Let your awareness settle into your body. Connect with your body. Let go of any mind activities.
- ❖ Imagine a hollow tube through the core of your body starting between your feet and legs through your Jewels all the way to the top of your head, sometimes called the "Inner Flute".
- ❖ Imagine your inbreath entering this Inner Flute at your heart and flowing upwards.
- ❖ When your inbreath shoots out of your head and your Inner Flute, stop breathing in through your nose and start breathing out through your open mouth.
- ❖ Imagine your outbreath cascading down around your body (front, back, and sides simultaneously) all the way below your feet.
- ❖ Start breathing in again through your nose, and this time letting your inbreath enter your Inner Flute between your feet and rising between your legs through your Jewels all the way to the top of your head.
- ❖ Once again, when your imagine your inbreath shooting out of your head and your Inner Flute, stop breathing in through your nose and start breathing out through your open mouth.

~~~~~~

- ❖ When you feel comfortable in visualizing the flow of your breath through and around your body, do the above cycle for about four to six complete breaths.

The Donut

- While breathing in and out, keep looking at your Mandala with soft eyes and blurry vision (this one comes quite natural to those of us who are near sighted without our glasses!)
- Add self pleasuring to your breath. You might want to close your eyes. Give yourself as much sexual pleasure as you want to, but hold back on having an orgasm.
- When you get really close to the edge, look at your Mandala again.
- Charge up your Mandala with sexual pleasure energy by looking at it while feeling turned on. Keep breathing in through the nose, and out through your open mouth, but breathe faster than before.
- If you want to, you can now go for the big "O" (orgasm). Keep looking your Mandala, if you are able to. Connect the vision of your Mandala with your orgasm.
- Or you can just stay with the charged up sexual energy, breathing slow and slower while looking at your Mandala.
- Keep breathing and looking until your feel soft and at peace while st charged and juiced up.

Suggestions

Charge up your Mandala with sexual pleasure energy like I just described, let's say, six to ten times. Eventually there will be a direct link between pleasure, full body donut breath, and the Mandala. It is then also called a Yantra. A Yantra is an image charged with some form of energy through repeated practices connected with the image.

Once you turned it into a Yantra by charging the image up with pleasure energy, all you need to do is look at your particular Mandala and get a full body pleasure charge. You can then place copies of the Mandala on the steering wheel of your car, your bathroom mirror, or your refrigerator door, and look at it any time you need a full body energy jolt! The above described practice is part of "sex magic" practices, bringing together some of the magical practices of pagan traditions with sexual energy.

It also charges up your full body breath with pleasure. Anytime your need an energy boost, start breathing the full body donut breath and it will be charged with your sexual pleasure energy. The prerequisite is regular practice. The more often you combine these three elements (Mandala, Donut breath, and sexual pleasure) the more powerful, that is charged up, your Yantra or your Donut breath will become.

Partnered: Sensuous Whole Body Pleasuring

Preparations

- Create some time to explore other than late at night just before going to sleep.
- Decide who will be the giver and who will be the receiver.
- Both giver and receiver: close your eyes and connect with yourself.
- **Giver:** Find your love for yourself and your partner inside of you.
- **Receiver:** Lie down and relax. Ask yourself how much pleasure are you willing to receive.
- Have some silk scarves, a piece of fur, juicy fruit pieces, good massage oil handy.

Exercise

Man Pleasuring Woman

Start by using your silk scarves and fur pieces to wake up your lover's skin. Very, very slowly move these different textures across all her body parts, gently across her face, across her neck, over her breasts and nipples, across her belly, between her legs, down her legs and over her feet and back up again. (Use the scarves and/or furs first as they do not mix well with oils).

Once her skin has been thoroughly awakened, use some massage oil and start connecting with her heart first by pouring some of the oil slowly over her heart area and her breasts. My suggestion is to use the Taking Touch (1 Loving Fullness), that is, to focus on your own sensations while touching her skin and body. Start spreading the oil all over her chest and over to her arms. Go back and forth between her heart, breasts, neck and the arms and hands.

Take some more oil and pour it on her belly and between her spread legs. Let it drip slowly down her Pearl, her Labia, and her Yoni. Again using the Taking Touch technique and spread the oil all over her belly and stomach, across her pubic hair. Ever so often dip down into her Jewels to slowly waken them up.

The Donut

You can focus more on her Jewels, but only just for a short while. Just enough to give her a taste of the turn-on to come. Use your hands and spread that turn-on energy all over her body, into her legs and feet, back to her Jewels, up into her hands, back to her Jewels, again down to the other leg and her foot, and back to the Jewels etc. Start touching her faster all over her body, but always come back to dip into her juices, and give her some sexual stimulation, but just enough to have her want more. You can even take some of her juices and move your hands all the way up across her breasts and nipples to her face, caressing her mouth, letting her taste and smell her own turned-on juices.

Invite her to breathe deeply into her belly with an open mouth, to make sounds, to moan, to sigh while you are touching all of her body parts and her Jewels. At some point you might want to feed her some juicy fruit pieces, while you are still touching the rest of her body and dipping into her Jewels.

When she is thoroughly turned on and juiced up, hold her in your arms and tell her that she now has several options. List them for her:

- ❖ You might just want to stay with that alive tingling whole body pleasure while I'll keep holding you and gently stroke you to allow you to come down from that high in your own time.
- ❖ You might want me to bring you to orgasm by honoring you manually or orally, and then switch roles.
- ❖ You might want to make love with me, to invite me to enter your Yoni, which will be a real pleasure for me, now that you are all juiced up and open and ready to burst.

While you are telling her what her options are (and you might come up with some other options I have not thought of!), watch her face for the smile that will tell you which of the choices is the right one at that moment.

No matter what she chooses, make sure to stay connected with her when she is coming down by holding her while gently touching her. Some hard pressure on her Pearl with the heel of your hand might help her ground. She might have an emotional release for the sheer joy of feeling so much pleasure!

Woman Pleasuring Man

Start by using your silk scarves and fur pieces to wake up your lover's skin. Very, very slowly move these different textures across all his body parts, gently across his face, across his neck and chest, across his belly, across his Lingam, down between his legs across his Twin Globes, down his legs and over his feet and back up again. (Use the scarves and/or furs first as they do not mix well with oils).

Once his skin has been awakened, use some massage oil and start connecting with his Lingam by slowly dripping some of the oil slowly all over his Jewels. My suggestion is to use the Taking Touch (Solo Pleasure Exercise in Loving Fullness) that is, to focus on your own sensations while touching his Jewels. Start spreading the oil all over his pubic hair, his Lingam, his Twin Globes. Just tease him a bit and then move your hands all over his body. Spread that turn-on energy all over into his legs and feet, back to his Jewels, up into his hands, back to his Jewels, again down to the other leg and his foot, and back to the Jewels etc. Start touching him faster all over his body, but always come back to touch his Wand, and give him some sexual stimulation, but just enough to have him want more. You can even take some of the oil and rub it on your own breasts and slide them all over his body, and especially around his Lingam.

Invite him to breathe deeply into his belly with an open mouth, to make sounds, to moan, to sigh while you are touching all of his body parts and his Jewels. At some point you might want to feed him some juicy fruit pieces, while you are still touching the rest of his body and occasionally gripping his Jewels.

When he is thoroughly turned on and juiced up, he most likely will want to make love with you, and to fell you around him now all turned on and tingling. But you might tell him that he now has several options and list them for him:

- ❖ You might just want to stay with that alive and tingling whole body pleasure while I hold you and gently stroke you to allow you to come down from that high in your own time.
- ❖ You might want me to bring you to orgasm by honoring you manually or orally and then switch roles.
- ❖ You might want me to make love with you, to have you enter my Yoni, which will be a real pleasure for me, now that you are all juiced up and open and ready to burst.

No matter what he chooses, make sure to stay connected with him when he is coming down by holding him in your arms and his Jewels in your hands. He might feel very emotional and vulnerable.

Suggestions

Here are a few suggestions on how to increase the high energy state, and/or make use of it:

- ❖ Combine this exercise with the one from the Gratitude Fullness Chapter: Touching My Partner's Body with Gratitude (Partnered Pleasure Exercise in Gratitude Fullness)), that is, while you going back between touching your partner's body and touching the Jewels, tell him or her all the things that you are grateful for. Or how beautiful and wonderful your partner is. Or how much you love your partner and his or her body. Or how much you are enjoying seeing her or him in so much pleasure.
- ❖ This is a great time to do the High Energy Oracle (Solo Pleasure Exercise in Knowing Fullness) if there is some knowing you (or your partner) are looking for, maybe a decision that needs to be made and you want the bigger picture.
- ❖ If you want to increase the openness and vulnerability, wash his or her Jewels (Partnered Pleasure Exercise in Knowing Fullness).

Mind

The Organizing Principle behind the Twelve Aspects of Fullness

The twelve Aspects of Fullness used in this book are based on my own interpretation and experience of an ancient East Indian system called the Chakras. I used the chakra system as an organizing principle. The word chakra is Sanskrit for wheel or disk and has been used for thousands of years to describe seven main energy centers in the human body. These seven Chakras correspond to seven glands in the human body, seven levels of consciousness, colors, sounds, body functions, and much more.

The Chakra System is based on the belief system that the seven chakras represent seven hierarchical levels of consciousness. Chakras one to three and their attributes are considered lower levels, while the attributes of chakras four to seven are seen as higher levels. There are numerous variations of the Chakra system, different interpretations of the function of each chakra, even the existence of more than seven chakras. They all have one thing in common though: they share the belief that we can move up and through these levels, one after another, through lifetimes of yoga, study, meditation and, most often, celibacy. Only when we reach the higher levels, do we become enlightened. This makes it a hierarchical system with a built-in value assumption that the awarenesses associated with the higher chakras are more desirable than the ones of the lower chakras.

The Chakra system is also a system based on an energy exchange between enlightened gurus, and followers on the path to enlightenment. The enlightened guru awakens the energy of the followers when Shaktipat is given in the Third Eye. Through Shaktipat the dormant coil of the Kundalini (at the base of the spine) wakes up and begins to rise through the body into the head and out. That awakened Kundalini energy is passed on by the follower to the guru when it shoots out of the head. The guru in turn offers guidance for the follower to reach his/her own enlightenment.

I believe that a different approach is appropriate for our times: in order to experience a life lived from fullness, all aspects of our lives deserve to be experienced equally in a balanced way. The different theme here is balance compared to hierarchy, a circle compared to a line, circulating flow compared to upward and outward flow.

If you have read through the Breathing Exercise for this chapter (see Body Section) you will see that all of the fullness aspects do come together in one big continuous circle. The Whole Body breath takes the shape of a (human size) Donut, which in the mathematical terms is called a torus. This Donut shape starts inside the body at the heart, moves all the way up out of the body above the head, all the way down around the body below the feet, and back up again inside the body all the way up into the heart.

A continuous circle is being created here, that offers an experience of the human body and its surrounding energy field as one unit comprised of equal parts. This circle offers the breadth of the whole human experience inside this marvelous container called a body.

Here is an overview of how the twelve Aspects of Fullness correspond to the East Indian Chakra System:

	Aspects of Fullness	Body Parts	Symbols	The 7 Chakras	Main Attributes
1	Loving Fullness	Heart	Your Own Color	4 Heart	Love & Intuition
2	Community Fullness	Collarbones & Throat	Peace Room & Ray	5 Throat	Communication & Creativity
3	Inspirational Fullness	Third Eye	Vessel	6 Third Eye	Vision & Clarity
4	Gratitude Fullness	Crown	Fountain	7 Crown	God
5	Heavenly Fullness	3 Feet above Head	Inverted Tetrahedron	N/A	N/A
6	Guidance Fullness	Back of the Neck	Sofa	N/A	N/A
7	Connecting Fullness	Hands	Hands & Jewels	N/A	N/A
8	Earthly Fullness	3 Feet below Feet	Tetrahedron	N/A	N/A
9	Laughter Fullness	Soles of the Feet	Bubbles	N/A	N/A
10	Security Fullness	Pelvis & Back	Seat	1 Root	Survival & Sexuality
11	Feeling Fullness	Belly	Anemones	2 Belly	Emotions & Sensuality
12	Knowing Fullness	Stomach	Caves	3 Solar Plexus	Ego & Power

At the same time the self-contained circle serves as a starting point from which we can reach out to other self contained units, and to which we can always return. Within the fullness of this human body the whole spectrum from such basic human instincts as procreation and survival to the God realization within us is possible as an internal and deeply personal experience. When "the cup runneth over," we give back where inspiration guides us, passion points us, and help is needed. But all of it starts within our own internal world inside our bodies. All of it inside mirrors the universe out there, and all of it out there is at our disposal, but only after we are finding fullness inside.

Fullness is awakening from the inside out, independent from a teacher or guru and his or her human whims and frailties, prescriptions and rules to follow. (It took probably lifetimes of guru dependent awakenings on my soul's part to dare this one without a guru, and probably many lifetimes of missing the awakening boat...)

This circular movement makes fullness available to everyone for the asking just by turning inward. What a grace to be given the chance to bring this knowing into human experience and into a shape and words. No wonder that I had to do this without a partner at my side, who fully matches me. I would have never tried to reach out for the words to translate my internal experience to those not already in it.

~~~ A deep sigh out ~~~

Soul

In the last gathering of the book
the leaves reassumed their imperial purple,
the final exultant psalms were again inscribed in gold,
and the psalter ended with a painted page
in which an empyrean of hovering angels,
a paradise of haloed saints,
and a transfigured earth of redeemed souls
all together obeyed the psalmist,
and praised God in the firmament of his power,
with every instrument of music known to man.
And all the quivering wings, all the haloes,
all the trumpets and psalteries and harps,
the stringed instruments and organs, the timbrels
and the load cymbals were of burnished gold,
and the denizens of heaven and paradise and earth alike
were as sinuous and ethereal as the tendrils of
rose and honeysuckle and vine that intertwined with them,
and the sky above them as blue as the irises and
periwinkles under their feet,
until the tips of the angels' wings melted
into a zenith of blinding gold,
in which the ultimate mystery vanished from sight.

~~ Ellis Peters, The Heretic's Apprentice ~~

~~~~~~~~~~

More

Margo Anand. *The Art of Sexual Magic*. The Western European version of Tantra.

Neale Donald Walsh. *Conversations with God*. All of his books have been at times my daily companions. www.cwg.org

Chakras: If you want to know more about the chakra system, there are numerous books, videos, and websites available. Just look for "Chakras".

Ellis Peters. *The Heretic's Apprentice*. See my book review of Ellis Peter's books in Chapter 3 Inspirational Fullness.

Just Fullness

Come Heart and Speak to Me

Come heart and speak to me of the unspeakable
Come heart and sing to me of songs unsung
Come heart and be with me in ways that being had not been

I ask for solace in my own arms
I ask for joy from groundless wells
I ask for living way beyond myself

I am the unborn essence
I am the unseen trace
I am the one I am
I AM

~~ Ulla! ~~

Just Fullness

This is one place where there is room for what I call The Mystery. Living in Just Fullness is not very conducive to putting many words to it, as it can be so elusive that verbal descriptions prove to be only rough sketches. I have again and again tried putting words to it and I have two languages available as I speak fluently German. But I find both languages inadequate. I am aware that what I am offering in this final chapter in terms of words is just an approximation.

~~~~~~~~~~

> The most beautiful thing we can experience is the mysterious.
> It is the source of all true art and science.
>
> ~~ Albert Einstein ~~

~~~~~~~~~~

I had to learn to be at ease with not knowing the hard way in a very difficult, long winter where reasoning, understanding, and words failed me and I felt very close to madness because of it. I had to learn the hard way that I actually do not need the use of words and thus the need to understand all the time. I had to learn the hard way that there is room in my life for mysteries that remain unexplained and unsaid, and that I am safe nevertheless.

Sometimes we just have to be with an experience and accept the fact that we are and will remain speechless in the face of it. In our word oriented culture that is not the easiest thing to do. But it is very rewarding as it opens up a whole other dimension of experiences.

My invitation here is to make some room, maybe in small corners first, for the unexplainable, the irrational, the mysterious in our lives. It can be a gateway to a whole new world, well worth the scare or madness or fear it may bring up. It can enter through any of the Fullness aspects I have described in this book. And part of it will hopefully always remain a mystery.

~~~~~~~~~~

> "…a mystery wrapped up in a riddle inside an enigma…"
>
> ~~ Terry Pratchett,? ~~

~~~~~~~~~~

Fullness No Matter What

Guess what, fullness in its deepest sense can only be received. There is nothing we need to do. It is a Grace. It visits us unexpectedly. It is where we come from. It is where we return to, either while we are still in a body, or in death.

Another way of saying this is my adaptation of a saying I found in Neale Donald Walsh's book "Conversations with God". For a long time this saying was my daily companion:

~~~~~~~~~~

> Fullness is the understanding
> That there is nothing to do
> Nowhere to go
> And nobody else to be
> Except who I am
> Right now, right here.

~~~~~~~~~~

And so often truth reveals itself in the form of a paradox, that is, two opposite ideas, truths, concepts, turn out to be equally true. (To me that paradoxical knowing points to a truth larger than our mind can hold.) This means, it is true that we can both receive fullness as an internal Grace, and manifest fullness externally in our lives.

Allowing ourselves the joy of exploring fullness externally opens up several benefits: it helps us to remember our original fullness. We all come from fullness and will eventually return to fullness, at least in my universe. It also helps to get us closer to the state of Grace, but in the paradoxical way of the following mathematical axiom:

> Let's divide a given length in two parts. Then divide one of the parts again into two parts. And again divide one of the parts into two parts. And so on and so forth. Ultimately we will get very, very close to one of the ends of the given length. But we will never quite make it. There will always be, by definition, another length left that can still be divided, once again, into two parts, even if it is infinitesimally small.

Here is another way of saying this: We can get very, very close to fullness but we do not quite experience fullness—until we do.

Just Fullness

~~~~~~~~~~

Baddabing, Badaboom.

~~ Terry Pratchett, Thief of Time ~~

~~~~~~~~~~

When I was living in Lahaina on Maui I had a dream one morning about a huge tsunami like wave. Tsunamis are ocean waves that can reach heights of up to 100 feet (30 meters) when they hit land. You know there is a tsunami coming towards you, (if you happen to be on a beach) when you watch the ocean water all of a sudden move very far out into the ocean, showing the beach and the corals and the rocks and the floor of the ocean. When you actually can see that much exposed ocean floor it is already too late to run, because this retreating of ocean water is the build up for the biggest and most likely last wave you will ever see.

I dreamed that I was swimming out in the ocean. In the dream a huge tsunami like wave came rolling up towards me, picked my up on its crest, carried me like a surfer towards the shore, and safely deposited me on the beach. In hindsight this dream told me all I needed to know about my journey into fullness. And it even gave me a metaphor for the events leading up to writing this book. I have referred to the nine months prior to writing my first pages a couple times in previous chapters as to the Madness or the Tunnel of Not Knowing. Those nine months were the build up of the tsunami, the emptying out of everything, the letting go of anything far out into not knowing. And the writing of the book is the wave coming back in. It is allowing me to surf on fullness so high, that it feels like in the dream. I am very curious to see on what shore the wave will end up safely depositing me, this time with a completed book under my arm.

~~~~~~~~~~

And it came to pass that in time the Great God Om
spake unto Brutha, the Chosen One: "Psst!"

~~ Terry Pratchett, Small Gods ~~

~~~~~~~~~~

Fullness No Matter What

What an amazing journey into fullness: to find my self at a point where my whole life makes sense, where it all comes together. Finally there is a rhyme and a reason for everything in my life right now. Literally everything, every wounding, every perceived shortcoming, every detour, every perceived failure, catastrophes, or fiasco. Every lover and their gifts, even if just for a short while. Every joyful high, every blissful moment, every ecstatic encounter. Every step along the way. All of it is making sense. To experience this clarity after the long winter of not understanding a thing is quite a gift. I still don't understand. And it does not matter anymore. I just know that it was right and necessary.

~~~~~~~~~~

"While I'm still confused and uncertain, it's on a much higher plane, d'you see, and at least I know I'm bewildered about the really fundamental and important facts of the universe."
Treatle nodded. "I hadn't looked at it like that," he said,
"But you're absolutely right.
He's really pushed back the boundaries of ignorance."

~~ Terry Pratchett, Equal Rites ~~

~~~~~~~~~~

Here are a few more fullness pointers:

Fullness offers a sense of being complete in any given moment.

Fullness is a pitcher being filled up
until it spills over,
and spills over,
and spills over.

Fullness is saying Yes in every single moment that we are able to until all that is left is one single big Yes to life.

Fullness spills over either into a sharing from that fullness with others, or into creation of more fullness.

Fullness is independent from any monetary expression of wealth like material possessions or financial security.

Just Fullness

Fullness brings with it a quality of "enoughness",
of having enough,
of being enough,
of doing enough.

When there is fullness, there is pleasure.
When there is pleasure, there is fullness.
Pleasure is another sign that we are actually living in fullness.

Fullness is when the cup runneth over and we give back
where inspiration guides us,
passion points us,
and help is needed.

~~~~~~~~~~

A BREAST IN THE SKY

I hear about the famous.
I hear talk about different cities.

The most intimate events of families come to my ears.
I hear about temples and
mosques and
saints.

All that can be said I have heard.
All that can be wanted I
have seen.

My interest in this world has waned, though
not because I am
depressed.

A fish in a bowl I was,
a bottom feeder,

but now I nurse
upon a breast

Fullness No Matter What

in the
sky.

~~ Rabia (Landisky Translation) ~~

~~~~~~~~~~

More

Neale Donald Walsh. *Conversations with God.*

Terry Pratchett. *Thief of Time.*

Terry Pratchett. *Small Gods.*

Terry Pratchett. *Equal Rites.*

Art Notes

Technique

For the Fullness Mandalas in this book I used water based, light grey pastels to cover every bit of white of the Bristol paper. Then totally cover up the water based pastels with black oil based pastels. This has to "sit" for about 2 days, until the oil pastels do not smear anymore. Using a compass, ruler, and scratch knife, (which looks like a little spoon with sharp edges in a pen holder), I created the images and patterns.

Design Elements

When I was looking for a graphic representation that would encompass all Fullness Aspects in this book, I was lying in my tent ready to go to sleep. All of a sudden I "saw" the solution: if I imagined myself looking down upon my head or up at the soles of my feet, all fullness symbols (like the Vessel of Inspiration, the Tetrahedron, or the Feeling Anemones), could be fit into a circle. All images that I so whimsically tossed into this book, some for the sheer joy of it like the Sofa of Guidance, actually came together and fit into one structural design. Every one of the 21 images (for 19 chapters plus front and back cover designs) could be constructed by using one or more of the following graphic elements:

- a tetrahedron,
- an inverted tetrahedron,
- three different size circles (the small Vessel circle, the medium sized Peace Room circle, and the large Body circle),
- six small circles,
- bubbles,
- a straight line, and
- the six petaled "Flower of Life" pattern.

All art images (except for Just Fullness) have the following elements in common:

- ❖ the diamond shape,
- ❖ the small white inbreath circle,
- ❖ the large white outbreath circle,
- ❖ a visitor from our natural environment (like a gecko, a cat, a whale tail, a creek, or a spider web complete with spider) placed outside the body circle, but always reaching in,
- ❖ and the direction: the top most corner of the diamond represents the front of the body, the bottom one the back and the left respectively right corners are the left shoulder and arm respectively right shoulder and arm.

The Front and Back Cover share the diamond shape and the large circle.

Individual Mandala Designs

Here are the 19 art pieces and their individual design elements:

Introduction
The large circle is a representation of the human body, with the small center circle being the inbreath, and the larger outer circle the outbreath. Both inbreath and outbreath are present in each design except in Just Fullness and the cover designs.

Basic Assumptions
The six basic assumptions show up as six small circles neatly fit into the body circle and surrounded by a school of fish.

Fullness Meter
The Fullness Meter design takes its 12 spokes from the two tetrahedrons creating the six pointed star you see in Loving Fullness plus six more lines at the half point (which does not quite fit the basic design elements—oh well!). A branch with ripe cherries reaches into the Fullness Meter.

Art Notes

1 Loving Fullness
Loving Fullness takes it six pointed star shape from the two tetrahedrons: the Earthly Tetrahedron and the Heavenly inverted Tetrahedron.

2 Community Fullness
Community Fullness uses the medium sized circle, the Peace Room, and a straight line from the tetrahedron for the Ray of Creativity.

3 Inspirational Fullness
The Vessel of Inspiration is the made out of the small circle and has a snake meandering through it.

4 Gratitude Fullness
The Fountain of Gratitude shows up as the six petaled "Flower of Life" design created by using six precisely overlapping semi circles. The gecko is seeking cover in the right corner.

5 Heavenly Fullness
The inverted tetrahedron is depicted here as if you are looking up into it with its base in the heavens and its tip in the body. It is accompanied by a flock of birds.

6 Guidance Fullness
The Sofa of Guidance design uses the parts of all three circles, and two partial small circles. Looks like a comfy sofa surrounded by a stylized rainbow on top.

Paradoxing
Paradoxing takes its straight line from looking down upon the pentagram drawn from the heart to the right hand, down to the left foot, up to the head, down to the right foot, up to the left hand and back to the heart. The dark shape on the left in the Mandala was actually a technical mistake (I had not covered up the paper all the way with light gray crayon before applying the black cover) and I first had wanted to put that piece aside, till I realized that it provided the perfect symbol for the shadow as part of the paradoxing balance.

7 Connecting Fullness
For the Web of Connection I used the paradoxing or pentagram line, and parts of the two tetrahedrons, and the spider offered her web as a symbol.

8 Earthly Fullness
The tetrahedron is the basis of this design, completed by crystals growing in the Earth.

9 Laughter Fullness
The Bubbles of Laughter nicely filled up the foot shapes. The fantastic mountain range and caves around the feet surprised me when they showed up to complete the design.

10 Security Fullness
The Seat of Security was created by using the small circle, parts of the medium sized one, and parts of two small circles for the arm rests. The spruce tree took a while to make an appearance.

Pleasure Fullness
The three pleasure spheres were complemented by a sleepy cat and the symbolic representation of a Lingam inside a Yoni.

11 Feeling Fullness
The six small feeling circles are grouped around one symbolic representation of an anemone in the center.

12 Knowing Fullness
The three Caves of Knowing share the same circles sizes as the three Pleasure spheres. And the whale tail told me a whale of a tale about cetaceans being the historians on the Earth, collectively remembering all that ever happened on Earth since the beginning of their presence in the oceans.

The Donut
Here all shapes came together to form one intricate yet simple white design being scratched into the black surface.

Just Fullness
Because Just Fullness is the state where all has changed and nothing is different, I took the same design made out of all shapes as in the Donut, but made it part of the background. It came to light by scratching the flowing fire design into the black cover, shining through darkness in its softer shape.

Appendix

A Word Concerning the Verbal Gems in the Soul Sections

Some of the verbal gems in this book have lost their owners over the years, that is, I have lost track of who wrote them. If you in reading them recognize their owners, please let me know (my contact information can be found on http://www.FullnessNoMatterWhat.com), so that I can give due credit in future editions of this book.

I have run into some difficulties obtaining written permissions for the quotes that I have added into the fullness of this book. It looks like you need a publisher to receive those written permissions and I do not have one as this book is self published. My apologies if anyone concerned feels that I have abused the right to quote materials. At least I have made sure that due credit has been given whenever I had a name to the quoted item.

Contact Information

Sending me an email to ulla@FullnessNoMatterWhat.com is the best way to contact me. For news, updates, private sessions, and book readings check out the website for my book at http://www.FullnessNoMatterWhat.com.

0-595-34081-4

Printed in the United States
98220LV00004B/1-9/A